NEW EDITION

This Is
Our Heritage

By

Sister M. Hugh, C.S.J., ED.D.
Mary Synon, LL.D.
and
Katherine Rankin

IN ACCORDANCE WITH THE EDUCATIONAL PLAN OF
RT. REV. MSGR. GEORGE JOHNSON, PH.D.
AND
VERY REV. MSGR. THOMAS OWEN MARTIN, PH.D., S.T.D.
THE CATHOLIC UNIVERSITY OF AMERICA

Ginn and Company

BOSTON · NEW YORK · CHICAGO · ATLANTA
DALLAS · COLUMBUS · PALO ALTO · TORONTO · LONDON

Acknowledgments

For kind permission to reprint copyrighted material, acknowledgment is made to the following:

William Collins Sons & Co., Ltd., for "The Crowning of Dreaming John," from *Poems, 1908–1914*, by JOHN DRINKWATER; Doubleday & Company, Inc., for "Prayer of a Soldier in France," from *Poems, Essays and Letters*, by JOYCE KILMER, copyright 1914, 1917, 1918, by Doubleday & Company, Inc.; *Extension* and the author for "Damascus Road," by SISTER M. DOROTHY ANNE, C.S.C.; Ginn and Company for "Two Long Miles Apart," by LYDIA LION ROBERTS, from *The Children's Bookshelf*, and "The Bravery of Elizabeth Zane," from *Short Stories from American History*, by ALBERT BLAISDELL and FRANCIS K. BALL; Houghton Mifflin Company for "Books," by ABBIE FARWELL BROWN; The Macmillan Company for "Hidden Things," from *North America*, by LUCY SPRAGUE MITCHELL, copyright, 1931, by The Macmillan Company and used with their permission; A. D. Peters for "Crusade," by HILAIRE BELLOC; Rand McNally & Company and the author's estate for "Silver Ships," by MILDRED PLEW MEIGS; Sheed and Ward, Inc., for "The Kingdom of God," from *The Flowering Tree*, by CARYLL HOUSELANDER, copyright, 1945, by Sheed and Ward, Inc.; The Talbot Press for "I See His Blood upon the Rose," by JOSEPH MARY PLUNKETT; MONSIGNOR HUGH F. BLUNT for his poem, "Our Lady's Dying"; FRANCES FRIESEKE KILMER for her poem, "Grace"; NANCY BYRD TURNER for her poem, "Washington"; SISTER MARYANNA, O.P. for her poem, "The Knight."

The authors also wish to make grateful acknowledgment to Sister Mary Daniel, C.S.J., Television Co-ordinator for the Archdiocese of St. Louis, Fontbonne College, for the dramatic and choral arrangement of "Son of Thunder."

The pictures in this book are by Dale Nichols, Forrest Orr, Charles Kerins, Cheslie D'Andrea, Heman Fay, Cleveland Woodward, Bruno Frost, C. A. Murphy, Milburn Rosser, Will Huntington, Ed Bradford, and John Polgreen.

Faith and Freedom

Nibil Obstat:

HENRY J. BROWNE, PH.D., *Censor Deputatus*

Imprimatur:

✠ PATRICK A. O'BOYLE, D.D., *Archbishop of Washington*

WASHINGTON, NOVEMBER 1, 1956

COMMISSION		THE
ON		CATHOLIC
AMERICAN		UNIVERSITY
CITIZENSHIP		OF AMERICA

MOST REV. BRYAN J. MCENTEGART

PRESIDENT OF THE COMMISSION

VERY REV. MSGR. THOMAS OWEN MARTIN, PH.D., S.T.D.

DIRECTOR

MARY SYNON, LL.D.

EDITORIAL CONSULTANT

SISTER MARY JOAN, O.P.

CURRICULUM CONSULTANT

PUBLISHED FOR THE CATHOLIC UNIVERSITY OF AMERICA PRESS
WASHINGTON, D. C.

Contents

I · Faith

II · Freedom

4

III · Chivalry

5

IV · Learning

V · Science

VI · Patriotism

VII · Justice

VIII · Unity

II

Faith

The Lord, Shepherd and Host

The Lord is my shepherd; I shall not want.
In verdant pastures He gives me repose;
Beside restful waters He leads me;
He refreshes my soul.
He guides me in right paths
for His name's sake.
Even though I walk in the dark valley
I fear no evil; for You are at my side
With Your rod and Your staff
that give me courage.

PSALM 22

Credo

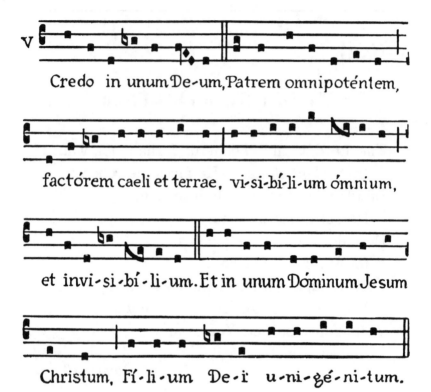

Credo in unum De-um, Patrem omnipoténtem,

factórem caeli et terrae, vi-si-bí-li-um ómnium,

et invi-si-bí-li-um. Et in unum Dóminum Jesum

Christum, Fí-li-um De-i u-ni-gé-ni-tum.

I believe in one God,
the Father Almighty, maker of heaven and earth.
and of all things visible and invisible.
And in one Lord Jesus Christ,
the only-begotten Son of God.

Miracle at Black Mountain

I. *Timothy Meets Paul*

Timothy was the son of a Jewish mother and a pagan father. He lived in a little town, a Roman colony, in Asia Minor that rested in the shadows of the wide Black Mountain. The town rose up a steep hill, from the crowded Jewish quarter toward the camp of the Roman soldiers, to their houses, and to their pagan temple. In the temple the Romans worshiped Jupiter, whom they believed to be the king of the gods, and Mercury, whom they thought was his messenger.

On a Monday, which was a market day, Timothy walked with his mother along a road that led through the Jewish quarter toward the market place. He saw a crowd gathering before the door of his friend, a cripple. "What has happened?" he asked his mother.

Timothy ran, fearing for his friend. His mother hurried after him. In the road, in front of the home of the cripple, stood two strangers. One was a tall man, broad of shoulder, with sad, dark eyes and a flowing beard. The other man, who was speaking to the crowd, was small and slender. The Jews were listening with keen attention to his message.

"Who is he?" asked Timothy.

"He, too, is a Jew," said his mother, "but I never saw him before."

The crowd grew larger. This was a new story that the stranger was bringing to them. The people stood silently and asked no questions as he told them that God had sent a Savior to Israel and that the Savior's name was Jesus. He spoke of the birth and life and death of Jesus, and his voice was deep with sorrow as he described the final, dreadful hours upon the Cross.

The Jews of the little mountain town had never heard of Jesus Christ. One man spoke. "Do you believe that Jesus Christ is truly our long-promised Messias?" he asked.

"I do believe," said the stranger.

"Were you there when men crucified Him?" asked another.

"I did not see Him die," said the stranger.

"Then why do you believe in Him?"

"I believe because I have seen the Light," he told them.

"Who are you?" they demanded.

With pride the stranger faced the crowd. "I am Paul. I was once called Saul," he said.

The Jews did not know him and cried out, asking him to tell his story. He spoke, and in silence they again listened.

Paul was born in Tarsus, a city that lay beyond the Black Mountain. His parents were strict Jews who sent him to a school that was taught by rabbis. By trade he became a tent-maker, but when he was old enough he went to Jerusalem where he hoped to become a rabbi. By the time he reached Jerusalem, belief was growing that the crucified Christ was really

the Messias. Paul was there on the day when Stephen, who was one of the disciples of Christ, was taken by the Jews.

"I even followed the mob to the outskirts of the city and held their garments while they clubbed and stoned Stephen to death," he admitted.

Timothy clutched his mother's hand in horror.

Paul went on. "I acted in ignorance," he said. "I did not even weaken when Stephen cried out, 'Lord Jesus, receive my spirit.' I even asked the high priest at Jerusalem to give me a letter to the Jews at Damascus. I wanted to go there to arrest the Christians in that city and to return them to Jerusalem for punishment."

Then Paul told the people what happened to him on the road to Damascus. For eight days he had traveled across the dry hills of Palestine. As he went, he kept thinking of the Christians in Damascus and how he

13

would punish them. Under a bright blue sky, through burnt grass, past dusty villages, he nursed his hatred. It came to pass, however, that as he drew near to Damascus a light from heaven suddenly shone round about him. Its brightness blinded him. As he fell to the ground, he heard a voice saying, "Saul, Saul, why dost thou persecute Me?"

He answered, "Who art Thou, Lord?"

And the voice said, "I am Jesus Whom thou art persecuting."

Paul trembled and said, "Lord, what wilt Thou have me do?"

Jesus answered, "Arise and go into the city, and it will be told thee what thou must do."

Still blinded by the light, Paul trembled as he rose from the ground. Then men led him by the hand into Damascus, past the gate with the tower and up to a house on the Street called Straight. There he was found by a disciple of the Lord, who gave him his sight once more and baptized him.

The Jews in the little mountain town drew closer to Paul. "Go on," they said breathlessly. "Tell us more."

Paul reached out and placed his hand upon the shoulder of the tall man beside him. "This is Barnabas, another Jew who is a disciple of Jesus," he said. "Three years after I left Damascus he befriended me in Jerusalem. He took me to Peter the Apostle, who told the Christians to forget my part in the stoning of Stephen. I was now, like the Christians, a true

14

believer in Jesus Christ. Through Him forgiveness of sins is proclaimed to you, and life everlasting."

The Jews were stunned by the story. They had known nothing of the death upon the Cross of a man named Jesus. Some of them began to mutter. What was this man saying? It was too new, too daring. For centuries men had been told that a Messias would come and that they would be free, but they could not believe that this man in the road was telling them the truth. Who was he? How could he promise them a spiritual kingdom that would last forever?

The crowd grew angry. Seeing their disbelief, Paul spoke again. "Everyone who believes in Jesus Christ will be justified," he said.

From where he stood Timothy saw the cripple in the doorway lift his hand. He seemed to be calling for help. The boy rushed toward him. "What can I do?" he asked.

The cripple raised his arm. "Lift me! Lift me!" he cried. "I must speak to Paul."

Timothy struggled to raise the cripple to his feet, but he could not do it alone. "Help me!" he shouted.

It was Barnabas who came to his aid. The tall, strong stranger and the boy carried the cripple through the crowd.

"Where are they taking him? What does he want?" muttered the Jews.

The lame man was brought to Paul. As Paul spoke to him, his voice rang above the rising jeers of the

15

crowd. "This man has faith," he said. Then Paul gave the command, "Stand up on your feet."

"You are cruel," sobbed a woman. "That man cannot stand. He has been lame from birth."

Paul lifted his hands above the head of the cripple. "Stand upright on your feet!" he commanded.

Timothy, holding the shoulders of the lame man, felt swift movement beneath his hands. The cripple was rising. He was standing. Then, as the crowd gasped, he began to walk!

A shout rang out, a shout that echoed through the Jewish quarter, up the hill, past the camp and the houses and to the temple of the pagan gods.

"Hush! Hush!" warned Timothy's mother. "Do not let the pagans hear of this miracle. They will not believe us and they will kill the Jews." Her warning was too late; the pagans had heard the shouts.

II. Day of Sacrifice

Down the hill the pagans came, running, rushing, stumbling in their haste. Timothy's father, who still believed in the pagan gods, was the first to break through the excited mob. "What has happened?" he demanded.

There was silence.

He shook Timothy. "Tell me the truth," he thundered. "Who are these strangers among you and what have they done?"

Timothy, for once unafraid of his father's anger, pointed at the cripple, now standing erect. "See him," he said. "He can walk!"

The cripple walked, past Paul, past Barnabas, past Timothy's father. "I am healed," he said, and his eyes glowed with joy. "I am no longer helpless. I knew that God would one day send help to me."

"Who did this for you?" demanded Timothy's father.

The cripple pointed at Paul. "This man is the healer," he said.

To a pagan there could be but one source of help—the gods on Olympus, a mountain in Greece where the ancient gods came down to earth in the likeness of men. Now, knowing that a miracle had come to pass, Timothy's father turned toward the Romans. "The gods have come down!" he shouted, as the cripple leaped and walked.

Through the town and up the hill, other pagans

caught up the cry. "The gods have come down in the likeness of men!"

The Jews fell back as the pagans surrounded Paul and Barnabas. The roar of pagan voices drowned out the protests of the disciples of Christ.

"We are not gods," cried Paul.

"We are not gods," echoed Barnabas.

The pagans neither heard nor heeded them. To them, only one of their gods could perform this miracle. These strangers must have come from the home of the gods on Mount Olympus.

"The one who spoke to the Jews is surely Mercury," said a pagan, pointing at Paul. "We all know that the god Mercury is gifted with the power of speech."

"He must be Mercury," agreed another, "for only Mercury has the power to make men strong of limb and vigorous in health. Is not Mercury the god of boxing and running and throwing the discus?"

The pagans shouted at Paul, "Are you Mercury?"

"I am not Mercury!" Paul's voice lifted in sharp, angry protest. "I am not a god. I am—"

The excited crowd would not listen. They turned to Barnabas. Seeing his flowing beard, one pagan cried, "See! He is Jupiter!"

Timothy trembled. How could these people believe that this quiet stranger was Jupiter, whom they worshiped as the supreme god of light and rain and thunder and lightning?

"Jupiter is here!" screamed the pagans. "He has come to give us special protection!"

"Stop! Stop!" Paul called out to them, his arms outstretched in a plea for understanding. "We are not your gods of Greece and Rome. We are Jews who bring tidings of the death of Jesus Christ and of the salvation of man!"

None but the Jews listened to him. More men came rushing down the hill, through the town, up to the Jewish quarter, crying aloud, "The gods have come!"

Suddenly, high on the hill, the doors of the temple swung wide. The temple courts were in an uproar. A high priest stood by the open gates. "Why are you shouting?" he asked the people.

"Come! Come!" the pagans cried. "The gods Jupiter and Mercury are here!"

The great bronze doors of the temple gleamed in the sunlight as the pagans surrounded Paul and Barnabas and led them up the hill. "We are not gods!" Paul repeated over and over, his voice hoarse from useless protest.

The high priest, hearing the voice of the disciple of Christ, welcomed him. "What I have been told by my people is true. You are the first to speak, so you must be Mercury."

"And see this man," called out the pagans, bowing low before Barnabas. "See his height! See his beard! He is Jupiter!"

"I am not a god," shouted Barnabas.

The high priest would not listen. He saw the man's height and his beard. "You are truly Jupiter!" he said.

"We must make sacrifice," shouted the pagans.

The high priest, with a wide gesture of his hands, indicated the open bronze doors of the temple. "Bring me the sacred bulls," he commanded. "They will be slaughtered to do honor to the gods who have come down from Olympus."

The Jews, standing on the edge of the pagan crowd, tried to make themselves heard above the clamor. "No! No! These men are not pagans. They do not come from Olympus."

"Bring out the bulls!" shouted the pagans.

Timothy knew what would happen. The sacred bulls, wreathed in flowers, would be led from their shelter beyond the city gates. They would be brought to the altar of the pagan temple. There, with cere-

mony of fire and sword, the bulls would be killed in the hope of pleasing Jupiter.

"They must not do this," protested Timothy. Who, though, could stop the pagans?

It was Timothy's father who braved the anger of the unbelievers. He had once taught Timothy all the beliefs of the pagan world, but now he stood erect on the steps of the temple and cried out, "Wait! Wait until you hear what this stranger has to say! He is not one of us. He is not a god. He is a Jew who preaches salvation. Give him a chance to speak!"

"Traitor!" shrieked the pagans, and spat upon Timothy's father.

It was Timothy's mother who found the way. She turned to Paul and said, "There is but one proof to them that you are a Jew. Rush toward the high priest and tear your garments, lamenting. Then they will know."

Paul and Barnabas obeyed her. They rushed forward, tearing their garments in the Jewish gesture of sorrow. Then Paul spoke to the great crowd which had gathered. "Men, why are you doing this? We also are men, who tell you to turn away from these superstitions. . . ."

"He says we are superstitious," muttered the pagans, growing angry.

Paul, facing them, went on, "Turn to the living God, Who made heaven and earth and the sea, and all that is in them. . . ."

21

The pagans roared with anger, but Paul would not be stopped. He told them in a loud, clear voice of the living God Who sends rains and fruitful seasons. He spoke of the Son of God and the promise of eternal salvation. The pagans were not listening to him. From the inner temple came the sound of flutes. From the streets below came the roar of the sacred bulls being led to slaughter. One by one, their garlanded heads bright in sunlight, they were guided toward burning torches and gleaming knives.

Paul, in sadness, turned to Barnabas. "Is there no one in this colony, but the cripple, who believes me?"

"I believe you," said Timothy's mother.

Timothy clutched the hem of Paul's garment. "I believe you," he said, "and I would like to follow in the steps of the risen Christ."

Paul placed his hand upon the head of the boy. "Bless you," he said. Perhaps he knew at that moment that Timothy would be his first missionary.

The pagans went into the temple. The Jews turned toward their homes at the foot of the hill, ready to give sanctuary to Paul and Barnabas. At that moment, some Jews from Antioch who once had heard Paul speak and hated him, came through the city gates. They set upon him with stones and clubs.

"They're stoning Paul," cried Timothy, as he rushed, weeping, toward the disciple.

Nothing could stop the attack. The Jews from Antioch dragged Paul outside the city wall. They kicked him, they stoned him, and they beat him. They left him lying on the ground as dead. Timothy kneeling over him, heard him repeat a prayer, "Lord Jesus, receive my spirit." It had been the prayer of Stephen the Martyr; it would one day be the prayer of Timothy.

The hour of Paul's martyrdom had not yet come. He stood up, bruised and wounded. There was a long road ahead of him, but he would not travel the road alone. Timothy, the son of a Jewish mother and a pagan father, would be with him, in joy and in sorrow, preaching the eternal truth of the kingdom of God.

ARRANGING EVENTS IN ORDER

Did you follow the author's pattern of thinking as you read this story? The seven sentences given below tell about the main events in the story, but they are not in the right order. Read them over and then copy them on your paper in the same order in which they occurred in the story.

Timothy's father begged the pagans to listen to Paul.

Timothy and his mother went to the market place.

The high priest of the temple ordered the sacrifice of the sacred bulls.

Paul told the Jews the story of his life.

The pagans surrounded Paul and Barnabas, calling them Mercury and Jupiter.

Paul healed the poor cripple.

The Jews from Antioch stoned Paul.

23

Damascus Road

What day it was I cannot now remember,
  I only know the sky was very gray;
I do not know what road my feet were treading;
  I only know somewhere I lost my way.

I had not thought how long I traveled on it;
  I kept my way, not glancing up or down;
My soul was stirred, when looking I discovered
  How near I was to this Damascus Town.

I knew without a doubt there was no turning;
  That signpost spurred me onward like a goad,
And all my heart was held with this one longing—
  To reach the Light before me on this road.

SISTER M. DOROTHY ANNE, C.S.C.

Prisoner on Patmos

I. *The Boy Slave*

Day after day, month after month, Jason, a Greek slave, had dreamed of the day when he would win fame and freedom.

Once every four years the young men and boys from all over Greece met at Olympia for the Olympian games. There they tried their skill in wrestling, in running, in jumping, in boxing, and in many other contests. The winners received prizes while the crowds cheered. When they went home, their cities and towns held celebrations in honor of the winners. One of the most important events was the foot race, and that was the event Jason hoped to win.

One day, two years before, the governor of Patmos had sent for Jason when he was running on the beach with Marcus, the governor's son. Jason wondered why the governor wanted him and was greatly surprised when he was told that he was to go to the Olympian games with Marcus. Now he would have a chance to win his freedom, for anyone who was a victor at the Olympian games would surely be given freedom if he were a slave. So for two years Jason had been playing and running with Marcus, thus practicing for the famous foot race.

Now, crushed and miserable, Jason sat on the high rock which looked out on the sea. His dream was dead, for today Marcus had told him the truth. Jason was to accompany Marcus to Olympia, but Jason could not run in the race. Only freemen, children of freemen, could enter the games; and Jason was a slave.

"I hate Marcus now as much as I once loved him," the boy told himself, as he stared down on the beach where he and Marcus had so often raced together. "He has known, all this time, that I could not go into the race, but he has kept me from knowing it so that I might help him to win. But I will find a way to keep him from winning. If I cannot win, neither shall he!"

Jason was still deep in the bitterness of his disappointment when he saw Marcus come upon the beach below. The son of the governor, looking up at a soaring bird, saw Jason on the rocks. "Come on!" he cried.

From the tone of his voice Jason thought that Marcus was making fun of him. "Come on!" Marcus repeated.

Instantly Jason was on his feet. With unbelievable swiftness he sprang down the cliff until he stood beside Marcus. "You cannot do this to me," he said. Almost without thought Jason struck the other boy.

Marcus struck back at him. The blow staggered Jason, but did not knock him down. Jason hit Marcus wildly. He drove at him a blow so hard that it took him off his feet. Marcus went down on the sand.

"Perhaps you will win at the games," Jason cried, "but I have won here."

A heavy hand fell on Jason's shoulder. Jason looked to see the captain of the governor's guard. He was looking down at Marcus.

"Can you get up?" the soldier asked the Roman boy.

"Yes," the boy said, rising to his feet.

"Come with me," the soldier ordered Jason.

27

No one spoke until they had entered the governor's house and had come before the governor. Then, in quick words, the captain told the story of how he found Jason, the slave, beating the governor's son.

"Is that true?" the governor asked Jason.

"It is true."

"Why did you do this?" the governor asked.

Jason could not speak. His misery, his bitterness, and—although he would have denied it—his old affection for Marcus choked him.

"Why did you do this?" the governor repeated. Marcus stared at Jason. The soldier moved nearer, but Jason said nothing.

"I am sorry," the governor said, "that I must punish you. You are a slave, Jason, but I have tried to treat you as the friend of my son. You have lost that friendship by what you have done. I must treat you now as any other slave. You shall go to work in the iron mines!"

The iron mines!

In them men toiled night and day. In them men grew old and sick. In them men died. In them his own father had labored and died.

The work was cruelly hard. The work was slave's work. "I cannot do it, I cannot do it!" the boy's heart cried; but "You must do it!" his mind told him. With one last look at Marcus, a look filled with hate, Jason turned away, and followed the soldier from the governor's house. His real slavery had begun.

Often the boy Jason had seen the slaves on their way to and from the iron mines of Patmos. Never, until he was one of the sad procession, did he fully realize the misery of their lives.

Now Jason knew what it meant to labor from dawn to dusk. Now he knew what it meant to be hungry, to be thirsty, to be hot, to be cold, to be sick without care, to grieve all the time.

In the shafts of the mines no one spoke but the slave drivers. The slaves labored without speaking, without pausing. Only when they came out of the mines and made their way to their miserable huts did they have any chance to speak with one another. Even then Jason had no desire to talk with his fellows. "Slaves!" he thought, despising them even more than he despised himself.

Sometimes Jason would go up on the cliff overlooking the beach where he had run with Marcus. From its rocks he would look down on the governor's house. One evening, as he watched, he saw Marcus come out. "I hate you," Jason flung at the other boy. "I shall never forgive you!"

Jason thought he was alone, but to his surprise a voice sounded close to him. He turned around to see an old man standing near him. He had seen the man before, a slave going to and coming from the iron mines.

The man was, Jason thought, almost unbelievably old. Deep lines marked his thin face. Wrinkled skin stretched over his bony hands. It was his eyes, however, which caught and held the boy's gaze.

They were joyous eyes for a man so old. Dark and brilliant, they shone from hollow depths. They were eyes filled with love, friendly eyes, which even now cooled the anger of Jason.

"Why are you sad?" the old man asked the boy.

"Because everyone is so cruel, so unfair to me," the boy cried.

"What has anyone done?"

As if his words were a river released from the holding of a dam Jason poured out his story. "I cannot enter the Olympian games because I am a slave, and the only way I can win my freedom is by winning a race. They will keep me a slave forever!"

"No one can keep you a slave," the old man said, "if you want to be free."

"You are a slave," the boy exclaimed. "Can you make yourself free?"

"I am a slave under the Roman law," the old man said slowly. "I am no slave under the law of God. For, no matter how men drive my body, they cannot say what my soul shall do. Therefore I am free. You too shall be free. The Truth shall make you free. It is God's promise."

"Which god?" Jason demanded.

"The one Almighty God," the old man said.

"The one God?" Jason repeated. "Who is He? Where is He?"

"He is the Creator of heaven and earth. He is in the earth, the sea, the sky. He is everywhere."

"Back to work!" shouted the slave drivers. The old man put his bony hand upon Jason's head. "May the peace of Almighty God be with you," he said and moved to go. "I shall see you again," he promised the boy.

Jason was eager to hear more about the one true God and the freedom which He gives to the souls of men. He was thinking of God's command to love one another when he was sent to the shaft where the old man was working. The slave driver let him take his place beside the other slave, and, even though they could not speak one with another while they worked, they became friends.

Sometimes Jason helped the old man at tasks which he thought beyond his strength. Sometimes the old man helped Jason with skills the boy did not have. In time, they came to labor as a team.

After the work of the day was done, they often walked together toward the huts of the slaves. More than once Jason went back in thought to the Son of God, the Christ, Whom the old man had known.

"You saw Him? You heard Him?" he kept asking the old man.

"While He lived on earth I followed Him," the old man said. "I knew Him and loved Him."

"If Christ loves you, why are you a slave, left here to suffer?"

31

"Suffering for the love of Christ is not slavery," the old man said.

"It is not freedom," the boy insisted.

"To suffer for Christ wins eternal freedom," the old man told him.

"How can I find this freedom?"

"In God," the old man said.

"And how can I find Him?"

"Pray, my boy," the old man said. "Ask God to come to you. Ask Him for the Light to see. He said, *I am the Light.*"

The days dragged into weeks, and the weeks went from new moon to new moon. Jason still slaved in the iron mines of Patmos, while Marcus, the son of the governor, ran upon the sands of the shore, making ready for the foot race of the great Olympian games.

II. *The Freeman*

The old man was ill. Jason missed him at the mines, and, when work was done, he went to the little hut. There was little he could do for his friend. He had no food to give him. He knew no way to help him. He could only bring him a drink of cool water from one of the island springs. The old man blessed him. "May God be with you, my son," he said.

"How shall I know God?" Jason asked himself, as he went up the rocks to the cliff. "How will He come to me?"

For a while the boy stared out over the sea, picturing again the sailing to the mainland of Greece of the boat which would take Marcus to the games. In a little while—perhaps tomorrow—the boat would go. He would not even see it, but he would know that Marcus had gone. Then, one day, Marcus would return. Would he wear the wreath of olive, the crown of the victor? "My crown," Jason thought sadly, and gazed toward the mainland, which he believed now that he should never see.

As Jason watched, he saw someone come out on the beach below. By his walk Jason knew him. Marcus! "I hate him," Jason started to say, then suddenly he thought of the old man's words *Love one another*. "I must not hate Marcus," he said slowly, "but I hope he cannot go to the games."

From the height Jason kept watching the other boy.

He saw Marcus plunge into the water and swim far out into the sea. There had been a time when Jason would have leaped down from the rock, would have run across the sands, would have flung himself into the sea to swim with Marcus. In spite of their differences in rank, Marcus had been his friend. Now Jason could only watch him from the high cliff. Marcus, the son of the governor, was no longer the friend of Jason, a slave in the mines.

After a time Jason saw Marcus turn back toward the shore. The Roman boy was swimming with difficulty. What was the trouble? Jason stood up as he heard a cry from the sea, a cry from Marcus, a cry for help.

For an instant Jason hesitated. What should he do? Marcus had taken from him the chance to win the race, but Marcus was calling for help. Marcus had taken from him the chance for glory, but Marcus needed him. Jason thought of the old man's teaching. Quickly he made his decision. He would go to the boy who had been his friend. He would go to the boy he must love. With a shout he leaped down from the rock and ran across the beach. He could see Marcus struggling in the waves.

"Marcus, Marcus!" he shouted. "I am coming to you." Quickly he swam, stroke after stroke, until he came beside the drowning boy. He seized him and held him up. "Do not struggle with me," Jason said. "I am trying to save you. I am taking you to shore."

34

Inch by inch, Jason made his way toward the beach. Suddenly Marcus ceased struggling. Jason was tiring, and he wondered how much longer he could hold Marcus. "O God," he prayed, "help me now, help us both!" He battled his way through the rough waters. Then, exhausted, Jason dragged himself and the other boy upon the shore.

Arms reached out to them. Cries greeted them. "You have saved him," a voice said. Along the beach Jason heard the shouts. "Jason, the slave, has saved the son of the governor. Praise be to Jason!"

He turned toward Marcus. The boy's eyes were closed. "Is he alive?" Jason asked a man who was bending over the other boy.

"Yes," the man said, "he is breathing."

"I am glad," said Jason.

A great cry went up along the shore as other men came running. A crowd gathered around the boys, but parted again as soldiers pushed them away with lifted spears. "The governor is coming," someone said, and Jason struggled to his feet.

The governor lifted his son's head. "You are safe, Marcus," he told the boy.

"Jason saved me," Marcus said weakly.

"Jason?" The governor stared down at the slave boy. "You saved Marcus? After all you have said and done against him, against me? Why have you done this, Jason?"

"I cannot tell," the boy said, unable to say all that

he felt. How could he tell men like these that he had saved Marcus because he loved him, and that he had prayed to God for help to love all men?

Marcus held out his hand to him. "I thank you, Jason," he said, but his eyes told more than his words. "Will you be my friend again?"

"I will be your friend," Jason promised.

The governor put his hand upon the shoulder of the slave. "Jason," he said, "I did you an injustice. I let you work with Marcus when I knew that only freemen could enter the games. I will try now to do you justice. From this day you have your freedom. You are free to go with my son to Olympia tomorrow."

"Free?" Jason could say no more for joy.

"Tomorrow," said Marcus, "we shall sail together. Will you come with me now, Jason?"

"I will come back to you," Jason said, "but now I must go to see someone who helped me."

Jason ran headlong through the crowd, not looking back. The crowd parted to let him pass. Men murmured words of praise to him, but he did not hear them. His one thought was to tell the old man of his great happiness, to tell him how God's love had led him to save Marcus from the deep waters of the sea.

The old man was seated just outside the door of his hut. He was writing with his reed pen upon the roll of papyrus. He did not see Jason as the boy drew near to him. He was so weary that the papyrus fell from his hand to the ground.

As the boy stooped to pick it up, he read the word at the top of the roll. It was the name of the writer. Jason did not know then or ever that it was the name of an Evangelist, a name by which men would find the love of God through long ages. All he saw was one word in Greek. It read:

JOHN

How well do you remember what you read? Number your paper from 1 to 9. Choose the best answer to complete each sentence and write the answer after the number on your paper.

1. The Olympian games were held (a) every year; (b) every ten years; (c) every four years; (d) every two years.

2. The Olympian games were held (a) in the city of Rome; (b) on the island of Patmos; (c) on the mainland of Greece; (d) on the shore of the sea.

3. The most important contest of the Olympian games was (a) a boxing match; (b) the foot race; (c) discus throwing; (d) long-distance swimming.

4. Jason lived (a) on an island; (b) on a houseboat; (c) on the mainland; (d) on a peninsula.

5. Jason wished to win the race in order (a) to wear the olive wreath; (b) to gain his freedom; (c) to get even with Marcus; (d) to win a prize.

6. The old man said he was free because (a) he had lived and talked with Christ; (b) he was not a Greek; (c) he was old; (d) no one could command his soul.

7. In saving the life of Marcus, Jason was influenced by (a) the governor's reward; (b) the hope of freedom; (c) love for all men; (d) desire for praise.

8. Jason won his freedom through his (a) practice with Marcus; (b) work in the mines; (c) charity and love; (d) running ability.

9. John the Evangelist had written his name on the papyrus roll in (a) English; (b) Greek; (c) Latin; (d) Spanish.

The Right Must Win

Oh, it is hard to work for God,
  To rise and take His part
Upon this battlefield of earth,
  And not sometimes lose heart.

Ah! God is other than we think;
  His ways are far above,
Far beyond reason's height, and reached
  Only by childlike love.

Workman of God! Oh, lose not heart,
  But learn what God is like;
And in the darkest battlefield
  Thou shalt know where to strike.

For right is right, since God is God;
  And right the day must win;
To doubt would be disloyalty,
  To falter would be sin.

                    FREDERICK WILLIAM FABER

Lucia Finds the Way

I. *A Lamp in a Dark Place*

Lucia, daughter of a Roman senator, heard the slaves talking as she sat beside the fountain in the courtyard of her father's house. At first she paid no heed to their voices, but little by little the meaning of their words entered her mind, and she moved unhappily away from the sound.

What they talked about was no secret. Everyone in the great house knew that the senator, Lucius Terrinus, was planning to divorce his wife, Emilia. There was no real cause for this divorce, but under the law of Rome a man could leave his wife whenever he desired. Emilia's sorrow and the unhappiness of her two children, Lucia and Titus, seemed to have no influence upon Lucius. Even the slaves could see that in a little while the home would be broken.

What would they do? Lucia wondered as she stared at the splashing waters of the fountain. Their father would send her away with her mother. She would no longer see her brother Titus day after day. And, even if she saw Titus at times, would she ever see her father again?

Lucia began to weep silently. She did not see the slave girl, Anna, until she heard her voice.

"Why do you weep?" the slave asked. "See, the sun is shining. The birds are singing. The flowers are blooming."

"You know why I weep, Anna," Lucia said.

"I know," said Anna, "but I know, too, that you will find comfort."

"How can I?" the girl protested. "If my father sends my mother and me away, I shall never be happy again."

"There is hope," the slave girl said. "The new religion, the religion of Christ, promises hope to all people, but especially to women."

"What does it promise?"

"It promises what no other religion promises," Anna said, "eternal life to all who deserve it by their deeds in this world. It offers, too, a better life in this world. It worships only one God, Christ, Who died upon a cross in Judea. He was the Son of God."

"Where have you learned these things, Anna?" her young mistress asked.

A look of fear came into the slave girl's eyes. She glanced quickly around the room to be sure they could not be overheard.

"You can trust me," Lucia said.

"Peter teaches us," Anna whispered.

"Who is Peter?" asked the Roman girl.

"He is an old man whom they call the Bishop of Rome. He stays in a poor house in a poor neighborhood. We Christians go to him there. He tells us of the Son of God, Christ, Whom he knew and loved and followed. He tells us of Mary, whom God chose to be the Mother of His Son. Because Christ respected His Mother, all women are respected. Peter tells us this, and tells us of the love of Christ for us all."

"Would you take me to Peter?" Lucia asked the slave.

Anna hesitated. "Your parents would not wish you to go to him."

"They are not thinking of me," Lucia said.

Anna sighed. She started to refuse Lucia's request, then she saw the tears in her eyes.

"It may be dangerous for you to go there," Anna warned. "Your father will not wish you to go among Christians."

"If he sends me away from his house with my mother, what is it to him where I go?"

"You should not speak like that of your father," the slave girl said. "Peter teaches us to love one another."

42

"Take me to Peter, Anna," Lucia pleaded.

"If you command me," said Anna, "I will take you to him tonight."

That evening, as the sun began to set, the two girls slipped quietly from the house. Lucia drew her robe around her as she followed Anna, the slave, through the narrow streets. Dark-eyed children in the misery of hunger stared at her. There was food, of course, for the free poor of Rome, food given by the government on certain days; but it was never enough for their needs. Everyone in the district, men and women and children, looked with the eyes of poverty at the Roman girl.

The woman at the door of the little house where Anna led Lucia had a different look. The place was just as poor as any other in the narrow street. There was no furniture but the benches along the wall. The only light came from slender wicks set in two bowls of oil. But there was a feeling of peace and happiness in the place. Men and women smiled gravely at one another as Lucia and Anna found places near the wall.

"Are they all Christians?" Lucia asked the slave.

"We are all Christians," said Anna. "We have been baptized by Peter in the religion of Jesus Christ."

"Is Peter a great speaker, like men in the Senate?"

"Peter is not like the men in the Senate," Anna said. "You shall see for yourself what he is like. He is coming now."

Peter came at the moment, an old man in a simple

43

robe. He was not tall, but he had a sailor's strength. His face was open and honest. His shoulders were broad and his arms were strong. His hair and beard were thick and almost white. It was his eyes that Lucia noticed most. They were bright and clear, and they were kind eyes.

The old man's voice was kind as he spoke to the people in the poor room. Some of them he called by name, asking them of their families. He smiled at Lucia as Anna said her name. Lucia sat back with a sigh as he passed. "He makes me feel strange," she said to Anna. "I want to cry, and I want to sing, and I want to be good always."

Peter stood near one of the lamps as he began to speak. "This lamp," he said, "shines in a dark place, even as the word of prophecy shone in dark places before the coming of the Son of God. Now the Son of God has been among us. He has lived with us, taught us, and died among us. I myself was with Him, and saw and heard His great love for us.

"I am, as you all know, only a fisherman. All my lifetime I have made my living with my own hands. But Jesus Christ, Our Lord and Savior, took me to His heart, as He takes all mankind. I tell you this, not to praise myself, but to prove to you that He lived, that through me He sends you a message. It is a message of hope to all the world. *Love one another*, He told us. That is our Law and our Gospel."

For a moment, as Peter paused, no one in the room spoke. Then Lucia lifted her voice. "Where is He?" she cried. "Where is the Son of the one true God? Where can I find Him now?"

Peter turned to her. His eyes were soft in the light of the flickering lamp. "The Son of God no longer walks the hills of Galilee," he said. "He suffered and died there in Judea. Men often failed Him. Even I, who loved Him, once failed Him, but He understood. He knew I was but a man, and that men sometimes fail. He forgave me, and He trusted me. 'Simon Peter, dost thou love Me?' He asked me.

" 'Thou knowest, Lord, that I love Thee,' I told Him.

" 'Feed My sheep,' He said to me. And that, my daughter, is why I have come to Rome. For the people of Rome are His sheep, even as were the people on the hills near Nazareth. Love Him because He has first loved you!"

Peter ceased to speak. Tears ran down his weather-beaten cheeks.

"Oh, how I wish I had known this Christ!" Lucia thought. "He would help me now. He would perform a miracle. He would keep my father and mother together. He would let my brother, Titus, be with me. He would keep us a family, loving one another because we loved Him!" She caught Anna's hand as people around them began to rise from the benches. "I must talk with this man who knows God," she said.

Lucia overtook Peter at the doorway of the little hut. She told him that her father wished to divorce her mother. Quietly, tenderly, he listened to her. When she had finished, Peter placed his worn hand upon her shining head. "Pray, my daughter," he said. "Pray for strength. Pray for grace. Pray for wisdom. Always pray."

"How shall I pray to the one God?" the girl asked.

"The Son of God has taught us," the Apostle said. Then, with the stars of Rome over them, he taught her

> Our Father Who art in heaven,
> hallowed be Thy name . . .

"When you are ready, my daughter," he told her, "ready to take up the cross of Christ, for you will suffer for your faith, even as I have suffered and hope to suffer more, then come to me for baptism."

"Where shall I find you?" Lucia asked.

"Somewhere among these poor," said Peter.

II. Nero's Torch

Peter was away from Rome when the persecutions of the Christians began. Lucia's brother Titus was the first to tell her of the danger. "Our emperor, Nero, hates the Christians," he said. "Do they not fear him?"

"No," she said.

"I admire them for that," said the boy, "but wait till we see what Nero will do."

Sooner than they thought, Nero struck. He gave the order that all the houses in the poorest quarter of Rome be destroyed. Before the people could leave them, a great fire broke out. Hundreds of stucco huts burst into flame. Within an hour the fire had spread toward other quarters, destroying hundreds of homes. Even faster than the fire, the rumor spread that Nero had caused it to be started.

Nero answered the rumor by declaring that the Christians had started the fire and ordering that they be punished. "Down with the Christians!" rose the cry. "Find the Christians!"

The search went through the city, past the house where Lucius' family lived. Lucia, frightened, sought her brother. "I cannot find Anna," she told Titus.

"We must find her," said the boy.

Quietly, so that they would not disturb anyone, the boy and girl crept from the house. Their own street was calm, for the mob had passed; but they overtook the crowds as they went down the hill.

Men and women from all lands, slave and free, were pushing and pulling. Shouts of "Kill the Christians!" rose in a dozen languages. The soldiers of the emperor made their way through the crowd. With sword and shield they pushed ahead, forcing men and women and children against the walls.

"They are taking the Christians," rose the cry of the mob.

Titus lifted Lucia up to a place of safety on a garden wall as the crowd drove them forward. He sprang up beside her as a group of soldiers rushed past them.

"Where will they take the Christians?" Lucia asked him.

"To the gardens of Nero's palace," Titus said. "See, they are all going that way!"

"Let us go after them, Titus," the girl pleaded; but the boy shook his head.

"It will do no one any good now, Lucia," he said. "Let us go home."

"But Anna—"

"Anna may be home before us," Titus told her; but she knew that he had no hope.

They turned their backs on the whirling mob and found their way through streets still lighted by the flames on other hills. "Do you believe that the Christians lighted the fires?" Lucia asked her brother.

"I do not believe it," Titus said. "I doubt if Nero believes it, but to save himself from the mob he must blame someone. He will kill the Christians for that."

"I am glad that Peter has left Rome," said Lucia.

Lucia and Titus found Iris, the Greek slave girl, weeping bitterly at the door of the courtyard. "The soldiers took Anna," the girl said. "They seized her just as she came to our wall. They asked her if she were a Christian. She could have denied it, but she said yes."

—"What can we do?" Lucia cried.

Her cry brought her mother from her own rooms. "What is it?" she demanded. Because Lucia was weeping, Titus explained everything to his mother. "No one can do anything for Anna," Emilia said. "Go to bed now, both of you."

"Let us go to the emperor's gardens," Lucia pleaded. "We can at least see Anna there."

"You can do nothing," said Emilia.

"I can pray," Lucia thought.

49

As she turned away, her mother cried out, "You shall not leave this house tonight. It is madness. You can do nothing for those poor unfortunates."

"I must do what I can to help them, for I will soon be one of them," Lucia said. "I will be baptized a Christian as soon as Peter the Bishop comes back to Rome."

"Lucia!" her mother cried.

"I, too, will be baptized," said Titus, "for I believe the Christians worship the one true God."

"What will your father say?" Emilia wrung her hands in misery, but dried her tears.

"Our father will at least be proud that his children have courage," Titus said.

"Go to bed," Emilia told them.

"I cannot sleep," Lucia said.

"Nor I," said Titus.

They went into the courtyard and sat in silence while they looked up at the sky, still red with the glow of fires. The glow might come, they thought, from the burning quarter of the city, or it might come from the gardens of Nero. As the night slowly turned to dawn, the boy and girl realized that the quiet of their own neighborhood meant that the city crowds still gathered in the emperor's gardens, that the Christians were still being tortured there.

"Who will care for them when they are dead?" Lucia asked Titus.

"I do not know," he said. After a long time he

spoke again. "Anna is our slave. It is our duty to care for her body. We must go there to find it, Lucia, and carry it to the funeral pyre."

"The Christians do not burn the bodies of their dead; they bury them," said Lucia.

"Then we will bury Anna," said Titus.

Lucia and Titus went from the house so softly that only the slave Iris saw them go. The glow in the sky had died down. The cries of the crowd had been stilled. Rome was dark and still and sad as the boy and girl went, hand in hand, to the gardens of Nero. There were guards at the gates, but they let Lucia and Titus pass without lifting their spears to halt them.

The crowds were gone from the hills around the gardens. Gone, too, were the emperor and his court, from the balconies. Gone were the savage dogs, the lions, the tigers. Gone were the flames that had destroyed the crosses and the men and women who had hung upon them. Only the bodies of the martyrs were left in the gardens of Nero.

Slowly, filled with horror, Titus and Lucia made their way around the gardens. Pictures, too dreadful for memory to hold, flashed upon their sight. Men and women and children had suffered persecution and death for the sake of their faith in Jesus Christ. Only by prayer could Lucia continue on the search. "O God, help me to find Anna," she pleaded. She had no thought of her own peril in seeking the body of her slave.

As the light grew, she saw that there were hundreds of men and women in the gardens, seeking, as did they, for the bodies of the martyrs. Sometimes soldiers came from the gates to stop them. No one came to Titus and Lucia; and, after a long, long time, they found the body of Anna.

Lucia took off her white mantle and put it over the dead slave girl. Then she and Titus lifted the body and carried it out of the gardens into the street. Men and women, bearing burdens like their own, passed them on the way to the Christians' cemetery. No one spoke to them until they came to their own house. There, at the door, they met their father.

Lucius Terrinus looked at them sternly as they carried the body of Anna into the courtyard. "What is this?" he demanded. "Where have you been?"

"We have been to the gardens of the emperor," Lucia said. "Anna, our slave, has been martyred. Titus went with me to find her body."

"Why?" the senator asked.

"Anna was a Christian. She must have Christian burial, in the earth, not by fire." The girl's gaze flashed across her father's as if two swords met. "I too shall soon be baptized a Christian."

"And you?" Lucius Terrinus turned to Titus.

"I shall be a Christian," said the boy.

"Why?" demanded his father.

"Because the Christians are brave. Because the Christians are good. Because the Christians have what

52

we do not have, happiness and peace, even in death. Like Anna, they were glad to die rather than deny they were Christians," answered Lucia.

"You are good Romans," Lucius said to their amazement. "Courage is the ancient spirit of Rome."

Lucius Terrinus moved away from them and pointed to the body of Anna. "Tell the slaves to bury her in our family tomb. She had courage to die for something nobler than life. That is Roman virtue. There is little of it in Rome today."

As he left the courtyard, Titus looked after him. "Wonderful!" the boy said softly.

"It is more than wonderful," Lucia said. "It is, perhaps, the beginning of the answer to my prayer."

III. *The Appian Way*

To the freemen of Rome time sped pleasantly enough as they watched processions, gambled on the pavements, idled around the slave markets, attended games at the great arena. To the slaves of Rome time dragged as they worked without ceasing in workshops and on docks and at the hard labor of road building. To Lucia time seemed to stand still as she waited for the return to Rome of Peter the Bishop.

While she waited, the girl prayed constantly. She felt that God had already answered her in the decision of her brother Titus to join the Christians. Lucia and Titus hoped, but they were not so certain that their father would change his mind.

53

Days ran into weeks. Rumors rose high in Rome. Every Christian in the city was to be found and put to death. There were to be new tortures for those rich and powerful Romans who had joined the new religion, for the many converts who were already declaring their faith.

"Where is this Peter whom you call the Bishop?" Lucius asked with scorn. "Why is he not in Rome to suffer with the Christians?"

"He will come," Lucia said. "Peter will come back to Rome."

Iris, the Greek slave, had the first news of him. Peter had been in a far land when he learned of the fire and the persecution of the Christians. He had started westward, but winds and waves had delayed him, but soon he would be in Rome. It was Iris, too, who brought the news of Peter's arrival. "He is at the house of Marcus," she told Lucia. "He is baptizing there."

"We will go to him," Lucia told Titus; but before they went, she told her father that they were going to be baptized. Lucius said nothing to keep them from their purpose. He stared long at his daughter as he spoke. "I may not be able to save you from death."

"I shall not expect to be saved," she told him.

"What is it these Christians have?" the senator asked. "I should like to see this Peter."

"Come with us, Father," Lucia pleaded. "Come with us to the house of Marcus."

"We must go at once," the senator said, "for the emperor has already given the order for Peter's arrest."

If Lucia had hoped that the sight of Peter would change her father, she was disappointed. Her own heart was filled with joy at the sight of the Apostle. The waters of baptism, cleansing Titus and herself of sin, gave them a grace which made her hopeful that one glimpse of Peter would bring their father to their faith.

Lucius Terrinus met the bishop with grave courtesy, but he showed no sign of becoming a Christian.

"Do you know that you are in danger?" he asked Peter.

"I have long been in what you call danger," Peter said.

"Do you not fear?" Lucius asked.

"Who is there to harm me," the Apostle asked, "if I am eager for what is good? Even if I suffer anything for justice' sake, blessed am I."

"A strange man," Lucius said to his children, as they went homeward, "but a great one."

Two days afterward all Rome rang with the news of Peter's arrest. In obedience to the commands of Nero, soldiers had taken him from the house of Marcus. He had been tried before the city judge and sentenced to die. He was now in prison, awaiting his death.

"Can no one do anything for him?" Lucia asked.

"No one," said her father.

"Peter will escape," said Titus. "He escaped from prison once before in Antioch. He was chained between two soldiers, but an angel came to him. His chains fell away, and Peter walked out of prison, free. He will escape again."

"Perhaps," said his father doubtfully.

Again the slaves brought news of Peter. He had, they said, gone forth from the prison, which had never let any man escape. He had walked through the streets, crowded with freemen and slaves, soldiers of the emperor, and the chariots of the wealthy, and had gone to the Appian Way. He could have kept on in safety to the seaport. Instead, he had come back to Rome.

"Why did he return?" Lucia and Titus asked.

"Men say," Iris told them, "that, as Peter walked away from the city, a light moved toward him on the road. The light came near. Peter saw that within the light walked his Lord, the Christ, coming toward Rome on the Appian Way. Then Peter said to Him, 'Lord, where are You going?' And his Lord said to him, *If you desert my people, I am going back to Rome to be crucified again.* 'No, no!' cried Peter. The light faded. Peter turned back to Rome."

"Where is he now?" Lucia asked.

"In prison," said Iris, "awaiting his own crucifixion."

Lucius Terrinus heard the story to its end. "It is the final test," he said. "Nothing else in the world approaches this faith of the Christians. I can do no less than my children. I too will become a Christian."

"O Father, Father!" Lucia cried. Tears came to her eyes, tears of happiness that this answer to her prayers had come at last, but tears, too, of grief that Peter, who had brought this grace, should soon leave them.

"Life may no longer be easy for any of us," her father said, "but it will, at last, be happy. We owe that to you," he told Lucia.

"No," she said. "We owe it to Anna, who died in Nero's gardens, and to Peter, who will die, as Christ died, for the sins of men."

They did not see Peter die.

They did not know that one day the Faith Peter had preached and had died for, the Faith of his Lord and Savior, Jesus Christ, would circle a vast empire, an empire greater than Rome had ever known.

Even the followers of Peter, the men and women

and children who believed in Christ, the Son of the one God, could not see that.

Like Lucia, they only knew that they had set their steps upon the Way of the Cross and that the Way would lead them to a land brighter and fairer than the Seven Hills of Rome.

ARRANGING EVENTS UNDER MAIN HEADINGS

Three main divisions of the story you have just read are given here. Below them are listed eleven events of the story. Read each event and place a number in the blank before it to show in which main division it belongs. The first blank is filled to show you how to complete the exercise. (Do not write in this book.)

I. Peter Meets with the Christians
II. Nero Persecutes the Christians
III. Peter Returns to Rome

Events

_II_ The soldiers take Anna
____ Peter explains the Gospel of Love
____ The soldiers arrest Peter
____ Lucia learns the Our Father
____ Anna takes Lucia to Peter
____ Lucia and Titus are baptized
____ Lucia tells Peter about her problem
____ Peter escapes from prison
____ Lucia and Titus go to the gardens
____ The Christians are tortured
____ Lucius becomes a Christian

58

Our Lady's Dying

Peter from Rome and mighty Paul,
John and the holy Apostles all,
Came at the Master's loving call,
   To see Our Lady die.

This is the story handed down:
When came they unto the Holy Town,
Our Lady lay in her winding-gown,
   To watch her hour draw nigh.

Out from the sky an angel throng
Fluttered to earth with joyful song,
And bore her soul, awaiting long,
   Unto the Savior's hands.

Peter from Rome and mighty Paul,
John and the holy Apostles all,
Bore her out by the city wall,
   While sang the angel band.

Monsignor Hugh F. Blunt

The Day the Sisters Went Away

I. *The Cathedral School*

Lent came late in that year, but springtime came early. The March skies were high and blue. Robins sang in budding trees. White starflowers bloomed in the convent garden. There was even a cluster of yellow primroses on the plant in the kitchen window of the tiny house near the cathedral.

Through the doorway, between her bedroom and the kitchen, Maria saw the blossoms as she awoke on the Wednesday of Holy Week. The sight of them, as bright as gold, fell like sunshine on the girl's heart. The flowers were beautiful, Maria thought, the most beautiful things —except the pictures of Our Lord and Our Lady—in the house. All the family, her father and mother, her brothers and sisters, even the baby Stefan, loved the golden blossoms.

Sister Teresa had given the little primrose plant to Maria. "For helping me dust the desks and clean the blackboard," Sister Teresa had said.

Now, as she looked at the flowers in the gray morning light, Maria thought with joy of Sister Teresa and the cathedral school. Under the old law of this Eastern European country, now behind the Iron Curtain, this school was a public school, but it was taught by the Sisters and attended by the Catholic children of the parish. To all the children, the school was a pleasant place.

No one in the school loved it more than did Maria. She had always enjoyed the school, but in these days she loved it more than ever. It somehow seemed like a peaceful island in a sea of trouble. Soldiers who were not the soldiers of her own country marched in the streets or went from house to house, telling the people what they must do. There were songs they must not sing. There were meetings they must not attend. There were newspapers they must not read. The Communists had taken over this old Catholic city.

Only the church and the school stood against these invaders, and they, too, were in danger. Last night Maria's father had said that it would not be long before there would be no freedom at all in their country.

"Then what shall we do?" Maria's mother asked. Her father did not answer.

Sadness hung like a cloud over the city as Maria hastened to school on the Wednesday morning of Holy Week. Shops were closed, their windows boarded up. People who used to smile no longer smiled. Even the children did not laugh and shout.

"But everything will be all right," Maria thought, as she joined a group of her friends.

Later when she saw Sister Teresa in the school-room, she was not so sure that everything would be all right. Sister Teresa, who had always started the work of the school day in gladness, sighed now as she looked down at the children. Once, as Maria watched her during Catechism lesson, she saw tears in Sister Teresa's eyes. What had happened, the girl wondered, to hurt Sister Teresa? Was it anything they had done, these children whom she loved and who loved her?

Through arithmetic and geography and Bible history, the sadness spread. Only Sister Teresa knew its reason, but every child in the room knew that something was wrong. They all watched Sister Teresa uneasily and stood up in relief when the cathedral bells began to ring the Angelus.

"The Angel of the Lord declared unto Mary," Sister Teresa began.

"And she conceived of the Holy Ghost," the children answered.

After the prayer, they sped homeward. There Michael lingered over the rye pancakes, without butter or syrup, which their mother had made. Barbara stayed to play with the baby; but Maria, with braids bobbing up and down as she ran, hurried back to school.

This was the time when the children who lived near enough to hurry back to school could talk to Sister Teresa, the time when they could listen to stories of books and pictures, of music and far places. Of all the happy hours, it was the happiest for Maria. That little time was to her like a window through which she could look out upon a world she never saw at any other time, a wide world of beauty. She ran toward it now in happy expectation; but, as she saw Sister Teresa at the teacher's desk, Maria knew that the time today would not be happy.

Sister Teresa was weeping, not quietly as she had wept through the Catechism lesson, but heavily. Her right arm rested on the top of the desk, and her head was bent low over it. Her sobs shook her. She neither saw nor heard Maria until the girl spoke to her.

"Oh, dear Sister Teresa," she said, "don't cry like that!"

At the sound of the voice Sister Teresa looked up. Then, clenching her hands, she arose. Her voice still trembled with sobs, and tears still ran down her cheeks, but she said, "I did not mean to let anyone see me cry. You will forget, Maria, that you have seen me weeping."

"I shall try, Sister," the girl said. "Is it because of anything we children have done?"

"Oh, no, no," said Sister Teresa. "You are good children, all good children." She tried to smile then. "Even John, whom I have to scold every hour to make him behave. No, Maria, that is not the reason why I weep today. You shall know, all too soon, but I cannot tell you now."

She took out a white handkerchief and dried her tears as other children came into the room. "What do you want me to talk about today?" she asked Maria. "The story of Saint Elizabeth? Or the story of Bernadette?"

"Oh, the story of Bernadette, Sister," Maria cried, and listened breathlessly to the tale of that other child of poverty who had seen the Vision of Mary which the great of earth had never witnessed.

"That Vision of Mary," Sister Teresa said, "was Mary's gift, not to Bernadette alone, but to all the

poor and humble of God's world. God knows they need the Mother of God in days like these!"

Like the morning, the afternoon dragged by, slowly and sadly. Then, just before the closing prayer, a messenger came into the room. Mother Agatha, the school principal, directed that all the children were to go at once into the cathedral where the Bishop would speak to them.

In the big cathedral all seemed quiet and peaceful. The Bishop was standing at the sanctuary rail as Sister Teresa led the children of her room into the gray old church. It seemed to Maria that the Bishop looked worn and tired.

"Perhaps," Maria thought, "that is his Holy Week look."

But when the Bishop spoke to them his voice rang out as clear and strong as a bell. "My children," the Bishop said, "I have often had to do things which were difficult for me. Never have I had to do anything as difficult as what I have to do today.

"Some of you already know that our Catholic Faith, which was once the savior of our country, is now the victim of our country's laws. Cruel and godless men have made these laws. There will come a time, I believe, when this persecution will be ended; but that time has not yet come. Today we face the unhappy fact that these evil laws, made by evil men, threaten the life of our Church here.

"Under these laws the Church must suffer." His

voice trembled now in just anger. "Her children must suffer with her, but we all know it is better to die for Christ than to live without Him."

The silence in the cathedral was so deep that Maria heard the fluttering of pigeons outside the open window. "To die for Christ," her thought repeated the Bishop's words. The martyrs in Rome, the soldiers in the Crusades, the slaves of the Moslems, all these had died for Christ—but how did anyone die for Christ in times like these? As if he had heard the question, the Bishop went on.

"You children may wonder what this means to you. My deepest sorrow is that it means so much. You, our Catholic children, are the first martyrs under the new laws, cruel and unjust laws. For these laws are changing our schools so that the Sisters can no longer teach here. They are being sent away from our country."

It could not be, Maria thought wildly. Even if the Bishop, who never spoke anything but truth, said this, how could it be true? There could not be a school without the Sisters, the girl thought. "Oh, God, don't let this happen," she prayed; but, as she looked at the face of the Bishop, at the bowed heads of the Sisters, she knew that it was true.

The children walked out of the cathedral, two by two. They did not run as they came into the street. They did not shout. They did not even speak. They walked silently to the houses of the neighborhood; but as they went, many of them wept.

II. *The Yellow Primrose*

Maria thought that the Sisters would surely stay in the city until after Easter. There was no school on Holy Thursday, but on Good Friday word sped around the parish that the teachers had been ordered to leave on Holy Saturday night. They would not even be allowed to remain for the Vigil Mass of Easter.

"May I go to say good-by to Sister Teresa?" Maria asked her mother as they walked home from the cathedral after Good Friday Mass.

"Not now," said her mother. "You must wait until tomorrow."

"But she will be busy tomorrow. I must see her, Mother," insisted Maria.

"You may go to the railway station."

"But there will be a great crowd there, Mother!"

"There is no other way," her mother said.

On Holy Saturday morning Maria awoke, as she had awakened on Wednesday morning, to see the golden blossoms of the primrose plant. The one yellow cluster had become a great bouquet of golden blossom. The flowers caught the morning sunshine and lighted the poor room.

"Oh, it is lovely!" Maria thought. Then, suddenly, remembering that it was Sister Teresa's gift to her, she sighed. Would she ever see Sister Teresa again? Where would she find the stories, the pictures, the music that had given such joy to her?

The day dragged by slowly for Maria, but in the afternoon she and her family left the house to go to the cathedral where the people would pray for the Sisters. The street before the cathedral was crowded as they came into it. It looked as if everyone in the city had come as a tribute to the Sisters for whom it would be the last service in their native land.

Maria found a way to join the children already in the church. Sister Teresa no longer knelt behind the pupils of her own room. With other Sisters, she knelt in one of the front pews. Maria saw her head bent as the people made the responses in the Litany of the Saints. "Pray for us, pray for us, pray for us," Maria repeated as the long list of martyrs rolled upward.

The prayers were over when, for the first time, Maria saw the little bundles and packages in the pews before her. With a terrible pang of misery she realized that nearly every other child in Sister Teresa's room was bringing her a parting gift. On the seats of the pews there were books, little statues, bright-colored holy pictures, and fruit. Soon all the children would march behind the Sisters to the railway station. There they would move forward, as the Sisters waited, and give them these gifts. Everyone but Maria had something to give, some token of the love, the gratitude, they felt. Only she had brought nothing. She must go home now to find something.

Maria held her breath as she thought of the one spot of beauty in the little house, the primrose plant in the kitchen. The primrose plant, the golden primrose! She would miss it dreadfully, almost as much as she would miss Sister Teresa; but it was all she had to give to the Sister she loved, the Sister who had brought so much beauty and brightness to her.

Her father had already returned from the cathedral and was sitting in the kitchen with Stefan, the baby, on his knee. Behind them bloomed the primrose plant, her beautiful primrose. Suddenly she saw how bare the house would seem without it, but she held to her desire to give it back to Sister Teresa.

"Oh, Father," she cried, "may I take this plant to Sister Teresa as a going-away gift? She gave it to me, but I have nothing else to take to her."

"Surely, Maria," her father said.

The primrose plant seemed almost like a friend as she picked it up. "I'm sorry," she said. "I'm sorry to take it, Father, but I have nothing else to give."

Swiftly she ran through the narrow streets, following the road which the other children and their elders had taken to the railway station. She reached it just as the crowd was pushing forward toward the platform where the Sisters stood. She could see them, excited and unhappy, with the children already giving them their farewell gifts. Past sobbing men and women, Maria made her way to Sister Teresa.

"Oh, Maria, Maria!" Sister Teresa said. Then she saw the golden flowers of the primrose that the girl held out to her. For an instant she looked as if she were about to weep. Then she smiled, but she shook her head. "No, Maria," she said. "I cannot take this from you."

"But it is all I have, Sister," the girl cried, "and

even if you gave it to me, I want you to have it. I have nothing else to give you."

"You have given me far more than the flowers, Maria," Sister Teresa said, "in your wish to give them to me. I shall always remember that. It is the finest gift anyone could have brought. But the plant itself— you must keep that, Maria. I could not take it. I want you to care for it so that in another year it will bloom again. Will you remember me then and say a prayer for me?"

"I shall always remember you, Sister," the girl said.

Maria stood in the crowd on the platform as the Sisters moved into the train. Sister Teresa was the last to leave. She leaned from the railway carriage to wave to the children. Maria lifted the primrose plant high above her head. It was her good-by. She never saw Sister Teresa again.

71

CAN YOU FIND THE MAIN IDEA?

Read thoughtfully from your books the page and paragraphs indicated below. Then choose for each the best *main idea* from those listed.

Page 61, first paragraph—(1) Maria's love for school
   (2) The Communists in control (3) The peaceful school
Page 65, the entire page—(1) The silence of the cathedral
   (2) The martyrs in Rome (3) The unjust laws
Page 68, fourth paragraph—(1) The Litany of the Saints
   (2) The service for the Sisters (3) Maria and the children
Page 70, first paragraph—(1) Gifts for Sister Teresa
   (2) Maria's great worry (3) The railroad station

HOW MUCH DO YOU REMEMBER?

Copy these sentences on your paper. Decide whether the sentence describes *Peter*, *Paul*, or *John*. Then write the correct name in the blank before the sentence.

1. _____ He was told, "Feed My Sheep."
2. _____ He was blinded on the road to Damascus.
3. _____ He was a tent-maker by trade.
4. _____ He worked a miracle by healing a cripple.
5. _____ He was an Evangelist.
6. _____ He heard a voice say, "Saul, Saul, why dost thou persecute Me?"
7. _____ He was a fisherman by trade.
8. _____ He said, "Suffering for Christ is not slavery."

72

I See His Blood upon the Rose

I see His blood upon the rose
And in the stars the glory of His eyes,
His body gleams amid eternal snows,
His tears fall from the skies.

I see His face in every flower;
The thunder and the singing of the birds
Are but His voice—and carven by His power
Rocks are His written words.

All pathways by His feet are worn,
His strong heart stirs the ever-beating sea,
His crown of thorns is twined with every thorn,
His cross is every tree.

JOSEPH MARY PLUNKETT

II

Freedom

Trust in God

The Lord is my light and my salvation;
    whom should I fear?
The Lord is my life's refuge;
    of whom should I be afraid?
Though an army encamp against me,
    my heart will not fear;
Though war be waged against me,
    even then will I trust.
One thing I ask of the Lord;
    this I seek;
To dwell in the house of the Lord
    all the days of my life.

PSALM 26

Vexilla Regis

Vexil-la Re-gis pró-de-unt: Fulget Crucis mysté-

ri-um. Quo carne car-nis cónditor. Suspén-

sus est pa-tí-bu-lo.

The banners of the King move by,
The Cross of Christ lifts to the sky,
The Cross on which the Lord Most High,
Who made all flesh, was nailed to die.

Sanctuary

I. *The Ascension Day Fair*

The great Ascension Day Fair of Paris brought traders from all over Europe. The Crusades, those wars fought by Christians to win back the Holy Places of Palestine, had opened trade routes from Asia and Africa. Silks, jewels, gold and silver plates, rugs, spices and other goods from the Orient poured into the Mediterranean ports. These goods were then carried by the traders to the fairs of Italy, Germany, and France. Of all these, the fair at Paris, in France, was the largest, the richest, the brightest.

Once every year the road to Paris from the south of France was crowded for days with men and women on foot, on horseback, and in oxcarts, all on their way to sell their wares. At night fires burned brightly beside their tents. Minstrels sang, and people danced. It was all a wonderful sight to Angelo, the son of Carlo, an Italian trader. The boy laughed happily as he talked with his father.

"But wait till you see Paris!" Carlo told him.

"What shall I see there?" the boy asked.

"Oh, the market place, and the Cathedral of Notre Dame, and the new chapel which they call Sainte Chapelle, and perhaps, yes, perhaps you will see the king."

"Shall I see the plays?" asked the boy eagerly.

"Yes, Angelo, I hope we shall see a play."

They had some trouble two nights before they reached Paris. Another trader, Malek, tried to steal Carlo's fine spices. Carlo heard him moving around the shed where the spices were stored. By the light of a candle he saw Malek lifting a bag. Carlo rushed toward him, and Malek sprang at him, holding a knife high. The boy, Angelo, awakened by the noise, flung himself at Malek's legs and threw the thief to the floor.

"If you try that again, I shall take you to the traders' court," Carlo told Malek.

"I fear no court in France," said Malek.

"Every court in France has power since Louis has been king," Carlo told him.

The other man went out, muttering. Carlo drew Angelo near to him. "Go back to bed," he bade him.

"I will not leave you," Angelo said, "and I am thanking God that Malek did not hurt you." All through the night he sat beside his father, guarding the sacks of spices. "Soon," he thought, "we shall be in Paris."

Two mornings later, on the Feast of the Ascension of Our Lord, Angelo awoke in Paris.

It was still dark when Carlo called his son, but gray light began to come through the narrow window before they were ready to set out for their day's work. Carlo had stored his spices in the gatekeeper's room at the gate of the courtyard before he had taken his horse to a stable. Angelo helped to load the spices into a cart, and together the father and son dragged it toward the Square of Notre Dame.

The square before the cathedral was already crowded with people. The huge church, begun nearly a century before, was not yet finished but had long been used. Angelo stood in the gray light of the Paris dawn and stared at the power and beauty of the great cathedral.

Men and women, boys and girls, were moving toward the huge door of the cathedral. Their dress showed that they had come from many parts of France. There were people from England, Spain, Germany, and other countries of Europe in the crowd.

Among the crowd the boy saw Dominicans and Franciscans. Angelo longed to speak with them in his own language. They would understand him, would answer him as so few of the crowd could. They passed, however, moving swiftly toward the doorway of Notre

Dame, and were followed by long lines of students from the big University of Paris.

"When shall we go to Mass?" Angelo asked his father.

"You may go as soon as we have unloaded our goods from this cart at our stall here in the market place," Carlo said. "I shall have to wait until you come back before I can leave the stall."

They found the stall, vacant but cleaned for their use, in the space held for the sellers of goods from the Orient. In other stalls near their own they saw men setting up embroideries and ivories from China, swords from Damascus, rugs from Persia. The traders, most of them old acquaintances, called out friendly greetings to Carlo; but, to his terror, Angelo saw that Malek had the stall next to their own.

It was a stall so crowded with spices that Carlo's looked small beside it. "Never mind, Angelo," his father said, "we shall sell everything we have here to-day, for we ask much less for our goods than Malek will ask. If Malek had my stock of fine spices," Carlo added, "there is no telling what price he would demand from the people of Paris."

Even before Carlo and Angelo could put the spices in order, men and women had come to their stall. Already they had heard that Carlo would sell at honest prices. Angelo could see Malek watching them slyly as they waited on customers.

"Aren't you afraid?" the boy asked.

"I do not fear Malek here," said Carlo. "Run along now to Mass," he told the boy. "I shall go when you come back." He took out a bag of silver coins and gave Angelo two pieces. "Take this money, my son. You may need it for something before the day is over."

"Thank you, Father," the boy said. He looked back once at the stall as he crossed the cathedral square. Carlo was too busy to be watching him, but the boy waved his hand to his father. What happy hours they would have together, here in Paris, when their goods were sold!

The crowd outside the door of Notre Dame looked so large to Angelo that he wondered how all the people could get inside. But when another crowd came out from Mass and this one went in, the church was not filled. Even though the boy had seen the bigness of the church from the outside, he was not prepared for the greatness of Notre Dame from within its walls.

The height of the cathedral, lifting the faith and hope of man toward God, made the boy feel tiny, but the sight of the rose windows and the flame of candles surrounding the tabernacle made him feel at home. There was singing too, but he could not see the singers.

Devoutly the boy prayed as the priest at the far altar said the Mass. Through *Confiteor* and *Kyrie*, through *Gospel* and *Credo*, through *Offertory* and *Sanctus*, through *Pater Noster* and *Agnus Dei*, he forgot all but his nearness to God in this, the Sacrifice of the Son of God for the saving of all mankind.

"O God, I thank You for all You are to me," he said in a prayer of his own when the Mass was over.

The crowd, moving out from the vast church, swung along beside the boy into the square. The sun had come up over the roofs of Paris and had brightened the market place. Colorful awnings and banners waved in the breeze. The birds, which the people of Paris called the doves of Saint Genevieve for the girl saint who had once saved their city, fluttered over the stalls. People were talking and laughing as they moved toward the fair.

A group of Dominicans, in their white-and-black habits, passed Angelo. The boy stepped aside for a big young man among them, but the young man bowed to him with courtesy and waited for him to go his way.

"You are too humble," another friar said in Italian.

"No one can be humble enough," said the big young Dominican.

He also spoke in Italian. Angelo's heart leaped at the sound. To think that here in Paris men could speak his language! Angelo turned to a sandaled Franciscan at his side.

"Who is that Dominican?" the boy asked and pointed to the big young man.

The Franciscan smiled. "Wherever he goes, people ask that," the friar said. "He is Thomas Aquinas, from Italy, and he has come to Paris to study."

"Is he the Thomas who is cousin of the king of France?" the boy asked.

82

"Yes, he is," the Franciscan said. "He is one of the great nobles of Italy, but here in Paris he lives like any Dominican student."

Angelo pushed his way through crowds of people toward the stall where he knew his father would be waiting. If he hurried, perhaps his father could go to the next Mass. The crowd grew greater as the boy went on. Near the stalls it was a pushing mob. People around him were shouting and yelling. Angelo could not understand the French cries, but he knew that something was happening to excite the people. What was it? he wondered, as he forced his way toward his father's stall. Had anything happened to his father?

His anxiety drove him through the mass of people until he came in front of the spice booth. There he saw his father standing with hands outspread, his face dark

83

with misery. Before Carlo, on the pavement, lay the body of Malek. Angelo's father was speaking in French, but somehow his son knew that he was saying something about this man who had been his enemy.

"O Father!" the boy cried and rushed up to him.

Carlo put his hand upon Angelo's shoulder. "Malek is dead," he said. "When I was alone he rushed at me, his knife in his hand. I twisted his arm to save my life. The knife cut me as it fell. I struck at him so that he could not pick it up again, and he fell there. These people say I killed him, but I swear to you, my son, that I had no thought to take his life."

"He killed him!" someone in the crowd shouted. "The spice dealer has killed Malek the trader!"

"My father did not intend to kill Malek," Angelo cried, but no one understood him.

"Call the soldiers," the crowd began to cry. "Call the soldiers of the king!"

"I did not kill him," Carlo said. "I struck him, but I had no weapon. The knife was his. I ask only justice."

"The soldiers will give you justice," someone cried.

"Let us not wait for the soldiers," another voice shouted. "Let us give him our own justice!"

"No, no!" Carlo cried, but the crowd began to move upon him. Swiftly he turned to Angelo. "Here," he said and held out to him the leather sack of coins he carried. Someone in the crowd reached forward and snatched it from the boy.

"Follow me!" Carlo called to his son and plunged toward a place where the crowd had thinned.

"Get him, get him!" rose the cry. "Get the murderer!"

Like a frightened fox dodging the hounds, Carlo ran, with Angelo at his heels. Around the edge of the crowd they made their way. In and out of stalls they ran while the cry rose, "Get him!"

As they turned toward the Cathedral of Notre Dame, Carlo called to Angelo. "Sanctuary!" he said. "I will seek sanctuary, Angelo." He rushed toward the door of Notre Dame. "I shall find it here!"

"Not here!" Angelo cried. "There are soldiers already standing beside the door. We must find another church."

Through a narrow street, past houses and courtyards raced the man and boy. Sometimes one of their pursuers almost overtook them. Suddenly, at the end of the street, Angelo saw a little church with a high steeple, a church which seemed like a gray candle pointing to the sky. Through the open door he saw a long room, rich with paintings and carved wood. It was the lower chapel of Sainte Chapelle.

"Here!" the boy cried to Carlo.

"Here!" said his father and ran into the church.

Carlo had reached the altar when the crowd came to the door of the church. "Sanctuary!" he cried to them. "Sanctuary!" With arms outspread he stood at the foot of the altar.

Swiftly the crowd filled the nave of the church. Men pressed up toward Carlo and Angelo, but no one dared set hand upon them. The right of sanctuary was more than law. It was sacred to the man who claimed it. For thirty days he could stay within it in safety. Church and king must protect him through that time. For thirty days, at least, Carlo was safe.

Slowly, in noise and confusion, the crowd moved away from the church.

"Where are we?" Angelo asked his father. "What is this church where no Mass is being offered on this Ascension Day?"

"We are in Sainte Chapelle," said Carlo. "This is the church King Louis has built for the Crown of Thorns. Only once a year, the king has said, is it to be open for service. There are two churches under this roof, the upper church, where the Crown of Thorns is guarded, and the lower, where I am in sanctuary. We may go to the upper church by means of that narrow stairway behind you. The king and his court enter from the palace. This lower church has the only door to the street. Luckily today the door was open. Here we shall wait and pray for justice."

"But what will you do for food, Father? And for the help you will need?"

Carlo lifted the boy's chin in his hands. "Listen to me, Angelo," he said. "My life now depends upon you. You must bring me food. You must find someone to take my cause to the king of France. There is no one but you to help me."

"I will do it, Father," Angelo said. But, he wondered how he should be able to do anything. With only two silver coins, with no knowledge of French, with no friend in Paris, how could he save a man hunted by the crowd, even a man in the sanctuary of Sainte Chapelle?

Again and again the boy went from the sanctuary to the door, hoping each time to find that the last of the angry mob had left Sainte Chapelle. Three men, who lingered long after the others had gone, still stood watching the door that led to the street. At last they went away, and Angelo could see no one but the men who were at work near the building.

"O Christ, Who wore the Crown of Thorns," he prayed, "help us, Your children, in this, Your shrine!"

II. *The Cousin of the King*

With a heavy heart Angelo went out from the king's chapel to seek aid for his father.

The fair was still being held in the square before Notre Dame, but Angelo dared not go to the stalls. His father had friends, the boy knew, among the traders; but most of them were, like himself, strangers in Paris and would fear to do anything to aid a man in sanctuary. Some of them would surely take care of Carlo's stock of spices and of the horse that Angelo had ridden into Paris. No one, however, would risk being seen with Carlo's son while Carlo stayed in the shelter of the church.

Slowly, cautiously, the boy made his way toward the square through narrow streets that were hardly more than lanes. Between tiny gray houses and past locked courtyards he walked, looking over his shoulder at every turn to see if he were being watched. He knew that he was near Notre Dame, for he could sometimes see the great towers and hear the sounds of the crowd in the square, but he had to keep away from the square itself as he sought someone who might help his father.

Through a street so narrow that it seemed an alley, Angelo caught sight of the crowd in the square. He crept toward it, keeping near the walls of the houses, until he could see the stalls, the puppet shows, the tumblers and jugglers, and the minstrels.

People were beginning to come away from the

square. Angelo dared not stay in the neighborhood. Sadly he turned back toward Sainte Chapelle. On the way he went into a tiny shop. There he bought a long thin loaf of bread and a bottle of wine. Then, keeping back his tears, he returned to his father.

A little crowd of men and women stood before Sainte Chapelle. They were admiring it with such close interest that they did not notice the boy, and he slid around the side of the lower church toward the small door which had saved Carlo. There were workmen near that door who smiled at the boy as he passed. If the church gave sanctuary for thirty days to a hunted man, who were they to deny entrance to this boy?

Carlo was on his knees before the altar when Angelo came to him. Quietly, the boy knelt beside him. When Carlo arose, Angelo followed him to the side of the sanctuary. The boy gave him the wine and the loaf of bread, but he shook his head when his father asked, "Did you find anyone to help us?"

"No," replied the boy sadly.

"You must find someone," Carlo cried. "The traders will stay here only for a little while. When they have gone, there will be no one who knows me. You must find a way, Angelo, to sell the spices and get money for us. You must find someone to plead my cause in the courts when I have to leave this shelter."

"But I can't speak French, Father."

"You must find someone who knows Italian, Angelo. I have no one but you, my son."

89

Slowly Angelo went out again into the streets of Paris. From the square of Notre Dame he could hear the sound of music and the shouts of the crowd, but the city looked cold and dark and lonely to him. Then, growing desperate, he tried to go into the square toward the stalls of the traders, but someone recognized him, and he ran to hide in a little courtyard.

When it was nearly dark, he came out again. He went from inn to inn, looking for someone he might know. He found no one. Torches blazing in the square showed that the fair was still being held there. Twice he met traders who knew Carlo. Twice he asked their help. Twice help was refused him.

He found Sainte Chapelle again by its high-pointed steeple, a finger pointing to God. For a moment he was seized with terror when he saw that the workmen's door was closed. But the door was not locked, and he crept through the darkness to the altar steps. There, upon them, he found Carlo praying. Angelo told his father of his failure to find help; then, worn out by weariness and worry, the boy fell asleep.

The next morning was the first of many mornings of the same pattern. Day after day the boy went out from Sainte Chapelle to buy food with the little money he had and to look for someone to bring help to Carlo. Day after day he came back disappointed. The traders had gone to a fair in a far-away city, and no one in Paris knew Carlo. No one in Paris could understand the few questions in Italian the boy dared to ask.

Three days before Pentecost, Angelo was watching some people going into the Cathedral of Notre Dame when he heard, close to him, a voice speaking in Italian. He turned around quickly to see two Dominicans waiting, as he was, for the company to pass by. One of them was, the boy saw, a thin little man. The other was the tall, big young man whom the Franciscan had pointed out to him as Thomas Aquinas, cousin of the king of France.

For an instant Angelo hesitated. How dared he speak to a man so great, so wise, so powerful, a man who was one of the great nobles of Europe? Then, looking up, he saw the kindness in the Dominican's gray eyes, and he cried out, "Will you please help one of your countrymen who needs help?"

"I will help anyone who needs help," the big young man said. "Who are you, and what can I do?"

Swiftly Angelo poured out his story. Thomas listened in silence until the boy came to the end.

"Is your father in Sainte Chapelle now?" he asked.

"Yes, he is there in the lower church," Angelo cried. "There, and only there, is he safe; and he will be safe only a little while."

"He did not mean to kill Malek?" Thomas asked.

"He is not guilty!" cried Angelo. "He struck him to save himself. My father was only defending his own life."

"I will go with you," said Thomas.

"Thomas Aquinas forgets everything but good thoughts and good deeds," Brother Reginald told Angelo.

"What else is there worth remembering?" asked Thomas.

He took Angelo's trembling hand in his own big hand as they turned toward Sainte Chapelle. For the first time since the Mass at Notre Dame Angelo felt safe. Here, at last, in this strange city, he had found a friend. He could not yet know how powerful a friend Thomas Aquinas would be to him, but he already knew the truth and strength of this young friar. He moved a little closer to Brother Thomas and smiled up at him. Brother Thomas smiled back, and Angelo sighed in the first happiness he had known in days.

The workmen near the door of Sainte Chapelle bowed to the Dominicans. One of them smiled at Angelo. "So you have found help?" his smile said as plainly as words. From the steps of the altar Carlo, pale and worn, saw them coming.

"Will you help me?" he cried in French.

Brother Thomas answered in Italian. "We have come to help you," he said. "Tell us your story."

As Angelo had done, Carlo poured out the tale of his misfortunes without stopping until he had come to the end. The friars listened closely.

"Do you think he tells the truth?" Brother Reginald asked Thomas.

"I believe him," Thomas said. "Malek tried to ruin his business because this boy's father, Carlo, is an honest seller of goods. When Malek could not ruin this man, he attacked him. Carlo only tried to save his own life. He did not intend to kill the other man. He will pay for that misfortune in grief all the days of his life, but he should have a fair trial."

"Where will he get it?" asked Brother Reginald. "He is a stranger here in Paris."

"He will find justice in the king's own court," Thomas said.

"But you cannot take him to the king," Brother Reginald declared. "He is not safe except here in sanctuary."

"No, but I can bring the king to him," Thomas said.

"Brother Thomas!" the other friar cried. "How can you do that?"

"I can take to the king the one who brought me here today—this boy."

"But the king is at his palace in the country," said Brother Reginald.

"Then we shall go there," said Brother Thomas. "Brother Reginald, you stay here with Carlo. Angelo will come with me."

"Do you think the king will help us?" asked Angelo.

"He is greater than any other man in France," said Brother Thomas, "not because he is the king, but because he is good and holy. Once, when he was a boy, his mother, Queen Blanche, said to him, 'I would rather see you dead at my feet than guilty of a mortal sin.' Louis has always remembered that. His whole life has been a life of goodness. He has built schools, churches, and hospitals. He is kind to the poor. More than that, he is just to everyone. He holds a court, not for the nobles of his court, but for people like your father. I am sure he will help us."

The walk to the summer palace was long. The May sunshine grew hot. Angelo, matching his steps against the large firm steps of the big Dominican, grew tired, but he said nothing.

Soldiers stood at the gate of the king's palace, but they lowered their spears as they saw the friar. In the shady grove lords and ladies in beautiful silks and velvets and muslins moved down pleasant paths. One of the courtiers bowed as he passed.

They went through the grove toward a great oak tree where the king held his court of justice. Lords and ladies stood a little way back from a table beneath the tree. Behind the table, upon a high-backed chair sat a man, slight and frail, but with the same look of dignity and power which marked Thomas. He looked up as they came near the table.

"Ah, Cousin Thomas," he said, "what cause of justice brings you here today?"

"This boy will tell you, sire," Brother Thomas said. "Tell the king just what you told me," he directed Angelo. For a moment the boy could not speak. "Do not be afraid," Thomas said, "King Louis wants only the truth."

"It was this way, sire," Angelo said. He told in Italian, as he had told Thomas, the story of Malek's desire to make Carlo join him in raising the prices of the goods they were bringing to the Paris fair. He told of the finding of Malek in a shed, stealing spices from Carlo's sacks. He told of Malek's attack upon Carlo there. He told of what he had seen when he came from Mass at Notre Dame on Ascension Day. "My father did not mean to kill Malek," he said.

The king turned to the Dominican. "I should like to hear the story from Carlo himself. Bring him to me tomorrow."

"Even for you, he cannot come here, sire," Thomas said. "You can free him after you have heard him, but until he has been freed, he dare not leave sanctuary."

"And he is in Sainte Chapelle?" the king asked. "My beautiful Sainte Chapelle which I have said should be kept so sacred that it is to be opened to the people of Paris only once a year?"

"How can it be too sacred to give justice to a child of God?" Brother Thomas asked.

"You are right, Cousin Thomas," the king said. "Tomorrow I will go to Sainte Chapelle with you."

"But my father, sire? He is alone, there in the church."

"No," said the king. "He is not alone. Brother Reginald is with him. Stay here with Brother Thomas. We will go to Paris tomorrow."

They went to Paris the next day, with soldiers and courtiers, with lords and ladies who rode behind the king's carriage. Angelo rode with Brother Thomas, but this time he paid no attention to the procession. He could think only of his father, waiting there in Sainte Chapelle. What would the king say to him? What would the king do? Refuse him a hearing in his own court? Send him to the Court of the Traders? Let him come out of sanctuary to meet a mob that sought his life?

Angelo could answer none of these questions as he went with Brother Thomas into the lower church, while the king and his court went into the palace on their way to the upper church of Sainte Chapelle. Carlo stared at the friar sadly as Brother Thomas led them up the little stairway. Angelo fought his tears as they moved upward, but even in his sorrow he gasped at the beauty and grandeur which met their eyes as they came into the upper church.

Through the door from the royal palace came the king, his courtiers, and the soldiers of the royal guard. The courtiers moved into the nave of the church, while the king sat upon a chair near the altar. Brother Thomas walked forward with Carlo and Angelo. Two soldiers stepped aside to let them pass. Angelo could not speak a word; but his heart leaped in hope as the king motioned to Carlo to begin his story.

Carlo told it clearly, just as he had told it to the friars. King Louis listened intently, asking questions here and there. "How do I know that you speak the truth?" he asked in Italian.

"My son knows that I am telling the truth," said Carlo. "Ask him, sire."

"Your son told me the same story yesterday," nodded the king.

"I speak the truth," cried Carlo.

"Will you swear to that?" asked the king. "Will you take an oath upon the Mass Book that this is the truth?"

"I will swear," said Carlo. He lifted his hand as Brother Thomas held the Book. He solemnly spoke the words of the oath. "This is the truth," he added, "as God is my judge."

"I believe you," said the king. "I believe, with Brother Thomas, that you did not intend to kill the trader. This was not murder, but you must pay some penalty. In your own country you are not a poor man. Will you promise me to give aid, great aid, to the children of God who need it?"

"I promise," said Carlo.

"You are free," said Louis. "You may go now, by order of the king."

Carlo knelt to kiss the king's hand, but Louis waved him toward Brother Thomas. "Not mine," he said, "but the hand of him who has saved you."

"God has saved you," said Brother Thomas. "You must find a way to thank Him."

"I have found a way, Brother Thomas," Carlo cried. He faced the altar of the sanctuary. "God willing," he said, "I will go with King Louis when he sets out from Paris to win back the Holy Places from the Saracen!"

"Pray for me," the friar told Carlo, "when you come into Jerusalem."

Together father and son went out from the upper chapel, down the little stairs, and into the street. As they left, Angelo looked back at the tiny building. Then he spoke to his father. "I think," he said, "Sainte Chapelle is the most beautiful church in the world."

NOTING CAUSE AND EFFECT

In Column I are listed some *reasons*, or *causes*, from the story you have just read. In Column II are listed the *effects*, or *results*, of the causes. Number your paper from 1 to 7 and copy the statements in Column I. Then choose from Column II the statement that tells the result of that cause and write its letter in the blank at the left of the statement.

Column I. Causes

1. __?__ the Crusades opened trade routes from Asia and Africa.
2. __?__ they had heard of Carlo's honest prices.
3. __?__ the sun had come up.
4. __?__ the friars spoke in Italian.
5. __?__ Malek had attacked him with a knife.
6. __?__ he was worn out by weariness and worry.
7. __?__ no one dared lay hand upon those who sought safety.

Column II. Results

a. The market place grew bright because

b. Angelo fell asleep because

c. Goods from the Orient poured into the Mediterranean ports because

d. Carlo twisted Malek's arm because

e. Men and women came to Carlo's stall because

f. Angelo's heart leaped at the sound of the friars' voices because

g. The right of sanctuary was more than law because

Crusade

The kings come riding home from the Crusade,
  The purple kings with all their mounted men.
They fill the street with clamorous cavalcade.
  The kings have broken down the Saracen.
Singing a great song of the Eastern wars,
  In crimson ships across the sea they came,
With crimson sails and diamonded dark oars
  That made the Mediterranean flash like flame.
And, reading how in that dark month the ranks
  Formed on the edge of the desert, armored all,
    I wished to God that I had been with them,
When Godfrey led the foremost of the Franks,
  And the first Norman leaped upon the wall,
    And young Lord Raymond stormed Jerusalem.

Hilaire Belloc

The Bell of Canterbury

I. *The Bell Is Made*

On a summer day in the year of Our Lord twelve hundred and fourteen a procession of pilgrims walked through the streets of Canterbury town as Alice Garland came out of the Garland cottage in the shadow of the new cathedral.

Every day men and women from all over England walked or rode to Canterbury. They came to pray in the chapel where Thomas á Becket had been murdered by soldiers of the king because he had defended the rights of the Church of Christ. The Church had declared Thomas a saint, and the people of England gladly came to do him honor.

Alice Garland was thinking neither of the pilgrims nor of Saint Thomas as she went through the gate into the garden of the cathedral. She was taking lunch to the workshop where her father and her brother Giles were working, with other men of the Guild of Our Lady, on the making of a bell. She was a little early on her errand; for, although a girl of thirteenth-century England was supposed to be interested only in sewing and embroidering, Alice liked nothing better than to watch the men who labored to finish the great bell for Canterbury Cathedral.

The Garland men were all bellmakers. A Garland had been a bellmaker before he had gone on the first of the Crusades, those great wars of the Christians to win

101

back the Holy Places of Palestine from the enemies of Christ. Alice's father, Roger Garland, had learned to make bells before he had gone on the Third Crusade with Richard of the Lion Heart. Richard had died in France, and his brother John was now king. "A bad king for England," said the men of Canterbury. But bad kings or good kings, the Garlands kept on making bells.

Alice heard the sound of hammers on metal as she went toward the workshop. *Clang, clang, clang* some of them sounded; and *cling, cling, cling* others of them answered. To Alice this sound was as sweet as the music of the choir in the cathedral. One day this bell of Canterbury would ring out its message of faith and freedom over the town and over the whole countryside.

"Cling-clang, cling-clang," the girl sang, as she walked through the cathedral garden.

Alice's joy died as she came to the door of the workshop and heard her father's voice raised in anger. "How can we go on?" Roger Garland was shouting. "How can we keep up our guilds if the king forces us to pay these high taxes?"

"Easy now, easy, Master Garland," another voice said. "There are worse things than paying taxes to the officers of the king."

"But these are unjust taxes," Alice heard her father say. "King John puts these taxes on our guilds because the guilds grow too strong for his liking. He wants to crush us."

"The king can crush us," a third voice, an old man's voice, declared. "King John has a way to win his will. See how he has made prisoners of the sons of the barons who have fought him! No, Master Garland, there is no use in going against the king."

"You said that, Parker," said Roger Garland, "when King John, against the law of the Church, tried to keep Stephen Langton, our Archbishop, out of England. The Pope was firm with the king and sent Langton to us, and so here today we work for Stephen Langton, Archbishop of Canterbury, the most just man in all England."

A murmur of voices then rose in the workshop in praise of the Archbishop, who had left a life of quiet study to take on a difficult and dangerous work as Archbishop of Canterbury. All the voices ceased as Alice reached the doorway of the workshop.

"It is only I, Father," the girl said.

Someone laughed, and the voices rose again. "Welcome, Alice Garland. . . . You are no soldier of the king. . . . No tax-collector, either. . . . That is a big basket for one maid to carry. . . ."

All the guildsmen were standing around the great bronze bell upon which they had been working. The bell was as beautiful to see as it was glorious to hear. Around its rim was set a procession of knights, riding splendid horses and bearing fine crosses. The bell glistened almost as brightly as gold. The workmen of the Guild of Our Lady, the guild of the metalworkers, could be very proud of their work.

"It is lovely," said Alice. She put down her basket and touched the bronze. "Will it soon be finished?"

"In a little while," her father said, "you will hear it ringing from the tower above us."

"It will be a great day for our guild," her brother said, "when our bell of Canterbury sounds the glory of God."

"It will be a great day for England," his father said, "and for her free men."

The great day seemed far off, however, as the demands of King John pressed down upon the bellmakers of the Guild of Our Lady. The struggle grew until the time when the officers of the king came to the workshop in the garden of the cathedral. They took Roger Garland prisoner because, as master of the guild, he refused to pay unjust taxes which the workers could not afford.

"The men of the guild will get him out," her brother Giles told Alice. However, the weeks went by, and Roger Garland remained in his cell.

Alice tried to comfort her mother. "Do not cry, Mother dear," she said. "Our Blessed Lady will hear our prayers."

Every day Alice knelt before the altar of Our Lady in the chapel of Saint Thomas á Becket. "Dear Mother of God, please send my father home to us," the girl prayed. Then, remembering how Saint Thomas had, on this same spot, given his life for their Faith, she always added, "And keep my father true to what he believes is right, even though he has to suffer for his belief."

When Alice came from the chapel, she went, as she had always done, to the workshop. The men were still working there, but no longer upon the bell. Alice moved her hands over the figures on the rim of the bell. "What a glorious sound it will make," she said, "when it rings in the high tower!"

"Yes, glorious when it rings, Alice, but the bell will never ring until our master is free," the men said. They had stopped work on the great bell when Roger Garland was arrested. "We will not finish this bell until we know that our master will be free," they declared. They continued to declare it, as every day they worked on other tasks in the shop.

"When will my father be tried in court?" Alice asked them one day.

"Perhaps he will never be tried," old Parker said.

"Doesn't every Englishman have a right to a trial by jury?" Alice asked the old man.

"He has a right," Parker said, "but King John does not respect that right."

"Do you mean," the girl asked, "that my father may be kept in prison without ever being given a trial?"

"Your father may be blessed if he is only held in prison," Parker said.

"What do you mean?" cried Alice.

The other guildsmen tried to warn Parker to silence, but the old man answered her. "I mean that by order of the king your father and the other men in prison may be put to death without trial."

"Put to death? My father!" Alice cried out. "That cannot be! That is not the law of England."

"Yes, but the law of England," old Parker said, "is being broken by the king of England."

"But my father! And the other men! Is there no

way to save them?" the girl sobbed. "What will the people do if no one can save them from the king?"

"There is little the people can do without a leader," old Parker said, "and the people of England have no leader to defend their cause against the unjust king who takes away their liberties."

"I believe," said Alice Garland, "that Our Lord and Our Lady will find a leader for us."

"Pray God that it may be soon!" the old man said.

II. *The Bell Waits*

The bell of Canterbury stood silent through many weeks in the guild workshop. All over England men were crying out against the king's deeds. His officers were making prisoners of the masters of the guilds in London and in other towns. The people rose in rebellion. The barons, noblemen of the lowest rank, joined with the town workers against the king. However, they had no real leader to make King John realize that the people of England would one day insist that even the king must obey the law of the land.

Roger Garland was still a prisoner. Giles and Alice knew that their father must be wretched, although they did not know, as their mother knew, that he was locked up in a damp and dirty dungeon where rats ran over him while he slept. The children realized, however, that their father was in great danger. On any day an order from King John might send Roger Garland to death without trial.

In every hour of daylight when she was not helping her mother, Alice Garland knelt in the chapel of St. Thomas á Becket, praying to God and Our Lady for help for her father. That was when she would see the Archbishop of Canterbury come in and kneel humbly —as humbly as did any pilgrim—before Our Lady's altar.

Because she herself was in sorrow, she could understand why the great priest was asking the help of God. There were times when she longed to speak to him, but shyness held her back. Once, as he passed her at the chapel door, the tall, white-haired man smiled at her. The kindness of the smile warmed her so that, for the moment, she forgot the greatness of the Archbishop. She smiled back at him as he went into the chapel, and she went toward the workshop in the cathedral garden.

Old Parker was alone in the workshop as Alice entered. He was standing beside the silent bell, his hand resting upon its gleaming bronze.

"Will it ever ring, Master Parker?" she asked him.

The old man shook his head sadly. "I do not know, Alice," he said. "I only know that it will not ring until the people of England have justice once more."

"Will the king never give us that?" the girl asked.

"The king will give nothing until he is forced to give it," Parker said.

"Who can force a king?" Alice sighed.

"Only one man can do that," said old Parker. "Only the Archbishop of Canterbury, Stephen Langton, can—"

"Who speaks my name?" a clear voice asked from the dusk outside the workshop. The old guildsman turned toward the door. "I speak it, Your Grace," he said. "Will you not come in?"

The Archbishop of Canterbury came through the doorway and moved toward the place where the last rays of sunlight gleamed on the great bell. As Parker had done, he placed his hand upon its shining surface. "When will it ring?" he asked.

"Not until Roger Garland walks out from prison a free man again. Not until we are sure that we will not be taxed without our consent. Not until we are sure that no one shall ever again be held in prison or put to death without trial by jury. Not until we are sure that these rights shall be protected will the great bell made by the men of the Guild of Our Lady ring from the tower of the cathedral of Canterbury."

"These are not new rights," the Archbishop said slowly. "They are old rights, given to man by God. Why can you not defend these rights?"

"We have no leader, Your Grace," the old man said.

"There are the barons," said the Archbishop.

"Yes," said Parker, "there are the barons. They are fighting, they say, not only for their own rights but also for the freedom of all the people of England; but the barons are not strong enough to win without a leader. The people of England will follow a man they know and trust. You are that man, Your Grace. You are our only hope."

The Archbishop stood for a long time, saying nothing but gazing at the great silent bell. Then, in the dusk of the autumn evening, he passed through the cathedral garden. Alice Garland and Parker stared after his figure.

"There goes," said the guildsman, "a great statesman, a great patriot, a great Archbishop. He is the greatest man England has ever seen, perhaps the greatest man she will ever see!"

Every pilgrim in Canterbury the last week of November had a story to tell of the sermon which Stephen Langton preached. All England, they said, even the far lands to the north and to the west, was repeating the words of the Archbishop, words that promised freedom to a people suffering from the deeds of an unjust king and his cruel officers. All England was rousing to action. In a little while, with Stephen Langton as leader, the people of England would again be free.

Giles had gone to Mass in the town church that Sunday in November. There he had listened to the words that were setting England on fire with hope.

Giles told Alice all about the sermon. "The Archbishop spoke about the law of England in which the rights of man are guarded. One of them was the right that no one should be taxed without his consent. The other was that no freeman should be held or sent to his death without a trial. I wanted to cheer; but I wanted to weep too. Something within me kept saying that this was for father, but that it was, too, for every man in England.

"Then, when he had ended, the Archbishop lifted his
right arm. 'Men of England,' he cried, 'what are you
willing to do for your freedom? Will you fight for it?
Will you die for it?'

"We were all up on our feet then. 'Yes,' we cried
in one voice.

"The Archbishop went on, 'The barons have promised to fight for the rights of the men of England. If I
pledge you that the barons will give you this freedom,
will you join with the barons against the king?'

" 'We will join,' we cried out.

"Then we all walked in silence to the altar rail.
There, one after the other, we knelt and promised to

give our lives, if need be, to win our liberties. And we shall win them, God willing, with His soldier, Stephen Langton, as our leader!"

"I know you will win them, Giles," the girl said, "but will it be in time to save our father?"

"It must be," her brother declared.

All England was aroused by the Archbishop's words; but the officers of the king were growing more cruel in their treatment of men who refused to pay unjust taxes. They were still throwing them into dungeons. They were still putting them to death without trial. England might cry out for justice, but John was king of England, and he refused to listen to the cry.

Alice Garland continued to pray for her father's life. Her prayers gave her comfort, but they could not take away the fears of what might happen to her father. Mistress Garland went again and again to the prison, but she was not permitted to see her husband. Giles went several times, but with no success. Old Parker went once, and with the aid of some old friendships that were stronger than prison rules, managed to get into the prison. He came back to tell the Garlands that Roger had not given up hope.

"Even the men in prison say," old Parker declared, "that Stephen Langton will prove himself a greater man than King John."

"Pray God that he may—and soon," said Alice's mother.

Day after day the Garlands waited and hoped. Unless the Archbishop won the cause from the king, Roger Garland would go to his death.

Easter had come and gone. The Feast of the Ascension had come and gone. In a little while a June Sunday would come. That was the day promised for the ringing of the great bell, the celebration of victory for the people. The bell would not ring, Alice thought sadly. The people were not yet free.

III. *The Bell Is Rung*

On a bright day in the last week of May, Alice heard the cling-clang of hammers upon bronze. The men were working on the bell. Quickly she ran through the garden and toward the workshop.

"Has he won?" she cried, as she came to the doorway. "Has the Archbishop won?"

Old Parker looked up from his work as the other men stared at her. "The Archbishop has not yet won," he said, "but we believe that he will win. This is our act of faith, Alice, not of triumph. Stephen Langton told the people that the bell of Canterbury should ring upon a June Sunday. Now they are saying that the Archbishop cannot make good that promise.

"But we men of the guild believe that he will," Parker went on. "That is why we are finishing the bell. It will ring out on a Sunday morning in June to tell Canterbury, to tell all England that the workingmen of Canterbury believe in their leader, the Archbishop of Canterbury."

113

"Perhaps when King John hears it," Giles Garland said, "he will know how strong is our cause."

By day and by night, under the light of candles, the metalworkers of the Guild of Our Lady worked on the great bell. At last they finished it and hung it in the tower. In the dawn of a June Sunday it rang out for the first time, rang over Canterbury town, over the countryside. To every man, to every woman who heard it, the sound was a voice of hope. To Stephen Langton, listening in the Archbishop's house, it was a voice of faith.

The story reached the king. "Langton has won," said the courtiers. "He would not have rung the bell unless he had won."

"Langton has not yet won," the king said gloomily; but, even as he spoke, the king knew that he could no longer refuse to sign the Great Charter, the Magna Carta, the paper on which Stephen Langton had written the rights of the freemen of England.

One June day the king of England met with the barons of England near Windsor, a place in later years would be known to all men as the birthplace of the Great Charter. John, dark and frowning, sat upon a throne. To his left stood his courtiers and his knights. To his right stood the barons with the men of the guilds of England behind them. Near the king stood Stephen Langton, Archbishop of Canterbury. Before the king stood a herald, bearing the paper on which was written the Great Charter.

"Read it," said King John.

The herald read. He read the first declaration of freedom for the Church. The herald then read the two rights that protected the freedom of the people: there were to be no taxes placed upon the people without their consent; and no freeman was to be held in prison or sent to death without trial.

One after another the herald read the provisions of the Great Charter that supported these first freedoms. The barons were to keep their lands. London and the other towns were to be given back their old liberties, liberties which protected the guilds. England was to be free again—when John signed the Charter.

At the final hour John hesitated. He looked at the barons and their followers. He looked at his courtiers and his knights. Which army was the stronger? In battle, who would win, the barons and their followers or his courtiers and his knights? The king waited.

Then Stephen Langton moved forward a little, just enough to be in sight of the king. "You will sign, Your Majesty," he said. His voice held not a question but a command.

Once more the king hesitated. The Archbishop reached for the Charter. He took it from the trembling hands of the king's herald. He held it up before the king. From the ranks of the barons came a clerk with a long quill pen. He handed it to the Archbishop, who passed it to the king.

"You will sign here, Your Majesty," he said.

For an instant the king of England stared at the Archbishop of Canterbury. Then the king took the pen in his hand and signed the paper which was to be the world's great charter of freedom.

"You have won," he said to Stephen Langton.

"Not I," said the Archbishop, "but God."

The Archbishop of Canterbury was praying when Alice Garland saw him, a few days later, kneeling before Our Lady's altar in the chapel of the cathedral. He was praying so devoutly that he saw no one. Alice wanted to thank him, for now her father, weak and ill but free, was home from the prison. She wanted to thank him because the men of the guild were once more safe. She wanted to thank him because the people of England were once again free, but Alice knew that this was no time to speak to him. She slipped quietly from the chapel, thanking God for the leader He had sent in their time of need.

PROVING YOUR STATEMENTS

Some of these statements are true; some are false. Copy *only* the true statements; then find the sentence in the story which proves your statement is true. Write the page and paragraph where you find the proof beside the statement.

1. The men of the guilds felt that the king taxed them unjustly so that he could do away with the guilds.

2. Alice loved her father so much that she wanted him released from prison, regardless of his beliefs about justice.

3. Stephen Langton was not only a great Archbishop, but he was a great Englishman as well.

4. The king signed the Great Charter because the strong will of the Archbishop overpowered him.

5. In his victory Stephen Langton realized that his success was due to his own wonderful ability.

DRAWING CONCLUSIONS

Select the *two* best answers from the following statements:

From this story we can conclude

1. that the Church always defended the rights of the working man;

2. that laboring men must fight for their just rights;

3. that we owe our wonderful freedoms to the courage of the brave men who have lived before us.

The Crowning of Dreaming John

Seven days he traveled
Down the roads of England,
Out of leafy Warwick lanes
Into London Town.
Gray and very wrinkled
Was Dreaming John of Grafton,
But seven days he walked to see
A king put on his crown.

Down the streets of London
He asked the crowded people
Where would be the crowning
And when would it begin.
He said he'd got a shilling,
A shining silver shilling,
But when he came to Westminster
They wouldn't let him in.

Dreaming John of Grafton
Looked upon the people,
Laughed a little laugh, and then
Whistled and was gone.
Out along the long roads,
The twisting roads of England,
Back into the Warwick lanes
Wandered Dreaming John.

Dreaming John of Grafton
Went away to London,
Saw the colored banners fly,
Heard the great bells ring,
But though his tongue was civil
And he had a silver shilling,
They wouldn't let him in to see
The crowning of the king.

So back along the long roads,
The leafy roads of England,
Dreaming John went caroling,
Traveling alone,
And in a summer evening,
Among the scented clover,
He held before a shouting throng,
A crowning of his own.

JOHN DRINKWATER

The Dawn's Early Light

I. *Flight to Freedom*

As long as I live, I shall remember my first day in America.

Daylight was creeping from behind dark clouds as our airplane circled Idlewild International Airport. The rising sun touched the tips of the great propellers with gold as the pilot brought the plane down smoothly on the runway. As the plane touched the earth, my mother made the Sign of the Cross. "Thank God," she said, weeping for happiness, "we have come at last to freedom's land."

We picked up our bags and boxes and came down the ramp. My father still wore his black uniform of the guards which had been given to him when he and other displaced Poles were hired by the United States in Germany. My mother and I wore the dresses we love so dearly, the red and white national dress of our beloved city of Krakow. My brother, Jan, wanted to wear the new American suit my father had bought for him in the post exchange at the American base in Germany, but my father said, "The guides who are to meet us must know at once that you are a Polish boy." So Jan wore a national costume of a Polish mountaineer.

Soon we were in the crowded terminal. Around us we could hear almost every language—German, French, Yiddish, Greek, Italian, and English. Jan and I had learned English in the years we spent in a displaced persons' camp. My father speaks it rather well, but my mother knows only Polish. In the terminal, when she heard no one speaking her native language, she grew alarmed. "How can I be understood?" she cried.

121

My father comforted her. "Zita and Jan will understand," he said, "when I am not near you."

"It is strange here," sighed my mother. "I wish I could see just one familiar face."

For a moment, as we stood among piles of bundles and suitcases, I felt strange, too. Children cried from excitement and hunger, women looked frightened, and most of the men gave loud, stern orders to hide their own fear of this new land. Suddenly, above the din of the crowd, I heard an announcement. "All passengers from Flight Eight are wanted in the reception center," said a voice over the loudspeaker.

We were among the passengers from Flight Eight. A guide led us toward a large room with long counters. After a short wait, my father showed his papers and answered many questions about the kind of work he could do. "I am a cloth weaver," he told the United States immigration inspectors. "I learned my trade long ago in Krakow."

The inspector examined another paper. "You are to remain in New York," he said, and wrote down an address on a card for my father.

Hours later, after my father had answered questions about our health, our money, our plans for the future, we turned away from the desk. My mother, tired from the strain of long anxiety, was trembling. Again she sighed and said, "It would be nice to see a familiar face."

There were no familiar faces, but there were

122

friendly ones. A lady in blue, who wore a badge, edged through the crowd. "I've been watching and waiting for you," she said, and held out her hand to my mother. She spoke in Polish.

My mother's eyes lighted with joy. "Who are you?" she asked, still clasping the hand of the lady in blue.

The lady smiled. "I am Irene Wayne, from the Bureau of Immigration of the National Catholic Welfare Conference in Washington. We meet immigrants when they reach our land and give them whatever advice and help they need."

"God bless you," said my mother.

Behind Miss Wayne stood a fine-looking young man in beautiful brown store clothes.

"This is Mr. Stanley," she said. He bowed politely. "I do not need to be told that you are from Krakow," he said. Then, as he shook my father's hand, he added, "Welcome to America in the name of the United Polish Societies. I, too, am here to help you."

"Thank you," we said in chorus, though all of us did not say it in English.

"First, we shall take you into the Chapel of Our Lady of the Skies," said Mr. Stanley.

There we prayed. Then we had breakfast. I sat next to Miss Wayne, and she told me I could order anything I wanted. I read the card. "What are waffles?" I asked her. I pronounced the word to rhyme with *maples*.

"You should have said it to rhyme with *raffles*," said Jan, who was on a bench at my left.

Miss Wayne laughed, but it was a kind laugh. "Both of you are wrong," she said. "That *a* in *waffles* is like the *a* in *wash*."

Jan and I repeated it after her, but I do not care how the word *waffles* is pronounced; after I ate them, I liked them.

"When breakfast is over, we will drive you into New York City," said Mr. Stanley. "This will be a very special day for you."

We did not know how special it would be until we drove past great sprawling suburbs and from the heights of a wide bridge came at last upon our first sight of the City of New York. There she spread— big and high and agleam with October brightness. Skyscrapers rose to the heavens. The roar of buses, taxis, and cars filled the streets. People—free people— rushed from one corner to another. Long, low whistles sounded from boats in the harbor. Planes flew over us.

"Where are we going?" I asked Miss Wayne who was driving the car.

"To Fifth Avenue and 28th Street," was all she told me.

I did not know why we were going to Fifth Avenue and 28th Street, and I did not ask her.

"Maybe we're going to live at Fifth Avenue and 28th Street," whispered Jan.

When we turned into Fifth Avenue, I was sure that this street would not be our home. It was too elegant, too busy, too important. Jewels glistened in shop windows; women in rich furs waited for traffic lights to change; great, long cars swung past us. I started to explain this to Jan, when suddenly I saw the flags! Whipped by the wind, rising high on standards that towered above the pavements, flew the Stars and Stripes, that I had come to know so well at the American bases in Germany. Beside the American flag flew the brave, bright old flag of Poland, its white eagle on a field of red! I pointed them out to my mother and to Jan. I could not speak in my excitement.

My mother gasped. "Why does the Polish flag fly here?" she cried.

Mr. Stanley leaned forward with pride. "This is Pulaski Day," he said, "and America does not forget her friends."

We knew about Casimir Pulaski, the Polish general who came to the help of the American colonies in their struggle for freedom in the War of the American

125

Revolution. We knew that he and his Pulaski Legion had nobly defended an American city and that General George Washington had praised him for bravery. We knew, too, that Casimir Pulaski, like generations of Poles who lived after him, had loved liberty and fought to preserve it.

"Pulaski Day!" echoed my mother, and her voice was singing.

"I'll let all of you off at the next corner," said Miss Wayne, "and I'll find a place to park."

I did not know what she meant, for I could see no "park," but we got out of the car. There were hundreds and hundreds of people standing in groups on the side streets of the Avenue.

"There's going to be a parade," said Jan.

"And we're going to be in it," said Mr. Stanley.

II. *The Parade*

A band began to play. People pushed their way toward signs that spelled out the names of Polish cities. "Others are proud of their birthplaces, too," said my mother, as women in their native costumes, orange dresses from the southeastern oil fields and red, white, and blue aprons from a city north of Warsaw, flashed past us.

"I'm staying with you," said Mr. Stanley. "My grandfather came from Krakow to America with nothing but strong hands and a faith in God."

The band kept playing. Miss Wayne found us in

126

the crowd. "Let's get into the line of march," she said, guiding us toward the Krakow banners. She spoke in Polish to the group around us, explaining that we had arrived that morning from Germany. "Welcome to America!" they called out to us.

Ahead of us, two men were carrying a banner. It read,

> Pulaski never went back to Russian enslavement.
> Neither shall we.

"Hurray! Hurray!" shouted Jan in excitement.

Behind us two young men were struggling to lift a larger banner. "Perhaps you could help them," I told my brother. He is young, younger than I, but he is strong.

The young men heard me. "Come along," they said to Jan.

I watched the three of them and read the words of their sign.

> We will defend America against her foes!

They were all proud when it rose above the heads of the marchers.

For a moment the band was silent, and then a shrill whistle blew. Standing on tiptoe I could see the first of the parade. "Who are the men in uniforms of the Polish Exile Army?" I asked my father.

My father lifted his head. "They are the men who fought under General Anders," he said.

"Did you fight under him?" asked Mr. Stanley.

"I did," said my father with pride.

"Then you should be in the front ranks beside them," said the man from the United Polish Societies. He clutched my father by the arm and rushed him forward through the crowd. "Look! Look! Jan!" I cried. "The general's soldiers and our father are going to lead the parade!"

We were starting! A guard of motorcycle policemen swung into perfect lines. A band blared loudly. Leaders moved into place. Some, like my father, wore the black uniform of the displaced Poles in Germany; others wore the blues of the British Royal Air Force. We began to move. I held my mother's hand as we marched proudly down the avenue of the biggest city in this great land we once feared we should never see.

The bands, many of them now, played familiar music, old marching songs, filled with the old hopes of the Polish people. My mother cried a little. "Do not weep," I said. "This is no time for tears."

She wiped her eyes. "I am crying," she said, "for those who are left behind, who will never see this blessed America."

The music of the bands changed into livelier tunes. Crowds on the pavements shouted greetings to us. Children waved American flags. Wave after wave of marchers surged ahead of us and behind us. Bright banners floated in the sunlight. Tramp, tramp, tramp went our feet, for history was marching along Fifth Avenue. History was marching, the history of a people who would never admit defeat. We Poles have known hunger and thirst and dreadful wars, but still we are proud, proud as our Polish eagle upon its field of red! Poland shall never die!

Down the Avenue rose the blare of another band. My mother's hand stiffened in mine. "It's the old Polish national anthem," she said, amazed to hear the familiar song in this new land.

I leaned forward. "They're dipping the flags at the church up ahead," I told her, standing on tiptoe to see the raised banners.

Miss Wayne smiled at us. "That is St. Patrick's Cathedral," she said, "and that is New York's own Cardinal Spellman on the steps, waiting to greet us."

"I can see him," I told my mother.

129

She is little, but she lifted her head high. "I see him," she said. "How kind he looks! How noble!"

"I can see others," I said.

Miss Wayne put on her glasses. "One man standing near His Eminence is the Governor of New York," she explained, "and next to him are the Governor of New Jersey and the Mayor of the City of New York. There is a prelate there near the Cardinal, but I do not know who he is."

My mother needed only one glimpse to recognize the spiritual protector of all the Polish exiles. "It is Archbishop Gawlina!" she cried. Her shout was caught up by the crowd.

"Archbishop Gawlina!" they cried, and the echoes rang down the bright avenue that is far from the land of our people.

Heads up, eyes front, we moved swiftly toward the cathedral steps. The bands again began to play, and this time it was that battle cry of freedom that lives in the hearts of the Poles. We sang as we marched, and our voices rang out loud and clear, for it was our old national anthem, "Poland Is Not Yet Lost!"

We stopped at the foot of the cathedral steps. For a moment, all was silence. Then there was a rising shout and a break in the ranks. I heard my mother say, "I have prayed to see a familiar face. At last I have found one!"

She was the first to reach the step where Archbishop Gawlina stood. She was the first to kiss his

130

episcopal ring. I raced after her and clutched her white skirt as the Archbishop held out his hand with its gleaming jewel; behind me swarmed hundreds of the marchers. "Where is my father? Where is Jan?" I cried.

"We are here." My father and my brother shouldered their way toward us.

We knelt then in the sunlight on the steps of St. Patrick's Cathedral in this land of the free. The Polish Archbishop gave us his blessing and the American Cardinal lifted his hand and added his prayer.

We rose from our knees. Pulaski Day was over. We stood, a closely united family, who had come to the end of a long journey. My mother spoke. "The years, the sorrows, and the grief are behind us. We have at last found freedom," she said.

Skimming is an important skill in reading. The exercises on this page will show you how well you can skim.

1. Skim page 128 to find the color of the British Royal Air Force uniform.

2. Skim page 130 to find the name of the Polish national anthem.

Now read pages 120–121 and then choose the correct answer to complete each of these sentences.

1. The family arrived at Idlewild Airport (a) in the evening; (b) in the early morning; (c) at noon.

2. The color of the father's uniform was (a) gray; (b) red; (c) black.

3. Zita and her mother wore dresses of (a) red and yellow; (b) blue and white; (c) red and white.

4. Jan wore (a) an American suit; (b) a German mountaineer costume; (c) a national Polish costume.

5. Jan's American suit was purchased in (a) New York; (b) Germany; (c) Poland.

What did you notice about your rate of reading in answering these questions? Now choose the correct answer to complete each of the following statements:

1. In skimming to find a certain fact I (a) scanned the page rapidly, looking only for key words; (b) read every word on the page carefully; (c) tried to get the full meaning of every sentence.

2. In reading pages 120–121 to find detailed information I (a) read very rapidly; (b) read slowly and thoughtfully; (c) read at the same rate as I did for pages 128 and 130.

For Travelers

Weary traveler, stop and pray
At a shrine along the way;
Dusty, weary road and street,
Endless roads, and broken feet,
Burdened backs and tired hands—
Broken homes in saddened lands.
Though your towns have gone in flames,
And your world is stranger names,
Though the road has not an end
There is still a traveler friend.

Weary traveler, fold your hands,
Think of old familiar lands.
Weary traveler, bow the head.
See the Savior's feet are red,
Red with Blood, and traveled far
Over ways where travelers are.
Yours are roads that He has worn
Smoothly, still of stone and thorn.
Yours the way that He has passed
Down your roads, but home at last.

RAYMOND KRESENSKY

IIII

Chivalry

The Guest of God

O Lord, who shall dwell in Your tent,
   or who shall live on Your holy mountain?
He who walks blamelessly and does justice;
   who thinks the truth in his heart
   and slanders not with his tongue;
Who harms not a fellow man,
   nor takes up a reproach against his neighbor;
Who, though it be to his loss,
   changes not his pledged word;
   who lends not his money at usury
   and accepts no bribe against the innocent.
He who does these things
   shall never be disturbed.

PSALM 14

135

Agnus Dei

VI

Agnus De-i, qui tollis peccáta mundi, mi-se-ré-re no-bis. Agnus De - i, qui tol-lis peccáta mundi, mi-se-ré-re no-bis. Agnus De-i, qui tollis peccáta mundi, dona no-bis pa-cem.

Lamb of God, Who takeſt away℘ the sins of the world,
have mercy℘ on us.

Lamb of God, Who takeſt away℘ the sins of the world,
have mercy℘ on us.

Lamb of God, Who takeſt away℘ the sins of the world,
grant us peace.

Nicolette

I. *How the Tapestry Was Started*

Nicolette did not know that the big piece of embroidery upon which the Lady Matilda and her court worked would one day be called the Bayeux Tapestry and rest in a museum in the town of Bayeux. She had no thought that thousands of people would crowd into the Bayeux Cathedral on the day, once a year, when the beautifully embroidered piece of linen would be placed high on the walls. She only knew that the Lady Matilda wished the work done speedily, and that she, Nicolette, wished to please the Lady Matilda.

The Lady Matilda was the wife of Duke William who had led hundreds of his knights away to war in far-off England. The Lady Matilda and the other women of her court had remained behind, grieving at this war. They had been sitting idly, weeping and worrying, when Bishop Odo of Bayeux, Duke William's brother, came to the court. "Why don't you do something?" he asked.

"What can we do?" sighed the ladies.

"I need something for the cathedral, something to place high on the wall and to reach all around the nave," suggested Bishop Odo.

"But that is too long for a tapestry," someone said.

"I don't care what you call it," said the bishop, "so long as you make a good religious picture. You could show Our Lord and some of the saints."

"If we make the tapestry," said the Lady Matilda, "we shall show why Duke William has gone to England and how he will defeat his enemies and become King of England."

Bishop Odo shook his head. "If you want to do it that way, go ahead. But get to work. Don't sit around moping."

"How large should the piece be?" the Lady Matilda asked.

"Two hundred and fourteen feet long and twenty inches high," said the bishop, "and I have not yet said I would put such a scene on the wall of the cathedral."

"We shall make it anyhow," said the Lady Matilda.

Immediately she sent for the linen and began to make patterns. She divided the work into sections and the workers into teams. Each team was to be responsible for the section given to it. The embroidery on the long piece of white linen was to tell the whole story—how this war was caused and how William had led his knights to England. Matilda even planned to show the battle in England, although it had not yet taken place.

"The Duke will win the battle and conquer his enemies," she told the ladies of her court, "and he will be the King of England."

"Then you will be Queen Matilda of England, milady," one of the ladies said.

"Do not say it so soon," Matilda warned her.

Nicolette remembered that even though Matilda was a duchess she wished them all to call her the Lady Matilda. "Then I feel nearer to you," she told them.

Nicolette knew much of the Lady Matilda, for the girl had lived for years in the great castle from which William ruled his people. Her father lived near the castle, but her mother was dead, and so the Lady Matilda had made the child part of her own family.

Nicolette had seen the wars that had swept to the gates of the many-towered castle. She had seen the knights put on their heavy armor and ride out to battle. She had stood in one of the high towers, watching for her father's return. She had knelt in prayer every morning and every evening with the women and girls. She had studied the lessons which Bishop Odo had recommended for the young so that she knew a little Latin, a little French, a little English, and something about the stars. She had learned to sew and embroider, although she could not do either very well.

What she knew best she had learned outside the great gray castle. She loved to walk in the woods and the fields and she made her way through them whenever the castle guard told her there was no danger from the enemy. She could call the flowers by name, and lingered over them even when she did not pluck them. She loved the Lady Matilda's roses, but even better she loved the wild flowers of field and forest.

While the artists drew pictures of the scenes which the duchess wished to show on the tapestry, and the cathedral architects checked them to make sure they were the right size, the women began to prepare the materials for the tapestry. There was the flax to be made into linen, and the wool to be spun into thread. Looms and spinning wheels were set up in the great hall, and the hum of work sounded under the high rafters. Everyone was busy, Nicolette thought—except Nicolette.

"Is there not something I can do, Milady?" she asked the duchess.

"Nothing," Matilda started to say, for Nicolette was not yet skilled enough in spinning or weaving to be trusted to work on anything as important as this tapestry. Then, seeing the eagerness in the girl's eyes, the kind duchess thought of something. "We shall need dyes for the woolen threads," she said. "We shall need plants of the crocus for the orange and yellow, madder roots for the Turkey red, and many other plants and flowers you know for different colors. You

140

are to find the roots and plants and flowers to make those colors. That is very important, Nicolette."

"Yes, Milady," said Nicolette.

"You are a good child," said the duchess, "and some day in England we will find you a splendid knight for a husband."

The artists colored the sketches they had made so that the women who worked on the embroidery could see the colors they should use. In the border they drew strange birds and animals and many kinds of signs which helped to explain the action of the picture. It all looked so jumbled to Nicolette that she decided to look at it only for the colors which the workers might need.

"Yellow," a woman could call, and Nicolette would run to the cupboard where she had put the plants of the crocus. She carried them swiftly to the dyers who were working over big iron kettles. Sometimes she waited to watch the bubbling liquid grow yellow and give color to the bits of linen thrown in to test the color.

"Turkey red," another worker would cry, and Nicolette sped for the madder root she had stored.

"Olive, olive," rose the order. What a lot of olive they needed, and how much brown!

Nicolette's favorite color was Turkey red, and for that the dyers needed madder roots. Nicolette went into the woods every day to look for the plants. "I'll bring you some tomorrow," she promised the dyers.

II. *How the Tapestry Was Finished*

Early the next morning Nicolette sped from the castle into the woods. She knew where the madder grew. She would fill her basket and hurry back to the great hall.

"I'm so glad that I can do something for the Lady Matilda," she thought. Then she saw the ragged little girl.

The child was pulling up the madder plants and dropping them into her apron. It was an old and dirty apron, but Nicolette grieved to see how the plants were staining it.

"Oh, don't do that," she said to the child.

"I have no other way to carry them," the child said.

"Why do you want them?"

"My mother sent me for them."

"Is she making something?"

"She's fixing her old dress so that I can wear it," explained the child.

"Oh!" was all Nicolette could say. For a moment she had the generous thought of giving her basket to the child, but she remembered her duty to take back madder to the castle. "Are you taking them all?" she asked.

"All of them," said the little girl.

"Then I'll have to go somewhere else," said Nicolette sadly.

She went through the woods, looking everywhere for other madder plants. She could find none, and she realized that the child must have plucked every plant she could find.

The sun rose high in the sky, and Nicolette grew hungry, but she kept on seeking the madder plants. The sun began to slide down toward the west, and Nicolette grew hungrier, but she kept on. She found no madder. Suddenly she realized that she was lost and that darkness was falling over the woods. "Oh, God, please take care of me," she prayed.

Meantime, back in the castle, the women at the embroidery frames began to call for red wool thread. The women at the spinning wheels had none. They called the dyers, and the dyers called Nicolette.

"Nicolette, Nicolette!" her name echoed through the great hall. No one had seen Nicolette.

"Not all day?" asked the Lady Matilda.

"Not all day," people answered.

143

"We must look for her at once," said the duchess.

The knights and the squires were all away with William, and so only the pages could take up the search. "Nicolette, Nicolette!" they called as they went through the woods. Darkness came, and they lighted torches to aid them in their search. Through the woods and fields they went, calling Nicolette by name.

For a long time Nicolette did not hear them. She heard, instead, the sounds of the woods, rustling leaves and the patter of animals' paws. Would some prowling animal harm her? the girl wondered, and prayed to Blessed Mother for protection. A small animal ran across her foot, and she almost screamed in fright. "Oh, Mother Mary, help me," she prayed.

Once she thought she heard the sound of a horn. Then it died away. Nicolette remembered all the stories of danger she had ever heard. At last she began to cry. Then, suddenly, she heard a shout, not far away. "Here, here!" she cried. "I am here!"

Three of the pages came running to her. "What brought you here?" one of them asked.

"I was looking for madder plants," she said.

Through the darkness they led her back to the castle. The Lady Matilda was waiting for the girl in her chamber. "Oh, Nicolette, Nicolette," she cried, "we have been praying for you. Where were you? And what kept you so long?"

"I was looking for madder," the girl sobbed, "and now I have delayed work on the tapestry."

"We can make up the time we have lost," the duchess said, "but we could never have made up our loss of you."

Later that night, as they all knelt in the great hall, the Lady Matilda thanked God that Nicolette had come back safe. "And do not worry about the madder," she told the girl after prayers.

The next morning, as Nicolette went out from the castle, she met the ragged child. The little girl was holding up her dirty apron, stained deep with the red of the madder plants. "My mother says," she told Nicolette, "that you wanted these for the picture."

"We do," said Nicolette.

"Then I am to give them to you. My mother says that my dress is not as important as the picture. Here they are." She thrust the apron at Nicolette, and started to run away, but Nicolette caught her by the arm.

"Come with me," she said, and led the child into the great hall. "This little girl has brought these for our tapestry," she told the Lady Matilda. "They are the plants she gathered to make the dye for her own dress. Should she not keep them?"

"You should not deny her the privilege of giving," said the duchess, smiling at the ragged child. "Why don't we divide the roots? Then we'll have some for the thread, and she'll have some for her dress." She called for a basket and put half the madder roots into it, giving the apron back to the little girl.

145

"We all thank you," she told her. "Let me show you how we will use your gift." She led her from table to table where the women worked. Then she called her maids. "Give her the best you have of sweets, and give her a pretty dress."

"She is generous," said Nicolette, "to give us these madder plants."

"And you are generous," said the Lady Matilda, "to give her credit." She looked thoughtfully at the people at the tables, the spinning wheels, the looms, the vats of dye. "This is a great work, little Nicolette," she said, "not because it will be beautiful, but because we have all worked on it together. I wish that all life were like that."

"Will it be like that in England?" the girl asked.

"Only if we do the will of God," said the Lady Matilda.

Neither of them went to England, although William won the battle which made him king. Matilda died before the news of his victory reached the castle. Years later, Nicolette married a Frenchman and stayed in France. Once, when she was an old woman, she went to Bayeux and looked at the tapestry on the cathedral wall.

"It is beautiful," she said, and she was proud that she had done something to make it beautiful, even though it was only finding the madder plants in the woods.

RECALLING FACTS TO PROVE A STATEMENT

Here are some statements about the people in the story you have just read. Read each statement and then write on your paper a fact you remember from the story which will prove that the statement is true.

1. Lady Matilda was humble and wished the ladies of her court to feel close to her.

2. Nicolette was not a skilled worker.

3. Lady Matilda grieved during the absence of Nicolette.

4. Bishop Odo was interested in the education of young people.

5. Nicolette was not easily discouraged by a difficult task.

6. The little ragged child had a generous heart.

Grace

O Lord of all things good,
Giver of grain
And harvester of beauty,
You Who have made the gold
Of sun and wheat,
Silver of moon, and grape,
Warmth of the hearth
And shimmer of white cloth,
Grant that we may remember
Here, seated at Your feast,
How You were cold and poor
And very small
And slept on hay
That we might have at last
Far more, far more than this.

FRANCES FRIESEKE

148

Richard's Minstrel

Queen Eleanor chose Blondel to be minstrel to her son, Richard, who would one day be Richard of the Lion Heart, King of England. "You will be the greatest of the minstrels," the old queen said, "as Richard will be the greatest of my sons."

"God willing," said Blondel. He knew that a minstrel was held in high honor, but to be worthy he must know how to tell stories of great battles and sing of high adventure and romance.

The boy quickly learned thrilling tales of heroes, repeating them over and over until he knew them well. He learned, too, the songs of England and of France; some were happy songs of the French troubadours, some were sad. Strangely, although Richard was not a gentle lad, both he and Blondel liked best one little French song, which they sang together. Then, as Blondel played upon his lute, they would laugh and talk of the future.

"Some day we'll go to Jerusalem on a crusade," Richard declared.

There had already been two Crusades which had set out from western Europe to win the Holy Places in Palestine which the Moslems had conquered. Once there had been hope of success, but now the Moslems again held the places where Christ had suffered and died, the Mount of Olives, the Garden of Gethsemane, the Holy Sepulchre, the streets of Jerusalem.

"We must win them back," Richard told his minstrel.

Blondel made songs about the victory they would win over the Moslems, but Richard would not let him sing them. "Wait until we win," he told the minstrel.

"But of course we shall win," said Blondel, "for you will be our leader."

"There are kings and princes in Europe older than I am," said Richard.

"But there is no man braver," said Blondel.

Before he became King of England Richard proved his bravery in the jousts and tournaments of knighthood. He could ride better than any other knight. He could fling his lance with surer aim. He could win every contest. He had, too, the best qualities of knighthood, for, although he was hot of temper, he was kind. He never struck a fallen foe.

When he became king, he helped all his people. Blondel sang of his good deeds, and the people repeated the songs. "Thank God it is Richard, not John, his brother, who is our king," they said. "John is cruel, but Richard is kind, and John is unfair, but Richard is just."

England was at peace, but Richard longed to go upon a crusade. "We must win back the Holy Places," he told Blondel again, and at last he won his wish. He became the leader of the Third Crusade and set out happily for France on the way to the Holy Land. There he joined forces with Philip, the French king.

It was a great spectacle. There were thousands of armored knights, waving the banners of Richard and the fleur-de-lis of France as they rode splendid horses. Their ladies, standing beside the roads, lifted white hands to bid them Godspeed. There was rejoicing, but

there was also sadness. When would they return? And who of them would never return?

Blondel was very sad, for Richard had refused to take the minstrel with him. "You are not a fighting man," he told Blondel. "Only the knights and squires and their servants may come with me. You will stay here with the pages until I return."

"The pages?" Blondel cried indignantly. "I am a minstrel, your minstrel. We have been companions since our youth. Once you said we would go together."

"Not on this journey," said Richard. "When I come back, you may sing the songs of my victory."

"You need me more than you need some of the knights," Blondel insisted. "There will be times when you will need my voice to cheer you, perhaps to save you."

"No," said Richard, but he put his hand on the minstrel's head. "Some day," he promised, "you and I will sing again."

"Good-by, my king!"

"Good-by, my minstrel!"

For a time all the news of the Third Crusade was good. Philip had returned to France, but Richard and his knights had stormed and won the port town of the Holy Land. In battle Richard of the Lion Heart had met Saladin, the greatest leader of the Moslems. They had fought, but they had respected each other, and finally the two leaders had signed a three-year peace. Soon Richard would be home in England with his welcoming people.

Then, in a little while, came terrible news. Richard had been captured by his enemies, not by the Moslem followers of Saladin but by the forces of the Emperor Leopold of Austria. No one knew where he was, but rumor said that he was being held prisoner in one of Leopold's castles. But where?

Hundreds of knights searched Leopold's empire for some trace of Richard. At home, in England, John took over the powers of the king. Under his unjust rule the people stirred in unrest. "There will be rebellion," men said, "unless Richard is found, and found quickly."

The old queen, Eleanor, sent for Blondel. "You must find Richard," she told him.

"I am no knight," he said, "only a minstrel."

"You are Richard's minstrel. He loved you and you love him. You will find him where others fail. You must go."

"But where?"

The old queen pointed to a map of Europe. Part of it, a large part, was black. "There is the empire of Leopold of Austria," she said. "Richard's ship was driven ashore upon its borders. He must be there. Go to him. Take a squire—or a knight, if you will."

"I shall ride alone," said Blondel. "I vow that I shall find him."

He left Paris, traveling eastward. He pretended to be a wandering French minstrel, but though he sought news of Richard everywhere he found none. He came at last into Leopold's empire and had to seek his information more cautiously. Day after day he rode on and on. There was still no trace of Richard.

Near every castle—and the land was full of castles—the minstrel asked about prisoners. Was there a nobleman imprisoned there? Often men said yes, but Blondel could not find the man he sought. Wearily, and sometimes hungrily, he kept on.

He came at last to the castle of Dürrenstein, set high on a mountain, above a rushing stream. There was no way to ford the stream, no way to reach the castle except by the guarded road which wound uphill. "Richard may be there," Blondel thought, "but how can I know?"

He went that night to a village tavern at the foot of the mountain. There, the half-dozen shepherds who had come together saw his lute and asked him to play for them. "I do not know songs in your language," he told them, but they insisted, and he began to sing in French.

"That sounds like the man in the tower," said one of the shepherds.

"Who is he?" Blondel asked, "a minstrel like myself?"

"Oh, no," said another shepherd. "He is a knight, but the Emperor holds him prisoner."

"Have you seen him?"

"No, but we have sometimes heard him singing."

The prisoner might—or might not—be Richard,

Blondel thought as he left the tavern. The night was dark, and he moved silently through the woods beside the road. The snapping of a twig under his feet made a loud noise, but no guard came. He grew bolder and climbed higher. He came at last to a point from which he could go no higher. What could he do, he asked himself. How could he find out if the prisoner in the tower was Richard? How could he let Richard know that he was there?

Then he thought of the song they had sung together. Softly at first, then louder, the minstrel strummed his lute. Twice he played the tune before he began to sing. Thrice he sang it. Then he paused, listening. From the height above him came the sound of a voice, echoing the words of the little French song.

"Richard, my king!" Blondel cried.

"Blondel, my minstrel!" Richard shouted.

They dared talk no more in the still night; but now Blondel was sure. Now he could sound the alarm, and knights from France and Italy, Spain and England, would ride to free Richard of the Lion Heart.

Blondel spurred furiously across the empire of Leopold, over mountains, through forests, across a sea, back to Eleanor in her castle. "Richard is alive," he told her, and drew a white mark on the black part of the map which showed Leopold's empire.

"We shall bring him back," she said, "and when Richard returns, he will make you an earl."

"I do not seek such honor," Blondel said. "I am proud to be Richard's minstrel."

The old queen smiled. "Perhaps you are right," she said. "Richard will have many earls, but he will have only one mother—and one minstrel."

IDENTIFYING CHARACTERS AND THEIR TRAITS

Copy this chart on your paper. Identify each of the principal characters in the story you have just read by giving an important fact about each. Then list as many character traits of each as you can.

Character	Identifying Fact	Character Traits
1. Eleanor		
2. Blondel		
3. King Richard		

Copy this outline on your paper. Then complete it by supplying minor ideas for the major ideas given below.

I. Skills a good minstrel must have
A.
B.

II. Places in Palestine held by Moslems
A.
B.
C.
D.

III. Proofs of Richard's ability to lead a Crusade
A.
B.
C.

IV. Virtues possessed by Richard
A.
B.
C.

V. Good news of Third Crusade
A.
B.

VI. Bad news of Third Crusade
A.
B.

VII. Efforts made by Blondel to find Richard
A.
B.
C.

Blondel

Within my heart I long have kept
A little chamber cleanly swept,
Embroidered with a fleur-de-lis,
And lintel boughs of redwood tree;
A bed, a book, a crucifix,
Two little copper candlesticks
With tapers ready for the match
The moment I his footfall catch.

He often comes, but sings no more
(He says his singing days are o'er)
Of Picardy and Aquitaine,
Blanche of Castile and Charlemagne;
Still, as he comes at candle-light
And goes before the east is bright,
He will not make the secret mine,
What song he sang at Dürrenstein!

Sleep, troubadour! Enough that thou
With that sweet lay didst keep thy vow
And link thy name with deathless art
With Richard of the Lion Heart!

CLARENCE URMY

The Long Crusade

I. *The Special Night*

Down Main Street, past the corner of Vernon and the large apartment building, around the hedge that fenced in the old Hawkins house, Steve hurried in the darkness toward the Boys' Club. "You'll be late," his mother had warned him, but for once Steve knew that he would be on time.

This was his night. The thought of what lay ahead of him made him speed past store windows, past the police station and the fire-engine house, past the Old Ladies' Home and the long row of neat, new houses that now spread across the old baseball lot. Tonight the Citizens' Committee of the Boys' Club would honor the members who had worked hardest for the club during the past year. Steve, a junior member, had brought in the greatest number of old newspapers. They had netted a large sum for the club fund.

"Maybe I'll have to make a speech," Steve thought and, with pride, began to rehearse the lines of the speech he had planned.

A traffic light halted him at Central Avenue. He stared for a moment into the lighted windows of the drug store. He could see Mr. Wilson behind the cigar counter and Nick the barber in front of the magazine stand. Steve kicked his right foot against the mailbox as the traffic roared past. "Guess the city ran out of green lights," he complained to himself.

When the light changed, Steve darted across the street and raced two more blocks until he came to the door of the Boys' Club. There was an air of unusual excitement about the place. It looked bigger and brighter. Bicycles by the dozen were already stacked against the side of the building and, at the curb, strange men were getting out of long, low automobiles. The club band was in final rehearsal as Steve stepped through the doorway. It was then that he saw Martie.

" 'Lo, Martie," Steve said, a little uneasily.

"Hi, Steve," Martie said, and smiled.

This was one time, Steve thought, when he could do without Martie. After all, he told himself, none of the other fellows in the club had much to do with Martie. There was nothing the matter with him, they said, but he was "different." He was too quiet. He hadn't joined any of their teams. He lived too far away from the rest of them. The clothes he wore were not like the warm jackets and bright scarfs of other juniors in the club. Even though his sweaters and slacks were neat and clean, they were old and worn. "Hand-me-downs," Martie had explained to Steve with a laugh.

Steve did not stop now to talk to Martie. "I'll be seeing you," he called back and walked, a little faster, toward the gymnasium. Martie made him nervous tonight. He was relieved when he saw Bill and Jim and Dave at the end of the hall. After all, he told himself again, Martie wasn't his best friend. They never sat together in Steve's house to watch television. They never went to the movies together, nor did they play football or baseball or basketball on the same teams. Martie didn't play on any team.

Once Martie had said to Steve, "You're my only friend." That was the day when he had agreed to take over Steve's paper route while Steve went on a plane with his parents to visit his grandmother. "I'll be glad to do it for you," Martie had told him.

Martie did lots of things for him, Steve admitted to himself. Martie fixed his bike when Steve didn't want his father to know it was broken. Martie took care of Crockett, his dog, when Steve went camping in the summer. Martie was the one who kept at him to collect newspapers for the club fund.

"I'd like to see you win," Martie said.

Now Steve had won. For months, pulling the old red cart across the city streets, he had delivered great

piles of newspapers to the club storeroom. The awards for work well done would be made tonight. Members of the Citizens' Committee would give baseball bats and gloves and football shoes and portable radios and cameras and all sorts of prizes to the boys who had worked the hardest.

"Wonder what I'll get?" Steve asked himself as he joined Bill and Jim and Dave. Martie did not follow him.

As they walked into the gymnasium Bill asked, "Are you scared, Steve?"

Scared? Why should he be scared? Steve looked around at the familiar room, hung tonight with bright flags, and he saw only familiar faces. What was there to alarm him? "I don't scare easy," he said, and slid into a chair just below the platform. As more than a hundred boys filled the room, Steve went over in his mind the reply he would make when an award was presented to him. He'd remember to be courteous and polite to the committee members; he'd give praise to Mr. Burns, the director; he'd tell what the Boys' Club meant to him and to the city.

Mr. Burns and the members of the Citizens' Committee came into the room. Behind them strode a newspaper photographer, pulling his camera out of its leather case.

"Maybe you'll get your picture in the paper," whispered Bill.

Everyone stood as the club band played the national

162

anthem. Then, as he sat down, Steve was startled to notice that his knees were trembling and his hands were icy. He clenched his hands as Mr. Burns made the opening speech and kept them clenched as members of the citizens' group expressed their pride of the accomplishments of the club and their hope for the future of the boys who belonged to it.

The older boys were honored first, but Steve paid little attention as their names were called out and their prizes awarded, though he had carefully examined the wide table that held the treasures.

"Carter got a tennis racket," murmured Bill.

At that moment, Steve neither knew nor cared what Carter had received; a queer, sick feeling made his throat dry and his spine tingle. His own turn to be called to the platform by Mr. Burns was drawing closer. He was sixth on the list. When his name was called, he mounted the steps in a daze.

"All of us are happy to honor Steve tonight," said Mr. Burns. "We have watched him through the months as he brought in pounds and pounds and pounds of newspapers. I was constantly amazed that one little red cart could carry so much weight."

Everyone laughed.

"I was more surprised," Mr. Burns added, "that one boy could have the perseverance to collect so many papers."

There was applause. The photographer focused his camera and fired a flash bulb. Steve blinked.

Mr. Burns pointed toward the center of the stage. "Stand here, Steve," he said, "and tell us about your work."

Steve moved across the stage, took his place, and bowed stiffly. He nodded politely in the general direction of the Citizens' Committee and Mr. Burns, then faced the room. In the audience he could see Bill and Jim and Dave. Bill gave him their secret victory signal, with the lifting of two fingers. Beyond them, smiling his friendly grin, sat Martie. Martie waved as Steve began to repeat his rehearsed speech.

"Speak a little louder," whispered Mr. Burns, "so that everyone can hear you."

Steve cleared his throat and started again. "I didn't think much about a prize when I started to collect newspapers for the club," he said. His voice rang with unnatural shrillness. He tried to lower it. "I just wanted to show the fellows that I'm a good member—"

Mr. Burns smiled. The members of the committee applauded. So did the boys.

"So I figured out that if I went to the places where people bought a lot of newspapers, and if I talked to them and told them about the club, they might—" Steve paused for a moment, then clutched at his words as if they were a life raft, "they might—they would—they could—" The room suddenly seemed to narrow before his eyes. No longer could he see Bill and Jim and Dave or the hundred other boys in the room. As if a spotlight had gone into swift reverse, all that Steve could see was Martie.

There sat Martie, the friendless boy who dogged his footsteps; Martie, the fellow who fixed his bike and cared for his dog. Martie had collected and hoarded all the newspapers and then turned them over to Steve to deliver to the club and get all the honors.

"Steve is nervous," whispered Mr. Burns to a committee member.

"Perhaps he has stage fright," said the visitor.

"It's more than that," said Mr. Burns, watching Steve, "but I don't know what's the matter." He rose and moved closer to the boy. He saw at once Steve's glazed eyes and trembling hands. He spoke in low tones, "Don't be upset, Steve." Then, turning toward the room, he suggested, "Let's give Steve a hand so that he will know he is among his friends." The gymnasium rocked with applause. Someone whistled. A boy whooped. Another called out, "Come on, Steve, we're your friends."

Steve locked his hands together to keep them from shaking. He looked at Mr. Burns and he looked down at the audience. There were tears in his eyes. "I shouldn't be here," he said simply.

"Why not?" There was a sharp note in the voice of the director.

"I shouldn't have any friends," said Steve.

"What do you mean?" Mr. Burns asked. His eyes were deeply troubled.

The photographer moved closer, but the committee members gestured him away. The room was still.

Then Steve lifted his head. "I don't deserve a prize," he said courageously, "I didn't earn it."

A gasp of surprise and a murmur of disbelief ran through the gymnasium.

Mr. Burns put his hand on Steve's shoulder. "Do you mean that you did not collect the newspapers?" he asked.

Steve nodded. "That's what I mean."

"Who did get them? Your father? Your mother?"

Steve shook his head. "Martie got them," he confessed.

The boys shouted their disbelief. It couldn't have been Martie! Martie, who always stood shyly on the sidelines of the club, who didn't play the games, who wore funny clothes, who was too bashful to talk to anyone but Steve! Martie could never have gone around ringing doorbells and asking people to save newspapers for him! "No! No!" they shouted.

Mr. Burns moved to the edge of the platform. "Is Martie here?" he asked and, as the boys pointed, he called out, "Come up here, Martie!"

There was silence as Martie moved slowly, timidly, toward the front of the gymnasium and up the steps of the platform.

"Stand beside Steve," said Mr. Burns, "and let us hear the story."

The photographer flashed another bulb.

II. *Steve Explains*

It was Steve who began the explanation. As if a great weight were being lifted from his soul, he said, "It all began no different from any other time. Ever since I've known Martie I've let him do the hard things, the things I don't like to do."

"Your homework?" asked Mr. Burns.

167

"No, not my homework," said Steve. "I do that alone. All the other things, though, delivering my paper along the route when I'd rather be doing something else, or taking care of my dog when I go away, or mending my broken bike, or even washing my father's car in the alley when I was supposed to be washing it. Martie does lots of things for me."

"But the newspapers," said Mr. Burns. "How did Martie happen to get them?"

Martie spoke. "It was nothing," he said humbly, in an agony of shyness.

"It was wonderful," said Mr. Burns. "How did you do it?"

"Let me tell you how he did it," said Steve. "Martie's too modest."

"Go ahead," said Mr. Burns.

Steve rubbed one cold hand against the other. "Martie has never made many friends among the boys," he began, "but, oh, Mr. Burns, you should see the way he gets along with other people. All of them want to help him. He started out with me on the only day I ever tried to collect the newspapers for the club. I rode up to one house on my bike and I rang the bell, quick-like. A lady came to the door and I began to talk to her as if I were her long-lost cousin. I was fresh. I was a smart-aleck. It wasn't the right thing to do, and she didn't like it."

"What did Martie say to her?" asked Mr. Burns.

Steve paused. "It wasn't just what he said to her.

I guess it was the way he said it. He just said we weren't doing this for ourselves, but for the club. He hardly lifted his voice, but you could see right away that she was ready to listen."

"Maybe she was sorry for me," said Martie.

Steve defended him. "It wasn't that; she liked him. Mr. Wilson, the druggist, saved all his papers for Martie. So did Nick the barber. The policemen kept their pile in the station for him each week, and so did the firemen. The janitor in the big apartment house on Vernon stopped giving his papers to the trash man, and old Mr. Hawkins and the matron at the Old Ladies' Home never threw out anything until they knew whether Martie wanted it. Nobody was sorry for him. They did it because they like him."

Mr. Burns again questioned Steve. "When did you stop collecting papers?"

Steve did not lift his eyes. "The first day," he admitted.

The director turned toward Martie. "Why did you let Steve take credit for the work you did?"

Martie faced him grimly. "He is my only friend in the club," he said.

A protest of sound filled the room.

"Did you ever try to be friendly with the other boys?" asked Mr. Burns.

"I thought they didn't like me," Martie said. "I didn't join the teams. I was afraid they'd make fun of me."

Mr. Burns spoke, and his voice was loud and clear. "This club was organized to help all you boys to lead happier, healthier lives. If you're on a team, that is good; if you just want to use the clubrooms to read or to play or to work on a hobby, that is good, too. It is our purpose to keep you strong and brave and honest and loyal. We want you to be kind to others and true to yourselves."

"We will," shouted the boys in the gymnasium.

Mr. Burns turned again toward Martie. "You proved your loyalty when you helped Steve," he said.

Martie's face flushed with pride and, for once, he was not too timid to speak. "Steve proved his goodness, too," he said. "He didn't have to give me credit."

"It's the last time I'll ever take credit that doesn't belong to me," said Steve, and those who heard him knew that he spoke the truth.

The photographer's flash flared again. The chairman of the Citizen's Committee arose. From the treasure-laden table he selected a portable radio. Then, walking across the stage, he handed it to Martie. "I think this prize belongs to you," he said.

The boys in the gymnasium applauded. So did the committee members and Mr. Burns. So did Steve.

Martie had no rehearsed speech. All that he could say was, "I don't know why everyone is making such a fuss. I was glad to do it for Steve."

The chairman smiled at Martie and at Steve, then spoke the final words. "I believe that all boys and

170

girls need constant help toward clearer thinking and deeper loyalties and better living. You learn this in your home, in your school, in your church, and in your Club, too. Some of you, because of your parents and teachers, learn these lessons earlier than others. Some stumble a little along the way."

The boys in the gymnasium listened attentively. Martie moved uneasily, and Steve did not lift his head.

The chairman went on. "Life itself, you will learn as you live, is a long crusade. You must go forth with honor and chivalry. Sometimes the way is lonely. It has been for Martie. Sometimes the way is rough. It was rough for Steve but, when he openly confessed his guilt to you, I knew that he was brave and strong of soul. I am happy to see that honor and chivalry did not die with the Middle Ages."

Steve looked up shyly.

171

The chairman reached across the table that bore the prizes. "I think that Steve deserves something, too, don't you?" he asked the boys in the flag-hung room.

The boys shouted, whistled, and applauded wildly.

Steve was so relieved and happy that he did not see the prize offered to him, nor did he know that the photographer had taken his last picture. All he knew was that he and Martie had won awards far greater than the treasure he had sought: they had been given the accolade of the bright band of knights who go forth with honor and chivalry to the Long Crusade.

WHAT DO YOU THINK?

Answer each question in one or two good sentences.

1. Did Steve treat Martie fairly in the first part of the story?

2. Do you think you could do what Steve did just before receiving an undeserved reward?

3. Why was that a very difficult thing to do?

4. Do you admire Steve for his actions? Why?

5. Do you think Martie deserved to receive the radio as a reward? Why or why not?

6. Would you like to have a friend like Martie? Why?

7. What makes you think Mr. Burns was really interested in helping the boys?

8. Why were the neighbors so willing to save paper for Martie?

9. What do you think about Steve's manner of asking people for their wastepaper?

10. What big lesson have you learned from this story?

The Knight

He rides no dashing charger in the tournament of life;
    No snowy plume waves o'er his helmet's crest;
His shield is moral courage midst the din of daily strife.
    He sings, as forth he fares upon his quest.

At dawn he seeks the Holy Grail, where waxen tapers
    shine,
    In dim-lit chancel, at a Royal Board,
Nor asks he sweeter guerdon at this ever-hallowed
    shrine
    Than to commune, in silence, with his Lord.

He clasps his lady's token now—a silver chain of beads,
    Then forth again, to jousts where lances ring.
His strength is turned to valiant acts, his hands to noble
    deeds,
    His eyes are ever fixed on Christ, his King.

SISTER MARYANNA, O.P.

IV

Learning

God's Glory in the Heavens and in the Law

The heavens declare the glory of God,
  and the firmament proclaims His handiwork.
Day pours out the word to day,
  and night to night imparts knowledge;
Not a voice nor a discourse
  whose voice is not heard;
Through all the earth their voice resounds,
  and, to the ends of the world, their message.

PSALM 18

Pange Lingua

Pange lingua glo-ri-ó-si Córporis mysté-rium,

Sanguinísque preti - ó si, Quem in mundi pré-

ti - um Fructus ventris generósi   Rex effúdit

génti - um.

Sing. my tongue, the Savior's glory
Of His Flesh the mystery sing;
Of the Blood, all price excelling,
Shed by our Immortal King,
Destined for the world's redemption
From a noble root to spring.

The Hill of Tara

I. *Brian and Donal Meet*

Brian, son of the king of Leinster, stood near the closed gate of his father's palace as a chariot came across the plain. The man driving the chariot was one of the chiefs of the Leinster clans. Brian hoped he was bringing with him a boy whom he could make his friend.

The palace was a lonely place for a lad without mother, brother, or sister. The king and the king's men joked and laughed with Brian, but he longed for friends and companions of his own age. This was the time when the chiefs of the clans of Ireland came to honor the rulers of the land. Brian hoped that the chief of the Leinster clan, now driving up to the palace, might have a boy with him. Then he would have a companion in his work and play. They could even work together to get ready for the contest to be held at the Fair at Tara.

More than anything else in the world, Brian wanted to be one of the winners in the contest. For then he would be admitted to the Fian, that noble band of youths, ready to fight and die for Ireland. With them he would be proud and busy and happy. Among them he would find not only fame and glory, but also friends, lads of his own age who would make him one of their splendid company.

It was not an easy thing to be admitted to this noble

company. There were many difficult tests, and Brian was finding some of them almost impossible to pass. If only this chief of Leinster had brought a boy who could help him! He watched the chariot in hope, but, as it drew near the gate, he saw in it only two men.

"Open the gate for Conor, chief of the Clan of the Lawgiver!" one of the men shouted.

"Open the gate yourself," Brian thought angrily, but he remembered the rules of courtesy which his father insisted that he must keep. He opened the palace gate as Conor leaped from the cart, tossing the reins to an old man beside him.

The chief of the Clan of the Lawgiver did not go through the gate at once. He turned back to the chariot, muttering low words to the old man. The old man looked down over his shoulder. For the first time, Brian saw a young boy sitting on the floor of the chariot. The boy was just about his own age. He was thin and pale, and his cheeks were hollow. In his gray eyes burned a flame which seemed to leap as the chief spoke.

"Remember, boy," said Conor, "to say just what I have told you when you answer the king's questions."

"I shall remember, sir," the boy said.

Brian let the gate swing shut after Conor. Then he went to a bench where there was a pail of fresh milk and a metal dipper. He filled two large cups and gave the old man and the boy a drink.

"May God and Mary bless you!" said the old man.

"What is your name?" Brian asked the boy.

"My name is Donal."

"Are you the son of Conor the chief?" Brian asked.

"No," said the boy, "I work for Conor."

"Donal is no ordinary worker," said the old man. "There is little he cannot do. He can make knives and swords. He can carve stone into statues. He can read anything you set before him. He can write on stone or on paper."

"He can?" Brian asked. These were talents he did not have. Then Brian began to boast. "I can stand in a trench as deep as my knees and protect myself against nine warriors with only a shield and a hazel staff," he declared proudly. "Can you do that?" he asked Donal.

"No, I can't," said Donal.

"With the head start of only one tree, I can run through a wood so fast that no one can catch me," said Brian. "Can you do that?"

"No," said Donal.

"Donal can do better things," said the old man.

Brian paid no attention. "I can pick a thorn out of my foot while I am running," he went on. "I can meet an enemy without letting the weapon tremble in my hand."

"My, you are a wonderful lad," said the old man. Brian knew that the old man's tone made fun of him, although his words praised him. "That makes you able to join the Fian, does it not? I suppose you are all ready to go into the contest at the next Fair of Tara?"

"I am almost ready," Brian told him.

"Almost?" The old man caught at the word. "What is it you cannot do?"

"I can say only nine of the twelve books of the history of Ireland," Brian cried.

"Nine?" The old man's tone still laughed at the boy. "What about the other three? A lad must know the twelve books before he may join that noble band. Donal knows all twelve of them."

Brian moved near to Donal, looking at him now with new admiration. For years Brian had been preparing for the tests of Tara. He was confident of his strength and skill and courage, but he was not sure of his memory. Over and over again he had tried to memorize the twelve books, but always he had failed to learn three of them. How could it be, he wondered, that the son of the king of Leinster could not do what this worker of Conor's household could do?

180

"Can you say them all?" he asked Donal.

"Yes," said Donal.

"Will you be going to the Fair of Tara?" Brian asked him.

"No," said the boy. "I cannot go to Tara. I am only a worker brought here by Conor to work for your father."

"But workers have as much chance as princes to join the Fian if they can pass the tests," insisted Brian.

"I am not strong in body like you," Donal said. He looked at Brian with friendly admiration. "Perhaps," he went on, "you would like me to help you with the three books of the Fian you have not yet learned?"

"Donal could really help you," said the old man. "Why don't both of you go to the school of the blessed Brigid at Kildare?"

"The School of Kildare?" Donal cried. "Oh, it would be wonderful to go there!" His eyes shone with joy, but soon clouded. "The School of Kildare does not teach the books of the Fian. It teaches the Gospel of Christ."

"Well, if you took Donal with you to Kildare," the old man said to Brian, "he could teach you the books of the Fian while he studies the Gospels. And perhaps, if you studied the Gospels too, you would be able to read so well that you would pass the tests at Tara."

"I will ask my father," Brian said, "to send Donal with me to the school of the blessed Brigid."

"You will not be sorry," Donal promised.

"The blessing of God be on you both," said the old man. He glanced toward the palace yard. "Here comes Conor now," he said.

The gate to the palace swung wide again as Conor, chief of the Clan of the Lawgiver, came out with the king of Leinster. Brian stepped near to his father. "O sir," he cried, "will you send this boy with me to the school of the blessed Brigid at Kildare?"

The king of Leinster laughed as he put his hand on Brian's head. "Since when have you grown so interested in a school?" he asked his son. Then, remembering the boy's ambition, he added, "Do you think you will learn the rest of the twelve books at Brigid's school? Kildare is no training place for a warrior."

"I think I can," Brian said, "if this boy may come to help me with the learning."

The king of Leinster looked closely at Donal. "What will you do for my son," he asked the boy, "if I send you with him to Kildare?"

"There is nothing I will not do for him, sir," Donal answered.

"That is a promise," the king said, "and a promise is a bond which no man breaks." He turned to Conor. "I will take the boy," he told the chief.

The king touched Donal on the shoulder, then whirled him around to Brian. "Tomorrow the two of you go to Kildare. The time is short before the Fair of Tara, and Brian has much to learn before he can pass the great test."

From the first day that they arrived at the school Brian, the son of the king of Leinster, began to learn more than the books which Donal taught him. The school was, first of all, for the training of young men and women who wished to become priests and nuns, but other boys and girls also studied there. Those who would be priests and nuns were taught Latin and Greek, the Scriptures, and the writings of the early Fathers of the Church. All the students were taught music, reading, writing, and the beautiful arts which were making the Irish monasteries famous throughout Europe—the making of glass, the making of ornaments in gold and silver, and the making of books called manuscripts because they were written by hand.

Mother Brigid herself taught the lettering of the manuscripts. Brian chose this study, and he and Mother Brigid became good friends.

Mother Brigid was working on the *Book of Kildare* one day when Brian came to the House of Writing. She was copying from an older book, a manuscript of the Four Evangelists, written by Saint Jerome. On every page she was painting letters and small figures in the loveliest of colorings. The letters and figures glowed like emeralds and rubies and sapphires. The gold gleamed like sunshine on the waters of a lake.

"That is beautiful," Brian said softly.

"All work that is done for God is beautiful," Mother Brigid told him. "What are you going to do for God, Brian?" she asked the boy.

"I will try to be a good king of Leinster," he said.

"King of Leinster?" she repeated. "There is a greater kingdom."

"Well, I may be king of all Ireland," said the boy.

"There is a greater kingdom than Ireland. It is the kingdom of God. Have you thought about that kingdom?"

From that day he began to see the young men who were studying for the priesthood not merely as students, but as soldiers, soldiers of Christ. Some day they would go out from the School of Kildare, ready to risk their lives as surely and as bravely as did any lad of the Fian. They would go to Britain and to those lands of the continent of Europe which waited in darkness for the Light these youths would bring.

Brian spoke one day to Donal of these young men. "Will you become a missionary, too?" he asked.

184

"If it please God to choose me as His messenger," Donal told him.

Donal advanced in his studies by leaps and bounds. He could read Latin and Greek. He knew the stories of the Old Testament. He knew the Psalms of David. He knew the Gospels of Christ. He could make bells of metal so beautiful that even the abbot praised him.

"When will you be able to do all this?" the bishop asked Brian.

"I shall be satisfied if I know enough to pass the tests of Tara," Brian said.

The abbot stared hard at the boy. "I wonder," he said, "if you will be entirely satisfied."

II. *The Great Fair*

The days, which seemed long to Brian when he had first gone to Kildare, suddenly seemed to grow short. All too soon he had mastered the books. In a little while he would go to the great fair at Tara to prove, if he could, that he was worthy to join the Fian.

The great fair was in full swing when Brian, the son of a king, and Donal, a scholar, came to Tara. For days the roads of Ireland had been black with crowds on their way to the place; for the Fair of Tara was more than a trading post, more than a show. It was the congress of Ireland.

At Tara the people of Ireland learned their laws, their rights, the history of the country, the warlike deeds of their brave ancestors. At Tara they found enjoyment in music, in poetry, in games, in sports. At Tara they exchanged their goods. At Tara they met in peace; for all knew that no man could break the peace without punishment of death.

The music had already struck up. Trumpets, harps, fiddles, flutes, and wide-mouthed horns were sounding. High above them all rose the shrill notes of the bagpipes.

"Listen, Donal," said Brian. "The bagpipes are calling the clans!"

From every part of the grounds of Tara the clans were answering the call. Warriors, bowmen, spearmen, men on foot and on horseback, ran across the grass. Jugglers and singers, sellers and buyers of goods, followed them. All of them started toward the place where rose the sound of the bagpipes.

Brian and Donal, hurrying after them, almost fell over an old man who was running on the heels of a younger man. The old man began to shout angrily at the boys, then suddenly changed his cry. "Glory be to God," he called, "here is Donal with the son of the king of Leinster!"

Brian recognized the old man who had come with Conor and Donal to the gate of his father's palace. "Here is your friend," Brian told Donal.

"Cormac!" Donal cried.

"I am so glad you are here," said the old man. "The march of the clans has already begun. Fall in with Leinster!"

Brian fell into step with Donal and the old man. The music of the pipes rose higher as the clans surged toward the highest of the seven mounds. Before the great banqueting hall of Tara, a high platform had been built. Upon it sat the five kings of Ireland, with the High King of all Ireland in the center. All of them wore crimson cloaks, fastened at their shoulders by round pins of gold set with precious stones, the Tara brooches. All of them wore golden necklaces and golden shoes. In the sunlight, the crimson and gold of the five kings shone like the brilliant letters on the pages in the *Book of Kildare*.

Brian, watching the kings as the men of the clans marched before the high platform, thrilled with pride that his father sat with the kings of Ireland. He must prove himself worthy of his father's high position, of his father's great trust. He must pass all those tests of the trial which would soon begin here on the plain of Tara. Because of the help of Donal and the lessons which Mother Brigid had given him, Brian felt ready for the recitation of the twelve books. Because of his old training he was ready for the physical tests. But would he pass them all? Silently he prayed for strength. "Christ be with me, Mother Mary help me, Patrick guide me!"

The men of the clans passed the platform of the kings and made a great semicircle in front of the banqueting hall. A trumpeter sounded a call. Then the herald of the High King arose and cried out an order. Again the sound of the trumpet pierced the air. The contest of Tara had begun.

Brian moved forward with hundreds of other youths as the heralds of the clans called for those who were to enter the contest. Sons of chiefs and of princes strode beside sons of poor men. Only eighty of them would be chosen from the hundreds; but each of them hoped that he would be one of the eighty.

To the right of the platform of the kings a trench had been dug. There a youth had to prove that he could hold off nine warriors with only a shield and a hazel staff for his protection. Lad after lad went down before the attacks of the warriors. But still there were many hundreds who had passed this test when the trumpet sounded; and Brian was one of them.

The wood-running came next. In the woods near the banqueting hall hundreds of boys went through the tests, proving that they could escape their pursuers. Not many of them could step so lightly that they broke no withered branch. Not many could jump over and stoop under branches without leaving a quivering branch in their passing. Hardest of all was the test which required them to pick thorns from their feet as they ran. Many failed in that; but Brian, son of the king of Leinster, did not fail.

Then came the most difficult of the physical tests. Warriors set upon those boys who had passed the other tests and tried to overcome them. The boys not only must win the contests, but must win without letting their weapons tremble in their hands. One after another, the boys dropped from the ranks as the fighting went on. Only a hundred of them were left on the field; but Brian was one of the hundred.

"I knew he could do it," Donal said.

"His hardest test is yet to come," said Cormac. "He has to show that he has mastered the twelve books."

"Brian will do that too," said Donal confidently.

The trumpets sounded to call the boys to the final test. On a platform below the place of the kings the hundred youths gathered. Around them grouped the bards, the poets, the harpers, the historians. The platform must have looked like this, Brian thought, on that day when Patrick came to Tara. On that day Patrick had preached to the assembly. He had won to Christ the king's poet and the king's spearman, the queen and many nobles of the court.

Patrick had also preached to a greater assembly. He had told the people of Ireland of the infinite love of Christ for them all, of the yearning of Christ to have them come to Him. He had told them of God, Who had sent Christ, His only Son, to save the world; of the Passion and Death of Christ; of Christ's glorious Resurrection; of His love for all mankind.

The people had listened to Patrick. They had knelt for his blessing. They had joined him in hymns to praise God. They had watched him light a fire to honor God. Brian was thinking of all this as he awaited his turn.

One after another, the youths on the lower platform had given answers to the questions of the bards and historians. There remained but one place to fill, and there were two boys, Brian and another youth, Finbar, waiting for the questioning.

"Brian will never win against Finbar," said Cormac.

"He has a chance," said Donal.

Through one book after another of the twelve books the poets and historians questioned the two boys. Sometimes Finbar hesitated. Sometimes Brian paused. They had to tell long stories, tales of the great heroes of the ancient Irish; they had to repeat the pledge of every man who joined the Fian: to choose a wife for her manners and her virtues only; to be gentle with all women; to fight against all odds for the sake of justice; and never to hold to himself anything which another needs. It was on the last verse of the pledge that Finbar stopped; he could not go on.

"Let me say it for him," Brian said to the bard who had given the question; but the bard shook his head.

"You can say that only for yourself," he told him.

Then Brian repeated the verse, "Never to hold to myself anything which another needs."

The bard lifted his arm to signal the heralds. "Brian, the son of the king of Leinster, is now one of the Fian," he said.

With a mighty cheer, nine thousand men of the Fian welcomed the eighty who had won the right to join them. Even the five kings joined in the great shout that rose from the plain. The king of Leinster moved near his son. "I am proud of you, Brian," he said. "You have done well at Kildare. But now that your time there is over—"

"My time at Kildare is not over, Father," Brian said. "I want to go back there—with Donal."

191

"Why should you go back?" cried the king. "You need no more learning now, not even to be king of Leinster."

"I shall never be king of Leinster," Brian said. "Here, at Tara where Patrick brought the Faith of Christ, I came to a decision. I want to go back to Kildare and study to become a missionary."

"Ireland does not need you as a missionary," said the king. "Ireland is now a Christian country."

"Just as Patrick brought the Faith to us," said Brian, "some of us must take the Faith to other lands."

The king of Leinster looked sadly at his son, but when he saw the light in Brian's eyes, he spoke firmly. "If it is the will of God," he said, "you may go."

Brian turned to find the old man and Donal close to him. Swiftly he told them of his decision.

"I have prayed for this," Donal said. "Perhaps one day we shall go together to far lands to preach the Gospel which Patrick brought to us."

They did not know, as they went forth from Tara, that the great days of Tara would come to an end, that the kings would pass, and the bards and the harpers and the heralds. They did not know that their Ireland would suffer through centuries to hold that Faith which Patrick had brought and which Brigid had spread.

They knew only that before them waited their mission. Knowing that, Brian, the son of the king, and Donal, the worker of Conor, were happy as they jogged along the road to the school of Brigid of Kildare.

Identify the characters in the story by writing the name of each on the proper line below. Then associate the speaker with the quotations by placing the name beside the number of the quoted passage. Number your paper from 1 to 10 for this work.

Characters	*Identification*
1. _____	Son of the king of Leinster
2. _____	Chief of the Clan of the Lawgiver
3. _____	Teacher at the School of Kildare
4. _____	A worker for the Leinster clan chief
5. _____	The old man
6. _____	King of Leinster

Quotations

1. "Since when have you grown so interested in a school?"
2. "Donal is no ordinary worker."
3. "May God and Mary bless you."
4. "My, you are a wonderful lad."
5. "With the head start of only one tree, I can run through a wood so fast that no one can catch me."
6. "But I am not strong in body like you."
7. "All work that is done for God is beautiful."
8. "That is a promise, and a promise is a bond which no man breaks."
9. "Never to hold to myself anything which another needs."
10. "Just as Patrick brought the Faith to us, some of us must take the Faith to other lands."

The Gaelic Litany

Saints of Four Seasons,
Saints of the Year,
Loving, I pray you;
    longing, I say to you;
Save me from angers, save me from dangers,
Saints of Four Seasons,
Saints of the Year!

Saints of Four Seasons,
Saints of the Year,
Patrick and Gregory,
    Brigid, be near,
Life in the Night, hold me God's light,
Saints of Four Seasons,
Saints of the Year!

SAINT ADAMNAN

Giotto of the Hills

There were many boys who tended the sheep on the Italian hillsides, dark-haired boys who rose at dawn and worked until darkness. Some of them were stupid and some of them were clever. Some of them would always be shepherds; others would own little farms. A few of them would go to the great cities, to Florence, to Padua, even to Rome. One of these boys would become so great that for centuries men have remembered him. That boy was Giotto.

Giotto did not seem much different from other boys when they all drove their sheep up from the sheds to the higher hills. He was kind and gentle and obedient to his father and mother, and sometimes he was careless. He would forget to watch the lambs, and the lambs would run away. Then Giotto's father had to come to his aid in finding them. Always, when this happened, his father said to the boy, "You have been drawing pictures again," and always Giotto replied, "Yes, Father, I have."

"But, why, my son?" his father would ask.

"I had to do it," the boy explained. "I see something, I keep watching it, and then I must set it down on the rocks."

"Where the rain washes it away."

"I know," said the boy sadly. "Some day, perhaps, I can draw pictures on something which will not be exposed to the rain."

"Paper is very expensive, my son."

"I know, Father, but perhaps—"

Giotto was on the hillside with his sheep one day when a splendidly dressed man on a beautiful horse rode up the hill. As usual Giotto was drawing his pictures on a rock. The rider stopped his horse when he saw what the boy was doing. "This is good," he said to Giotto, after he had looked at the sheep and lamb the lad had scratched on the flat rock. "Who has taught you to draw like this?"

"No one."

"Then this is more than good. What do you plan to do, lad?"

"I suppose I shall always watch the sheep, but I wish I might be an artist, a great artist like Cimabue."

The stranger laughed. "I know better artists than Cimabue," he said, "for I am Cimabue."

There was no greater artist at that time in Italy, and Giotto's eyes grew wide with wonder as Cimabue went on, "How should you like to come to Florence and to study with me?"

"If only my father would let me! But we are poor. He could not pay."

"Who said anything about paying? Where is your father?"

They found Giotto's father near the sheepfold. He thought carefully over the question Cimabue asked. Then he said, "I believe my son has a great talent. Our Lord has said we must not hide our talents under a bushel. I accept your offer, sir. Giotto may go with you."

A new life opened for Giotto when Cimabue took him to Florence. From the master and his pupils the boy learned much. He carefully followed the kind of painting the others were doing. After a time it did not satisfy him, but it was only when Cimabue sent him to Assisi to paint wall pictures of the life of Saint Francis that Giotto dared to paint in what he thought might be a better way.

From the time he had been a little boy Giotto had cherished a deep devotion to Saint Francis of Assisi. In his thoughts he saw the saint walking over the rough roads of the Italian hill country, with the soft blue skies of Italy over him and the silvery green of the olive trees around him. The birds hovered about him and the animals, even the wolves, followed him. Giotto always saw him like this; but when he came to the church in Assisi he found that Cimabue had painted Francis with a bright gold background.

"This is not right for Saint Francis," Giotto told himself. "He was not the saint of gold rooms and of rich people. He was the saint of the poor who walked the roads of our Italy."

He set to work removing the gold background. Then, when he had made the walls white and bare, he painted the hills as he saw them, soft green hills under the blue Italian sky. When he had finished, he sighed in pride. "That is right," he said. Then he began to worry about what Cimabue would say when he saw what his pupil had done.

Cimabue stared at the walls in wonder when he came to the church in Assisi. Then he flung his arms around Giotto. "Beautiful, beautiful," he cried. "That is right. That is the way to picture Saint Francis."

From all over Italy people flocked to see the paintings on the church wall. Today, hundreds of years later, people from all over the world travel to the town on the steep hill to look at the Giotto paintings. For those paintings were the beginning of modern art. The great painters who came after Giotto owed much of their greatness to the method he had used and which they copied.

Giotto went on to other triumphs. He went to Rome

to decorate the walls of St. Peter's. In the Chapel of the Arena in Padua he painted the famous picture of the Blessed Mother and the Child on their way to Egypt. There, remembering his own humble boyhood, he painted the picture of Joachim and the shepherds. Returning to Florence he designed the famous Bell Tower, and set in its lower part a marble carving of a shepherd, with his sheep dog guarding the lambs.

All Florence walked in procession to do him honor when the Bell Tower was finished. Giotto, the shepherd boy of the hills, had risen to fame and glory because he had shown the courage to set forth his vision for all men to see.

SENSING RELATIONSHIPS

As you read, do you sense relationships between sentences? There are many contrasts in the story you have just read. Write the sentences below on your paper and for each write another sentence that shows a contrasting thought.

1. Some of the shepherd boys would one day own little farms.

2. Some of the shepherd boys were clever.

3. At first Giotto drew pictures on rocks exposed to the rain.

4. Giotto carefully followed the kind of painting the others were doing.

5. Cimabue painted Saint Francis with a bright gold background.

Song of the Sun

Be praised, O My Lord, by all Your creatures,
And chiefly by the honored Brother Sun,
Whom You make bright for us within the day;
For fair and high he is and brightly shining.

Be praised by Sister Moon and Stars of Night;
In Heaven You made them, precious, fair, and bright!

Be praised, O My Lord, by Brother Wind,
By Air and Cloud and Sky and every Clime,
By whom You give help unto all kind!

By Sister Water, O My Lord, be praised!
Useful is she and lowly, precious and chaste.

Be praised, O My Lord, by Brother Fire,
By whom You brighten all our steps at night,
And fair is he and merry, strong and mighty!

Be praised, O My Lord, by our Mother, Sister Earth,
Who helps our lives upon her and gives birth
To many fruits and colored flowers and herbs!

O bless and praise My Lord and thankful be
And serve My Lord with great humility!

SAINT FRANCIS OF ASSISI

Conrad Humery and the Word of God

I. *The City of Saint Boniface*

Afternoon sunlight, hot and bright, shone over the valley of the Rhine on a September day in the long-ago year of 1454. It shone upon wheat fields and pastures, upon orchards and vineyards, upon little villages and great towns. It shone upon Mainz, the old city of Saint Boniface.

Its golden light seemed to pour into the room of the parish school of St. Stephen. Young Conrad Humery sat in dull silence, while around him five and twenty boys lifted happy faces to Father Cremer.

Father Cremer stood at the front of the room while boy after boy passed to one another the one book for the entire class. It was a block book called the *Bible of the Poor*. It had forty pictures, showing scenes from Our Lord's life. Beneath each picture were words to explain the pictures.

Conrad Humery knew how the block book had been made. He could have drawn the pictures and letters upon the block and cut away the wood from around them. He could have made the block ready for inking and placed it upon the pages of the book. But he was not able to put the letters and words together so that he knew what they meant.

"Conrad Humery," called Father Cremer, as the reading lesson went on. "What does the next picture show, Conrad?" Father Cremer asked.

"The picture shows the crowning of Our Blessed Mother in heaven," said Conrad.

"Read the words under the picture," said Father Cremer.

For a moment Conrad stood silent. Only yesterday Father Cremer told him he was giving him just one more chance to learn the lesson. If he had not mastered it by today, Conrad would have to go back with the younger children. Tears came to Conrad's eyes, but he fought them back before he spoke. "I cannot read the words, Father," he said.

"Conrad!" The tone of the priest's voice showed that he was annoyed. "Why do you not learn to read? If you were another boy, I might find some excuse for you. But you are the son of the greatest scholar in Mainz. What does your father say? Isn't he worried that his son does not yet know how to read?"

"Yes, Father," Conrad said. His voice trembled so that he could hardly speak.

Father Cremer looked at him sharply. "You will stay after school, Conrad," the priest told the boy.

As the other boys took up the reading of the book, Conrad fell back into silence. All too well he knew how his father grieved over his dullness. Doctor Conrad Humery, highest in rank of the scholars of Germany, could not understand why his son could not read. Day after day, when school was over, he tried to teach him, but in the younger Conrad's mind rose a wall which no teacher of reading could cross.

"I do not know what is wrong with me," the boy thought miserably.

He sat alone as the other boys filed out into the street. What would Father Cremer say to him? What would Father Cremer do to him? He looked up as the priest came toward him. Father Cremer's voice was kind. "Conrad, what do you like to do?" he asked, as he sat down beside him on a low bench.

"I do not know, Father," Conrad said.

"There must be something you like to do, something you want to be. Do you want to be a scholar like your father?"

"I could never be that."

"Do you want to be a goldsmith?"

"If I could be a goldsmith like Master John Gutenberg," Conrad said. His eyes brightened at the

203

thought. "Do you know what he does, Father? He makes letters—not a block of letters like the ones from which the *Bible of the Poor* is made, but separate letters of metal. First he made lead letters. These were too soft. Then he made iron letters, but they did not work. Then he mixed brass with other metals to make them hard. That worked. Master John made a little mold for each letter and poured the metal into it. Now he uses those letters over and over again."

"Master John is doing a great work," said Father Cremer. "If he can keep on with it, he may make it possible for every pupil in school to have a book of his own. How did you happen to see his work, Conrad?"

"My father took me to Master Gutenberg's shop one day. While they talked I went around, looking at everything."

"Did you like the shop, Conrad?"

"Oh, Father, I liked it better than any place I have ever seen." Suddenly Conrad sighed. "If only I could work there, I should be happy!"

Father Cremer looked at him closely. "I think you would be happy, Conrad," he said. The priest arose from the bench and walked toward the door. There he turned back. "Will you ask your father to come to see me this evening?"

"Yes, Father," the boy said.

"You will not forget?"

"I do not forget anything but words on the page, Father," Conrad said.

II. *The Gutenberg Bible*

John Gutenberg, a white-bearded man, studied Conrad closely as the boy's father told of Conrad's desire to work in the Gutenberg shop. "Do you wish to work with me?" he asked the lad.

"More than anything in the world," Conrad said.

Gutenberg laughed. "Even if I shall have work only for a little while?" He turned to Doctor Humery. "There is a lawsuit against me. I borrowed money from a friend. Now he sues me. If he wins the suit, he will take my type and my books. Then I must close the shop. Do you still wish to come with me, my boy?"

"Yes, sir," said Conrad. "When may I begin work?"

"Now," said the printer. He led the new apprentice

to the big wooden press. Slowly he made the Sign of the Cross. "Say these words after me," he bade the boy. "They are the prayer of the worker, the draftsman, the artist. In the name of the Father, and of the Son, and of the Holy Spirit!" he said, "let us offer to God, Who has given us everything, all the work of our hands and our minds."

Day after day Conrad worked in the printing shop on St. Christopher's Street. He learned how to mix tin and lead and brass and pour the mixture into the type molds to make letters. He learned how to take out the type when it cooled. He learned how to pick it out, letter by letter, and how to set it in the wooden frame. To his own surprise, he was learning to read as he put the type in the frames. As he put words together to make sentences, he realized what they meant. "Listen!" he would sometimes call out, amazed at his own progress.

Conrad learned how to ink the letters, how to set paper over them, how to move the big screw so that the paper was pressed down tightly upon the inked type. He learned how to take out the printed paper at the right time. Better than all, Conrad learned Master Gutenberg's standard of work. In his shop there could be no cheating on the quality of work. Every task must be made perfect. Everyone must do his best.

Master Gutenberg was never satisfied with anything as it was. He always wanted to make everything better. The boy labored over metal and inks and paper by sunlight and by candlelight. It was amazing to Conrad what Gutenberg did, but the boy knew that the master could do much more if he had the money. He needed metal, materials for ink, better paper, and parts for the printing press. "If only I had a few more tools!" the printer sighed over and over. "If only I had a little more money!"

Day after day the boy went from the shop to the cathedral to pray that no misfortune would come to John Gutenberg. Conrad had come to love the master. The boy had never been so happy before. Even the boys who had been with him at St. Stephen's School noticed the change in him. Not only was he Master Gutenberg's apprentice, but he was an intelligent apprentice. He knew the type by sight and feeling. He could read the words which he helped Master Gutenberg to print. He could read sentences, then paragraphs. Even Father Cremer shook his head in wonder when Conrad read for him the Gospel of Saint John.

"Excellent! Master Gutenberg is a better teacher than I," the priest told Conrad.

"Oh, no, Father!" the boy cried. "Do you not remember that you are the one who asked him to take me as an apprentice?"

"I am glad you are happy in your work, Conrad," Father Cremer said. "For that is one of the surest ways to win true happiness. Do your work for the sake of God, and God will reward you with peace of mind."

"He has rewarded me, Father," said Conrad. "I

only pray I may keep on with Master Gutenberg until I have learned all he can teach me."

"I too pray for that," said the priest.

For a time it seemed as if Conrad's wish would be granted. Then, like a clap of thunder, came the news that John Gutenberg had lost the lawsuit. The printer would either have to pay a large sum of money to his former partner or else turn over to him all the type for the Bible which Gutenberg was making.

"You will still have your printing press," Conrad tried to cheer the printer.

"But nothing to set upon it," said Gutenberg. "What can I do without type?"

"Can you not borrow the money?" Conrad asked.

"Where?" cried Gutenberg. "Who will lend money to a man who is being sued for what he has already borrowed?"

John Gutenberg went to men whom he thought could help him. He went to goldsmiths, who had been his fellow craftsmen before he had left work upon that metal to work on the making of type. In spite of all his efforts, he was unable to raise the money. On the day when officers from the Palace of Justice came to take the type from Gutenberg's shop, the printer was in the depths of misery.

"I am all through," he told Conrad. "I have done all I can. I can do nothing now but lock up my shop. I am sorry for you, Conrad, but perhaps you can find work with other masters."

"I will never work with them," Conrad said. "They are not like you, Master John."

"Thank you for your trust," the printer said, "but I fear that you and I can no longer work together, Conrad."

They stood alone in the shop while the officers took all the cases of type. Without the type the shop seemed cold and dreary.

"I feel as if my hands had been cut off," Gutenberg said. "Always before, no matter what happened, I felt that I could go on. Now I know that I can do nothing. Good-by, Conrad."

Suddenly Conrad gave a shout which echoed through the too-quiet shop. "I know!" he cried. "I should have thought of this before. But it is not too late. Wait here for me, Master John!" he called, as he ran from the shop out into the bright sunlight of St. Christopher's Street.

Swiftly he raced through the narrow street to the rectory of the Church of St. Stephen. He knocked at the door until Father Cremer himself opened it.

"O Father, Father Cremer!" the boy cried. "I have prayed that you would be here!"

"What is it, Conrad?" the priest asked.

"Do you know," the boy asked, "that the court has ordered Master John's type to be given to his old partner?"

"I know that."

"The officers have taken it. Master John says he can do no more. He needs money for new type. If he had that, he could go on. He could finish his beautiful book, the splendid Bible whose pages you have already seen."

"Has he no money at all?" the priest asked.

"He has nothing, and can get nothing. That is why I have come to you. Father, there must be a way to help him. If you could find a way for me, surely you can find a way for him!"

"Master John's case is not the same as yours, Conrad."

"But, Father, there must be some way. He is such a good man."

"Yes, Conrad, Master John is a true Catholic, even among men who are beginning to lose their Faith. He should have help—but how can I give it to him?"

"Can't you find a way?"

"I do not know what I shall be able to do, but I

210

will see what I can do. The Church of St. Stephen
has, like many other churches, a parish fund for the
help of those in need. Your Master John was born in
this parish. He has a claim upon our charity. I cannot give it to him without the consent of the board
which decides questions like this, but I will take it
up with the board."

"I know you will find a way to help him, Father
Cremer."

Conrad Humery was right. Father Cremer found
the way to help John Gutenberg. The printer was
provided with enough money to buy new type. And in
time there came from the shop in St. Christopher's
Street a Bible so beautiful that even today, over five
hundred years later, the few copies that still exist remain among the finest books in the world. For not only
did John Gutenberg make new type much better than
the old, but Father Cremer himself worked by hand
upon the book, making the glorious red and blue letters
which still gleam upon the pages.

"It is wonderful," Doctor Humery said, as he looked

upon the first finished copy. "It is the beginning of a time that will be altogether different from our own, a time when books will be in the hands of all men. It is a miracle you have performed, John Gutenberg."

"No," said John Gutenberg. "It is not a miracle. Only God can perform miracles." Again, as he had done on the day the boy had come into the shop, the printer placed his hand upon Conrad's head. "Conrad and I know what it is," he said. "Thanks be to God, it is a good job."

"A good job, Master John," said Conrad Humery.

SENSING THE FEELINGS OF CHARACTERS

To recognize and sense the feelings and virtues of the characters helps you to interpret the stories you read. Number your paper from 1 to 10 and after each of the words, or groups of words, below write the incident which caused Conrad to experience each feeling. The first one is completed as an example.

1. Sadness (*Conrad could not read the words under the picture.*)
2. Hope
3. Interest and curiosity
4. Happy amazement
5. Accomplishment
6. Loyalty to Master John
7. Security
8. Sudden inspiration
9. Confidence and trust
10. Faith in prayer

Books

Here's an adventure! What awaits
   Beyond these closed, mysterious gates?
Whom shall I meet, where shall I go?
   Beyond the lovely land I know?
Above the sky, across the sea?
   What shall I learn and feel and be?
Open, strange doors, to good or ill!
   I hold my breath a moment still
Before the magic of your look—
   What will you do to me, O book?

Abbie Farwell Brown

213

The Class at Collie Creek

I. *Margie's Summer Pupils*

Margie saw the children as she went down the road to the swimming pool. There were five of them, a tall boy, a tall girl, a small boy, and two small girls. They stood behind an old rail fence and watched her with solemn, unfriendly eyes. She waved to them, but they did not lift a hand in greeting. She called to them, but they scattered like frightened quail.

"Do they think I'd hurt them?" Margie asked herself, and laughed a little at their flight.

They were gone from sight when she came back from swimming, but the next day they were there at the fence. Margie walked a little nearer to them. "Where do you live?" she asked. They made no answer, but their glances shifted back over their shoulders toward a tumble-down cabin near the top of the hill.

"I live down the road," she told them, nodding toward the big white house that gleamed through the pine trees.

"You don't live there," the tall boy said suddenly. "You only come there in the summer. You're just a stranger."

"No, I'm not," Margie said. "Well, not exactly, anyhow. My grandfather lives here all the year round. What's your name?"

They were silent until she left them. Then the tall

214

girl spoke loud enough for her to hear. "That's a right funny dress you're wearing."

"It's my swimming suit," Margie said.

There was no reply. They all ran away, hiding in the thick woods. That night, in the candlelight of the old dining room of the big white house, Margie asked her grandfather about the youngsters.

"They are the Blakes," the old man said. "Wild as colts, but you can't blame them. Their mother's dead, and their father doesn't take care of them."

"Then who does?"

"No one," said her grandfather.

The answer troubled Margie but, she thought, there was nothing she could do about the Blakes. The next morning, however, she stopped again at the fence and met the straight gaze of five pairs of eyes. "Don't you ever go swimming?" she asked.

"Sometimes," the tall boy said, shifting bashfully from one bare foot to the other.

"What's your name?" asked Margie.

"Lem."

"What's your brother's name?"

"Clem."

The tall girl was Fern. The little girls were Linda and Lily.

"Where do you go to school?" asked Margie kindly.

"We go to the crossroads school," Fern said, "but there's no school in wintertime."

"Or in summertime," said Linda.

215

"Or in springtime," said Lily.

"You mean there's school only a little while each year?" Margie asked.

"September, October, November," said Fern.

The group moved a little nearer to her along the fence rail. "Do you know stories?" Fern inquired. "Can you tell stories?"

"I know some," said Margie.

"Could you tell"—the tall girl hesitated—"could you tell stories to the little ones? to Clem and Lily and Linda?"

"I suppose so," Margie started to climb the fence. "Let's go where we can sit down."

"There's a sitting-place by the creek," the tall boy said.

To Margie's surprise he and the tall girl came with the younger children. They led the way to a circle of rocks by the side of Collie Creek. Margie chose one, and the others found places near her. What story, she wondered, should she tell them? She started with the tale of Cinderella. Lem and Fern listened as closely as did Linda and Lily and Clem.

"That's a nice story," Fern said when Margie finished telling the old fairy tale. "I'd like to be a Cinderella sometime."

"We all would," said Margie.

"Do you know any more stories?" Linda inquired.

"Do you know a story about Jesus?" Fern asked.

"Don't you?" Margie questioned the girl.

"Our mother used to talk of Him," Fern said.

"Don't you go to church?"

"It's too far away. We can't walk so far."

Slowly Margie began to tell them of Christ. Wide-eyed, the Blake children listened as she told of the birth of Jesus in the stable of Bethlehem, of the wonder of the shepherds, of the coming of the Wise Men. They sighed as she spoke of Herod and the order to kill the babies of the land. They smiled as she described the flight of Mary and Joseph into Egypt with the Holy Child. They shared with her the story of the Boy of Nazareth.

"Could He read?" Clem asked when she had finished the tale.

"Oh, yes," Margie said, and added the story of Christ teaching the doctors in the Temple of Jerusalem.

They went with her halfway down to the swimming pool. There she said good-by to them, but she kept thinking about them during the day. "Why can't the Blakes go to a good school?" she asked her grandfather.

"Too far," he said, as Fern had said.

"But they can't learn much by going to school just three months a year."

"They know a lot you don't know," her grandfather told her. "They can hunt and fish and skin a rabbit."

"But they have no books." Margie could not imagine a world without books. Books to her were broad highways that led through bright valleys toward golden mountains. "Grandfather, couldn't we get some books and teach them?"

"Who'll do the teaching?"

"I'll do some," the girl said.

Her grandfather laughed. "What grade are you in, Margie?"

"I've finished sixth grade," she said.

The next day Margie took an armful of books to the fence where the children waited. She held out the books to the older boy and girl. They took them eagerly and began looking at the beautiful pictures.

"We don't know all the words in these books," Fern said.

"Then we'll have a reading class," said Margie, "and I'll help you with the words you don't know."

Margie wrote to her mother in the city and asked her to send some books. After that, each time she met with the children, she brought new books. Some of them were easy reading and some were more difficult. It made her happy to see the children enjoying the books which they were able to read without help.

On some days the children had to work at home and could not meet Margie. However, they met several times each week, and Margie tried to teach them as much as she could of religion. She was teaching them the Our Father, and they recited this prayer at the beginning of every story hour or reading period. She told them stories of the Blessed Virgin and she often sang one of Our Lady's hymns for them. The children loved to hear the stories of the saints.

One evening Margie spoke to Grandfather about the Blake children. "Don't you think the Blakes should go to school for more than three months a year?" she asked.

He looked troubled. "The nearest all-year school is the one next to the Catholic Church. That's a nine-mile drive. I travel it every Sunday and Holy Day."

"Are the Blakes Catholics?" Margie asked him.

"I don't know," he said. Her grandfather seemed to be thinking of the problem. "Let's ask Penfold," he suggested. Penfold and his wife, Elsie, kept house for Grandfather, and they had lived in the neighborhood of Collie Creek all their lives.

Penfold knew all about the little family. "Their mother was a good woman," he said. "Every one of those Blake children was baptized."

"That settles it," said Grandfather. "We'll take them to church next Sunday and ask Father Philip if they can enter school in September. We can surely arrange for some method of transportation for them."

The very next Sunday the Blakes climbed into Grandfather's station wagon and were soon at St. Joseph's Church. Everything in church was strange to them, but they carefully followed Margie's lead. When she knelt, they knelt. When she stood, they stood. They listened eagerly to Father Philip's sermon.

After Mass they waited while Grandfather spoke to Father Philip. They smiled as the young priest came toward them. "I did not know you were Catholics," he told them.

"Neither did we," said Lem.

"You must come to Mass every Sunday and enter our school in September."

"That will be wonderful," cried all the children.

II. *The Blakes' Summer Pupil*

Margie continued to meet with the children and tried to teach them even more of their religion and prayers. The children beamed when she told them how Our Lord went about the country and through the fields, teaching the people. She reminded the children that they were learning much about many of God's creatures just by living so close to them. Many boys and girls have to learn about plants and animals from books.

"Did you learn about them from books?" asked Clem.

"Yes, and there's much I don't know," admitted Margie.

"Then why don't we be teacher some day and give you a lesson?" suggested Fern.

"That would be fine. How about Wednesday?" said Margie.

Margie could hardly wait to get to the meeting place on Wednesday. She had no idea what the children would do. She had been there only a few minutes when she saw them coming. Lem and Clem were carrying a large wooden box. Clem also had a piece of cardboard and a large crayon. On the cardboard were printed in large letters the words *Right* and *Wrong*.

"This is the way we keep score at school," said Clem.

Margie was eyeing the box when Lem explained

that he would take the things from the box one by one, and Margie must tell what each thing was. Clem would record her score and Fern would be the umpire.

"Ready?" asked Lem as his hand went into the box.

"Number one," called Fern as Lem's hand came into sight holding a small mass of yellow fluff.

"A baby chick," answered Margie.

"Right," announced Clem as he put a check in the *Right* column, "but we call them biddies."

"Number two," called Fern, as the hand came up with a larger mass of yellow-green fluff with web feet and long bill.

Margie remained silent, but little Lily chimed in, "It's a little gosling!" Clem put a check under *Wrong*.

"Number three," and up came the hand with another web-footed mass of yellow.

"Another gosling," Margie gleefully called, but her glee faded when Clem called, "Wrong, it's a duckling."

Number four was a large egg with brown spots like freckles all over it.

"Don't know," admitted Margie.

"Don't you even know a turkey egg?" laughed Linda.

"I'll bet you won't know number five," said Lem.

Margie could hardly see the tiny blue egg which she recognized at once as a robin's egg. "I know the birds better than the others," she said, and was puzzled to hear Clem say, "Those were all birds."

"Ready with number six," announced Fern.

Margie almost screamed as she saw a slimy creature crawling up Lem's arm. "Lizard," she called and won another check in the *Right* column.

Margie feared to think what might appear next and almost before she knew it a bright-eyed, tailless, spotted green animal leaped to the ground in front of her. She recognized the frog, and the scoreboard looked better now.

"Shut your eyes for this one," came the command. "Now open them," and as Margie saw the thing moving slowly toward her she jumped from her rock and shouted, "Turtle!" After her score had been entered, Margie waited expectantly for the next test, but instead Fern ran to another rock and called, "Come over here for this one." Margie and the group followed her. Lem pushed the rock aside and Margie exclaimed, "Oh, what beautiful yellow spots! But what is it?"

"It's a salamander," said Fern. "We were sure you would miss this one."

Clem totaled Margie's score and told her the result

—six right and four wrong. The Blake children were delighted that they were able to tell Margie some things that she didn't know. They told her much about different plants and animals. They told her about the many snakes they had seen and how some of them grow a new skin and crawl out of the old one, leaving it turned inside out on the ground. Margie was thankful they had not included a snake in her lesson.

That evening Margie said to her grandfather, "You surely were right when you said the Blakes knew many things that I didn't know. But, Grandfather, are chickens and ducks really birds?"

"Of course," said Grandfather. "All birds have two legs and two wings. Some fly and some do not fly. How was your lesson today?"

Margie told him all about it, and Grandfather chuckled when she described the lizard.

"I'll be going home soon, Grandfather," she said. "Could I have the Blakes here for a farewell party?"

"Why, of course," said Grandfather. "Get Elsie to help you and get anything you want for the party."

Two weeks later everything was ready for the party. Margie was waiting for her guests when she saw them coming in the distance. Again Lem was carrying a large box. "Not another lesson for me today, I hope," thought Margie. As soon as the children reached the porch little Lily cried out, "Open your surprise." Lem placed the box on a chair and removed the cover. Margie peered cautiously into the box and saw the salamander. It was lying contentedly in the house that the boys had made for it. A pan had been filled with layers of gravel, sand, and soil, with some stones, moss, and fern in the top layer. The sides and cover were made of glass and in one end of the cage was a pan of shallow water.

"This is your present to take home with you," proudly announced Lily.

"Oh, thank you!" cried Margie, and she gingerly touched the creature on the head.

The happy afternoon passed quickly. The Blakes enjoyed the games Margie had planned, and their eyes opened wide when they saw the chocolate layer cake and ice cream Elsie had made for refreshments. After the thank-yous and good-bys had been said, Margie stood at the gate, watching her summer pupils walk down the road.

"I shall miss them, Grandfather," she said. "I wish I could stay longer to teach them more about religion. And I know there are many more things they could teach me about God's creatures."

Her grandfather patted her shoulder. "Don't worry, my dear," he said. "They are in good hands now. Father Philip will see that they get to church and school. The Blakes are on the way to better times."

Margie was surprised that ducks and chickens are birds. Do you think she could have classified the other animals? Fill in this chart, writing the name of each animal mentioned in the story under the group to which it belongs. You may refer to your science book and the encyclopedia for information.

1. Bird group
2. Reptile group
3. Amphibian group

NOTING RELATIONSHIPS

Can you note relationships? For example, shoe is to foot as hat is to head. Fill the blanks in the relationships listed below. Use your science book or encyclopedia if necessary.

1. Duck is to bird as lizard is to __?__.
2. Duckling is to duck as gosling is to __?__.
3. Feather is to chicken as __?__ is to turtle.
4. Flying is to bird as __?__ is to snake.
5. Speckled brown is to turkey egg as blue is to __?__ egg.
6. Leghorn is to chicken as copperhead is to __?__.
7. Corn is to chicken as insect is to __?__.
8. Tadpole is to frog as kitten is to __?__.

Treasure Island

Sultry and brazen was the August day
When Sister Stanislaus went down to see
The little boy with the tuberculous knee.

And as she thought to find him, so he lay:
Still staring, through the dizzy waves of heat,
At the tall tenement across the street.

But did he see that dreary picture? Nay:
In his mind's eye a sunlit harbor showed,
Where a tall pirate ship at anchor rode.

Yes, he was full ten thousand miles away!
—The Sister, when she turned his pillow over,
Kissed "Treasure Island" on its well-worn cover.

SARAH N. CLEGHORN

V

Science

Praise of God the Creator

Bless the Lord, O my soul!
  O Lord, my God, You are great indeed!
You fixed the earth upon its foundation,
  not to be moved forever;
With the ocean, as with a garment, You covered it;
  above the mountains, the waters stood.
At Your rebuke, they fled,
  at the sound of Your thunder they took to flight;
As the mountains rose, they went down the valleys
  to a place You had fixed for them.
You set a limit they may not pass,
  nor shall they cover the earth again.

PSALM 103

Veni Creator

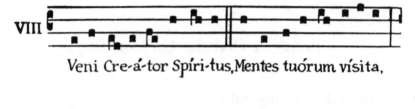

Veni Cre-á-tor Spíri-tus, Mentes tuórum vísita,

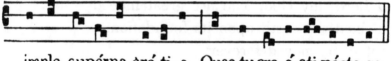

imple supérna grá-ti-a Quae tu cre-á-sti pécto-ra.

Creator Spirit, all divine,
Come visit every soul of Thine,
And fill with Thy celestial flame
The hearts' which Thou Thyself
didst frame.

A Day with Leonardo

Florence, a lovely city of flowers, spread like a great garden before young Bruno as he looked down from the balcony of his father's house. It was, you would have thought, a scene to make a boy happy, especially a boy who seemed to have everything; but Bruno was most unhappy this morning. Carefully and secretly he had been making a statue. He hoped it would be the finest statue which any boy in Florence would make. When it was finished, he would take it to the greatest artist of Florence, Leonardo da Vinci.

Bruno hoped that Leonardo would like the statue so well that he would ask the boy to work with him. Then—and Bruno's heart beat fast at the thought—Leonardo would take him out in the fields beyond the town and let him see the flying machine about which all Florence was talking. That had been Bruno's hope.

Now his dream had been broken. This morning Bruno had seen another statue, one which his cousin Roberto, the orphan who lived in their home, had made. It was a beautiful piece of work, much better than Bruno's statue, and Bruno was honest enough to know its worth.

"What are you going to do with it?" he asked his cousin.

"Show it to Leonardo," Roberto confided. "Will you come with me to Leonardo? Your father has already arranged a meeting with him."

"But why do you want me to go with you?" asked Bruno.

"Because you can talk better than I can," Roberto explained.

"Your statue will speak for you."

"Please come with me, Bruno," the other boy pleaded. "Leonardo is acquainted with your father, and he will be glad to see you."

For an instant Bruno hesitated, but at last he decided to go. Returning to his room he took from its hiding place the little statue he had made. It was a good statue, he realized, and, for a moment, he considered taking it to Leonardo. "But, even if it were the better statue," he thought, "it would not be fair to Roberto when he has planned this meeting." Slowly he put the statue back in its hiding place.

In the morning sunlight the two boys went through the streets of Florence. They passed the Foundlings' Home with its lovely white and blue decorations which della Robbia had made. They went past the Church of St. Michael with its great bronze statues.

"The artists of Florence are the finest in the world," Roberto said.

"Leonardo is the greatest of them," Bruno declared. "Just see all the things he can do! He is a painter and a sculptor. He has made a beautiful statue of the Mother of Christ holding the Child in her arms. He is working on a statue of Saint John the Baptist. And do you know what else he is doing?"

"He is painting a great wall picture," Roberto began, but Bruno interrupted him. "He may be doing that, too, but that is not the biggest thing on which he is working. Leonardo is an inventor too. He is working on a great machine that will fly through the air, the way a bird flies."

"Oh, Bruno, that is ridiculous," Roberto said. "You know that no machine can fly through the air."

"Why not?" Bruno cried. "If a great man like Leonardo thinks it is possible, then perhaps it is possible."

"Have you seen this machine which will fly?" asked his cousin scornfully.

"No," Bruno said, "but perhaps you will see it when he takes you as his pupil."

233

They entered the door of Leonardo's studio and climbed the stairs to a vast room. At first Bruno thought there was no one in it. Then he saw a man, holding a paint brush in his hand and standing before a half-finished painting which stood on the easel. He turned as the boys came into the room. "Ah, the boy with the statue," he said. He put down the brush and came toward them. "Is this yours?" he asked Bruno.

"No, sir, it is my cousin's," said Bruno.

Roberto held out the statue. Leonardo took it to a tall window. He examined it carefully, turning it over and over, holding it up to the light. "It is good," he told Roberto, "very good." Then he turned to Bruno. "Did you make a statue, too?"

"Mine is not like his," Bruno told him. "It is not so good."

"Where is it?"

"At home. I didn't bring it."

The artist studied him shrewdly. "Why did you make it?"

"Because I wanted to meet you," Bruno said.

"To see me working on my statues?"

"No, sir, to see you working on the machine that will fly."

"Ah, the machine!" Leonardo moved back from the window and stood closer to Bruno. "Do you believe my machine will fly?"

"I don't know, sir, but it might if it isn't too heavy."

Leonardo laughed. "Have you seen my model?"

234

"No, sir."

"Then come with me, both of you." He turned to Roberto. "If you will leave your statue with me, I shall show it to my council. If they like it as well as I do, I shall take you for a pupil. You may come back next Monday morning."

"Oh! thank you, sir," Roberto said.

All the way to the field at the edge of the town Leonardo talked of his dream of flight. "Think of it!" he cried. "Think of rising in the air like the birds, and flying over the woods and the rivers, even over the ocean!"

"Many of the men of Florence say that if God meant us to fly, He would have given us wings," suggested Roberto.

"What do you think about it, Bruno?" The great man turned to ask the youth's opinion.

"Maybe God wanted us to make our own wings," the boy said.

"Good lad!" Leonardo put his arm over the boy's shoulder. "God gave us brains, and He gave us hands, and He gave us eyes. He wants us to use them. That is why I make statues. That is why I paint. Most of all, that is why I wish to fly."

"Has anyone ever flown?" Roberto asked.

"The Greeks have a legend about a flight. They say that the father of Icarus made two great wings of feathers. Each feather was skillfully held in place with wax. He fitted them on the shoulders of Icarus, and the boy soared into the air. But, alas, the boy ventured too near the sun, and the heat melted the wax. One by one, the feathers fell from the wings, and Icarus plunged into the sea."

"Aren't you afraid?" asked Roberto.

"Would you be afraid to fly?" Leonardo asked Bruno.

"No." The boy's eyes lighted with the joy of the thought. "I think it would be wonderful."

When they came to the field they found a dozen men at work upon a huge machine. One of them, a blacksmith, was pounding the iron of the framework. Others were cutting wood, still others were spreading canvas into sails. "What do you think of it?" the artist asked the boys.

"It does not look much like a bird," said Bruno. "Look how thick it is here. If a bird were thick like that, how could it lift its body into the air?"

"The boy is right, sir," the blacksmith said.

"How would you lift it?" Leonardo asked Bruno.

"I don't know, but I know that when I fly a kite I run downhill, with the wind at my back. The kite begins to go up. If I didn't weigh so much, I would go up with it."

"Of course, of course, but how can a great machine like this go up like a kite?"

No one answered him, and he went among the men, instructing one after another about the carving of wood, the spreading of sails.

"Iron is too heavy," the blacksmith told him. "We need something lighter, but just as strong."

"That is a difficult problem to solve," said Leonardo, "but we'll do it."

The blacksmith shrugged his broad shoulders. "Not in our time, sir," he said.

Bruno listened eagerly to every word the men said, watching carefully every motion they made. Some day, he thought, this machine or some other machine would lift from the ground, taking men up into the blue skies. What a day that would be for the world— and if only he could be a passenger in that daring flight!

"I wish I could work for you," Bruno said to Leonardo.

"What could you do?"

"Oh, many things."

Leonardo did not answer, but turned away from the machine and the workers. He was silent as he crossed the field with the two boys. When they had come to the town, he spoke. "What are you thinking?" he asked Roberto.

"Of Monday, sir, and your studio."

"You may come Monday, and start your work. Perhaps some day you will be a good artist."

Bruno sighed. Roberto had been given the chance he had so longed for, the opportunity to work with Leonardo so that he might watch the making of the airship. Roberto did not care for machines, but what would that matter? He had won the prize by his art. To him would go the glory of working with the greatest genius of Florence. Perhaps, in time, he might even ride in Leonardo's ship.

Leonardo interrupted Bruno's thoughts by saying, "Bruno, you seem interested in the airship. Would you like to work with the men on the machine?"

"Oh, yes, sir!" Bruno stammered, too happy to say all that was in his mind.

"Then come to the field on Monday," the artist told him. As he left the boys, he spoke again to Bruno. "Perhaps we shall never rise to the sky, you and I," he said, "but other men will keep on trying, and some day one of them will do what we have tried to do. That is God's way. He lets us discover His secrets and use them for our benefit." He left them then, and the boys turned back to the hill.

"How can he waste time on a machine when he might be making a statue?" Roberto asked.

"How can you call it wasting time when he may be finding the way to fly?" Bruno asked.

But neither of them could answer the other's question.

FINDING PROOF

Number your paper from 1 to 12. Find one or two sentences from the story which will prove each of the following statements to be true. Write the sentences on your paper.

1. Florence was a lovely city.
2. Bruno had a fine sense of justice.
3. Roberto was sure no one would ever fly like a bird.
4. Leonardo da Vinci worked quietly.
5. Leonardo was not too busy to visit with the boys.
6. Bruno thought a machine for flying should be light in weight.
7. Many people in Florence thought that God never intended men to fly.
8. God wants us to use His gifts.
9. Bruno was not afraid to fly.
10. Bruno did not think the flying machine was being properly built.
11. Leonardo da Vinci was not discouraged because his flying machine did not give prospects of success.
12. God wants scientists to make new discoveries.

Prayer for a Pilot[1]

Lord of Sea and Earth and Air,
Listen to the Pilot's prayer—
Send him wind that's steady and strong,
Grant that his engine sings the song
Of flawless tone, by which he knows
It shall not fail him where he goes;
Landing, gliding, in curve, half-roll—
Grant him, O Lord, a full control,
That he may learn in heights of Heaven
The rapture altitude has given,
That he shall know the joy they feel
Who ride Thy realms on Birds of Steel.

CECIL ROBERTS

[1]From *Poems*, by Cecil Roberts; copyright, 1920, 1947, by Cecil Roberts.
Published by J. B. Lippincott Company.

Two Long Miles Apart

"Mr. Watson, please come here; I want you!"

It was a cry for help. Watson was standing in Bell's bedroom at the front of the house, waiting to see if the professor, in his laboratory at the back, could make his voice carry over the wire stretched between the rooms. The two men were trying out a new kind of battery which they hoped would make the sound travel.

It certainly had traveled! Not only could Watson understand what his friend was saying, but he could even recognize his tone of alarm. Rushing down the hall, he found that the inventor had spilled the acid from one of the batteries over his clothes. But the two young men were so excited at their success in sending a voice over the wire that the acid was forgotten and was left to spoil Professor Bell's suit while they took turns talking to each other. As yet the telephoning could be in only one direction.

This was in March, 1876. A month earlier Professor Bell had received a patent for his telephone, but the invention was still in the stage of experiment. By June, however, the experiments had gone so well that the young professor was able to show his telephone to the public at the Philadelphia exhibition. The famous scientists who were now given the fun of talking over it grew so excited and made so much noise that the police thought the building was on fire. And no wonder! It was necessary at that time to shout into the telephone mouthpiece. In fact, when telephones were first being used, it was said that people would rush to hold their horses if they saw someone preparing to talk over the telephone.

That same summer Professor Bell, while visiting his parents in Canada, got permission to connect his telephone instruments to the telegraph wires in a neighboring town. Messages still went only one way, and the answers had to be sent by telegraph, but the experiment proved that the telephone would work over a distance of miles instead of yards.

The next step was two-way telephoning. A day came in early October when Professor Bell said into the telephone, "If you understand what I say, say something to me." He was rejoiced to hear from Mr. Watson, in another room, "It is the best I ever saw."

At last they had been successful and they were ready, as Watson said, "to take the baby outdoors."

A manufacturing company had a factory in Cambridge, and a private telegraph line two miles long ran between the office in Boston and the factory. Bell got permission to use this line for his experiments when the office and factory were closed for the night.

Bell knew that his "baby" had been called a toy by some people, who thought that he was a crank. There were many persons who said that speech could not be transmitted by wire. One man even insisted that there must be a hole through the middle of the wire to make it possible for people to talk through it.

"If we can talk to each other over the telephone from a distance, people will have to believe that it is possible," said Bell.

"Yes," agreed Watson, "but it seems a daring experiment, even though you were so successful in telephoning along a telegraph wire this summer. You and I have never tried to talk over such a long distance. We shall be two miles apart."

"It will be an important test," said Bell, "but I have no doubt of our succeeding. We must keep an exact record of what we say. I have already announced this test, you know, and if we are successful our whole conversation will be published in the newspapers. Write down in parallel columns what you say to me and what you hear me say to you, and I will do the same. Then the doubters can compare them and decide for themselves whether or not I am right."

On the night of October 9, 1876, the inventor went to the office in Boston. Watson took the best telephone he had made and went to the Cambridge factory, where a watchman was in charge. The watchman must have wondered why the young man should disconnect the telegraph instruments and connect a crazy-looking instrument to the wire in their place.

Every part of the telephone was carefully adjusted after Bell had signaled by telegraph that he was ready. Watson drew a long breath and pressed the receiver to his ear. He was going to hear the voice of his friend, although they were two long miles apart. He listened, his breath coming quickly, but not a sound came through the telephone.

He thought that something must be wrong with the adjustment, and he went all over the instrument with great care. Everything was in perfect working order. He knew that Bell must be shouting to him from the other end of the wire. He shouted into his instrument and listened. There was complete silence on the line.

Could it be possible that all their work had been in vain? The telephone worked well in a house; why shouldn't it operate over an outside line? Were the doubters right after all, and was the instrument worthless except for short distances?

He tried again and again to get a connection with Bell, but he was unsuccessful. The telephone was dead. No sound or voice came over the line. What was Bell doing? What would he think if he did not hear from the Cambridge end of the instrument? Would his great interest in his experiment be crushed by this failure?

Suddenly an idea came to the discouraged man. He hurried into the hall to find the night watchman.

"I want to get into the other parts of the building," he demanded. "Our telephone does not work, and I think there's another wire here that interferes with it."

The night watchman hesitated. He plainly showed his disgust with a man crazy enough to try to talk over wires. As if anyone could hear what was said when the person who spoke was two miles away!

"I must find that other wire!" insisted Watson.

The watchman still hesitated. He was paid to look after the building, and he was not going to take a crazy man through it. There was no knowing what such a fellow might be trying to do.

Finally he was convinced that no harm was intended, and he led the way through the rooms, while Watson searched eagerly for the troublesome wire that might interfere with his instruments.

"I thought so! Here it is!" Watson finally shouted. With dull eyes the watchman watched the young man disconnect the offending wire. He couldn't see anything to be so excited about.

With the watchman at his heels Watson hurried back to the telephone. If the telephone would not work now, the greater part of Bell's work had gone for nothing. The long evenings together, the hours of thought, the years of hope and worry, would mean nothing. Unless voices could be heard over a long-distance line the telephone would never gain a world-wide success. If the interfering wire was all that had been the trouble, he should get an answer now.

Watson put his ear to the receiver and listened, hardly daring to breathe. A second of waiting, and then Bell's voice came plainly over the wire.

"Ahoy! Ahoy! Are you there? Do you hear me? What's the matter?" Bell's words were as clear as if he had been in the next room. Watson noticed that his voice was hoarse. Bell had probably been shouting for a long time, wondering why he received no reply.

"Ahoy! Ahoy!" replied Watson in ringing tones.

"Where have you been all this time?" asked Bell.

When Watson had explained, they congratulated each other that at last they were really talking together. Then they began the conversation which each copied down carefully. They knew that when it was published the following day it would astonish the whole country.

"What do you think was the matter with the instruments?" asked Bell.

"There was nothing the matter with them," shouted Watson. "Can you understand anything I say?"

"Yes," replied the inventor, "I understand every syllable. Now speak in an ordinary conversational voice."

"I am now talking in quite a low tone of voice," said Watson.

"The sounds are quite as loud as before, and twice as clear," said Bell. "We may congratulate ourselves upon a great success."

The two men were both excited, and they could not talk enough. It was sufficient reward for years of struggle to hear each other's words coming plainly over the wire. They talked for several hours, merely to enjoy the sound of their own voices, and Watson let the watchman listen. He still seemed to think it was all a trick.

Finally Watson disconnected the telephone and connected the telegraph instruments to the wire again. He hardly knew how he got back to Boston, for his mind was whirling with new ideas. Bell's face was beaming as they met in his room. He took his friend by the shoulders and whirled him around, while both laughed excitedly. Then the two men forgot that they were grown up, and they danced a wild war dance to celebrate the victory of the telephone over space. They had talked to each other through the telephone while they were two long miles apart!

LYDIA LION ROBERTS

FACT OR OPINION?

Facts are statements that can be proved or events that actually occurred, while *opinions* are beliefs or ideas not yet proved. Copy the statements on your paper and place *F* before those that state facts and *O* before those that express opinions.

- - - 1. A month earlier, Professor Bell had received a patent for his telephone.
- - - 2. Some people thought Bell was a crank.
- - - 3. "Our telephone does not work, and I think there's another wire here that interferes with it."
- - - 4. No sound or voice came over the line.
- - - 5. The night watchman hesitated.
- - - 6. There was no knowing what such a fellow might be trying to do.
- - - 7. A manufacturing company had a factory in Cambridge.
- - - 8. One man insisted: "There must be a hole through the middle of the wire to make it possible for people to talk through it."
- - - 9. "Bell has probably been shouting for a long time," thought Watson.
- - - 10. Bell got permission to connect his telephone instruments to the telegraph wires in a neighboring town.

DICTIONARY WORK

Find each of these words in your dictionary and write the definition which fits its use in the story.

public	spoil	vain	dead
crank	receiver	alarm	patent

248

Hidden Things

Under the sea, the silver sea,
the limitless, glittering, blue-green sea,
are treasures hid:
for there amid the swaying weed,
where fishes skim and corals breed,
are flowers strange;
and sea beasts range
in pastures hidden under the sea.

Under the ground, the common ground,
the piled-up, mountainous, tree-grown ground,
are treasures hid:
for there amid the rocks so old
lie pools of oil and veins of gold—
the precious stores
of metal ores
in places hidden under the ground.

LUCY SPRAGUE MITCHELL

A Man and a Microscope

I. *A Famous Man*

If you had been in any city or any town in France two days after Christmas in 1922, you would have heard a great ringing of church bells. It was not the usual quiet ringing for a church service. Every bell seemed to be turning over and over, as if something very unusual had happened. The ringing lasted for two minutes, without a single bell stopping.

Of course you would have asked, "What has happened?" And any French boy or girl would have told you, "We are celebrating the hundredth anniversary of the birthday of Louis Pasteur."

"What wonderful things Louis Pasteur must have done!" you would have thought. "Just think of every church bell in all the country ringing to remind people that he was born a hundred years ago!"

You have read stories about heroes who fought and killed giants and dragons. You have been thrilled by the victories of great soldiers and by daring deeds of great explorers. All these men and many, many others lived courageous lives. Louis Pasteur was not that kind of hero. In the wars he fought there was no din of battle and no bloodshed. His battlefields were quiet

[1]From *More Than Conquerors*, by Ariadne Gilbert; copyright, 1914, Century Company. Reprinted by permission of the publishers, Appleton-Century-Crofts, Inc.

laboratories; his guns were microscopes, test tubes, and other laboratory apparatus; his purpose was to save lives, not to destroy them. His faith was as strong as his science. A good Catholic, he prayed as he worked. Yet Louis Pasteur proved himself, in his quiet laboratory, as great a conqueror as any man who ever lived.

The enemies that Pasteur fought were not powerful giants or fierce dragons. They were worse than any such things. They were the terrible microbes or germs that cause disease, suffering, and death.

It was not easy for Pasteur to fight such enemies. Germs cannot be seen by the eye alone. Yet there are millions of them. They seem to be everywhere, even floating in the dust of the air.

And how fast they grow! In a few minutes one microbe grows, divides itself, and becomes two microbes. In an hour, if nothing stops them, a thousand germs may grow from just one germ. In another hour the number may be a million. Each hour a thousand times as many as there were the hour before! Pasteur needed as much power of mind and patience, strength and courage, as the bravest soldier or explorer.

After years and years of careful work Pasteur won his victories. And what wonderful victories they have been for everyone! It was his discoveries that taught doctors that it is necessary to keep wounds clean when they perform operations. From his work the world learned how to pasteurize milk to make it safe to drink. His victories showed doctors how to prevent many diseases. From his discoveries vaccines and antitoxins to control many dreadful diseases have been perfected. This great work has been carried on throughout the whole world at institutes which bear Pasteur's name.

Once the school children of France were asked, "Who was the greatest Frenchman ever born?" They voted "Louis Pasteur." The French government has issued a postage stamp bearing his picture. In France this is an honor given only to the most famous men.

What sort of person was Louis Pasteur? What can we learn about the way he worked and the discoveries he made? Let us see.

His father and mother were both industrious people. They taught their children the value of hard work done for the sake of others.

As a boy, Louis seemed like any other boy. He was fond of fishing. He liked to draw pictures of his friends and of his teachers. He liked to read stories about the great men of France, especially the scientists.

At school he was somewhat slow at first. This was not because he was stupid, but because he worked carefully. He would never give an answer to a question until he was perfectly sure that he was right.

As he grew older, Louis became fonder of study than of anything else. He put away his fishing poles and his crayons, and devoted himself to learning. He decided to prepare for the Teachers' Training College. He wished to be educated in order to please his parents, who had worked so hard for him. He wished to help his parents, too. And when in later years he received his first teaching position, he offered his small earnings to pay for the education of his youngest sister. He was ambitious for her as well as for himself.

In college Pasteur liked his chemistry class better than any other. If his chemistry professor had allowed it, Louis would have followed him about asking questions all day long. "Stop! Stop!" cried the bewildered old gentlemen one day. "I am the one to ask questions, not you!"

Pasteur worked many hours in the laboratory after the other students had gone home, or before they came to work. Once, he got up at four o'clock in the morning and began an experiment. When the clock struck four in the afternoon, he was just finishing that same experiment. He was tired, but happy, because he had found out exactly what he wished to know.

II. *Experiments of Pasteur*

France has always been a great wine-making country. The wine makers were once having a great deal of trouble in making pure wine. Their wine kept turning sour.

Pasteur, who was now a professor in an important college, made some experiments. By using his microscope, he found some very small jellylike balls in the sour wine. He also found that there were many more of them in sour wine than in good wine. By watching these carefully, he noticed that in a short time each one divided and became two. In that way the number of tiny bodies increased rapidly.

Pasteur wanted to find some way to keep the tiny bodies, or germs, as he called them, from growing. He tried the effect of chemicals, of heat, and of cold. He discovered that these germs could be destroyed by heating the wine to a temperature of about 145 degrees. The process that he invented is now called pasteurization. In a perfected form it is now used everywhere in the civilized world to keep milk fresh and pure.

The raising of silkworms is one of the leading industries of France. In some parts of France, all the people live on the money they earn from raising silkworms. When a man meets a friend in the morning, instead of saying, "How are you?" he is likely to ask, "How are the silkworms?"

When a disease began to kill off their silkworms, the people were afraid of losing their whole business. All sorts of unscientific remedies were tried, but the disease could not be stopped.

The French government asked Pasteur to help. "I have never even touched a silkworm," said he, "but I will try."

The silkgrowers did not believe he could help them. "What can a mere chemist know?" they asked. "Give us a man who has made silk farming a business."

But Pasteur went to work with his microscope. He found that there were two different germ diseases which were killing the silkworms. After more than five years of study, he found a sure method of curing both diseases. By following his directions, the silkworm diseases were soon wiped out of France. Another great industry was thus saved by Pasteur.

Several years later, the sheep all over France began to sicken and die. Pasteur searched for the reason. His microscope once more showed him what kind of germ it was that caused the disease.

Many years before, an English doctor, Dr. Jenner, had proved that vaccine made from the germs of smallpox can be used to keep people from catching smallpox. Pasteur believed that vaccine could be made which would prevent sheep from having anthrax, the terrible disease that was killing them everywhere. So he prepared a vaccine from the germs of anthrax and tested it until he was sure it would work.

When Pasteur announced that he could prevent anthrax in sheep, many people doubted him. He was asked to prove it by a public experiment.

Pasteur agreed to take fifty healthy sheep for the experiment. Twenty-five of them were to be vaccinated according to his instructions. The other twenty-five were not to be vaccinated. On a certain day, as soon as the vaccine had time to take effect, the strong germs of anthrax itself were to be injected into every one of the fifty sheep. After that the two groups of sheep were to be kept in separate pens, but otherwise were to be treated in exactly the same way.

Before the experiment began, Pasteur told what would happen. He said that within a few hours after the sheep were inoculated with anthrax germs, the twenty-five that had not been vaccinated would all be dead or dying; the other twenty-five would be alive and healthy.

The experiment lasted for three weeks, for the vaccination work took about that much time. During those days people became more and more excited. Would all the vaccinated sheep remain healthy? Would all the others die?

At last the day came that Pasteur had set to show the results of the experiment. A great crowd collected at the sheep pens. Scientists, doctors, newspaper reporters, and farmers came to see what would happen.

In a few hours the story was completed before their eyes. The twenty-five sheep that had not been vac-

256

cinated were scattered about the pen. Most of them were dead; the others were either dying or were very, very sick. The twenty-five that had been vaccinated were walking about nibbling the grass, as healthy and lively as sheep ever were.

Again Pasteur had proved himself right. From that time, the pastures of France, where there had been no healthy sheep for many years, were filled with vaccinated herds, safe from attacks of anthrax.

The discovery by which Pasteur's name became most widely known was made when he was sixty-three years old. That discovery resulted from years of experimenting to find a vaccine that would prevent hydrophobia, or rabies. This horrible disease was often caused from the bite of "mad" dogs or other "mad" animals.

Pasteur decided to try to prevent such torture and horrible deaths among animals. He knew that in experimenting he would have to handle the mad dogs and that if he were bitten, or became infected, he would die. But his zeal was so great he would not be stopped by possible danger to himself.

Month after month he worked with diseased and dangerous dogs in developing and testing the serum. Again and again he gave the serum to sick dogs and saw them recover. Again and again he gave the serum to well dogs, and afterwards inoculated them with the germs of hydrophobia. In all such cases the dogs did not have rabies, or go mad.

Pasteur was now certain that he had a vaccine that would prevent hydrophobia among animals. He thought that it would work with human beings, but he did not wish to experiment with human lives. The country, however, had heard of his wonderful success in preventing rabies among animals. Sooner or later he was sure to be asked to try the treatment on human beings.

One day, Joseph, a little boy nine years old, was brought by his mother to Pasteur's laboratory. Two days before, he had been bitten by a mad dog. A man found him knocked down, screaming, and trying to cover his face with his hands. By the time the man could beat off the dog, Joseph had been bitten in fourteen places. The disease, hydrophobia, however, had not yet set in when the boy was brought to Pasteur.

"Shall I risk trying on a human being the treatment that has always worked with animals?" Pasteur thought.

Pasteur was greatly worried by that question. But he knew that if he did nothing, little Joseph would surely die a horrible death. He called up all his courage and decided to inoculate the boy with the vaccine.

At the first inoculation Joseph was badly frightened. He cried bitterly as Pasteur made just a tiny pinprick in his side and injected a few drops of vaccine. But when the boy found that a little pinprick was all he had to bear, he dried his tears quickly.

Joseph was soon happy, playing with the tame rabbits, guinea pigs, and white mice that Pasteur used in his laboratory. But Pasteur was very anxious. It would take ten days to give the necessary number of inoculations. At the end of ten days if the vaccine worked, the boy would live and be healthy again. If it did not work, he would be tortured by the fever and agony of hydrophobia.

In all that time Pasteur hardly slept. Finally the day came when the result of the treatment would be known. Little Joseph awoke without any trace of fever. He began to call for his pets. The success of Pasteur's treatment was sure! From that day to this there have been few cases of hydrophobia in human beings.

In his remaining years, honors were heaped upon Pasteur. Patients flocked to him from every part of

Europe and from America. Hydrophobia was under control. Pasteur was a great citizen of France and a great benefactor to the world. But all his life he was a modest man. When he learned that a village in faraway Algeria had been named for him, he wrote these words to the governor-general of that colony of France: "When a child of this village asks the origin of its name, I should like the schoolmaster to tell him simply that it is the name of a Frenchman who loved France very much, and who in serving her, contributed to the welfare of humanity."

ARIADNE GILBERT

NOTING TIME RELATIONSHIPS

You will have a better understanding of what you read if you are alert to time relationships given in the story. Number your paper from 1 to 14 and copy the happenings listed in Column I. From Column II select the time related to the happening and place its letter in the blank.

Column I

1. __?__ Hundredth anniversary of Pasteur's birth
2. __?__ Date of Pasteur's birth
3. __?__ Time it takes one microbe to grow
4. __?__ Time it takes one thousand microbes to grow
5. __?__ Pasteur worked in his laboratory on one experiment
6. __?__ Greeting: "How are the silkworms?"
7. __?__ Pasteur found a method to cure diseases of silkworms

260

8. __?__ The experiment on the sheep
9. __?__ Discovery which made Pasteur famous
10. __?__ Pasteur worked with diseased dogs
11. __?__ Pasteur would be asked to try the experiment for hydrophobia on human beings
12. __?__ Time required for hydrophobia inoculations among humans
13. __?__ There have been few cases of hydrophobia in human beings
14. __?__ France has been a wine-making country

Column II

a. when Pasteur was sixty-three years old
b. always
c. lasted for three weeks
d. a few minutes
e. in an hour
f. December 27, 1922
g. ten days
h. sooner or later
i. from that day to this
j. in the morning
k. December 27, 1822
l. after five years of study
m. month after month
n. from four o'clock in the morning until four in the afternoon

Beauty[1]

Beauty is seen
In the sunlight,
The trees, the birds,
Corn growing and people working
Or dancing for their harvest.

Beauty is heard
In the night,
Wind sighing, rain falling,
Or a singer chanting
Anything in earnest.

Beauty is in yourself.
Good deeds, happy thoughts
That repeat themselves
In your dreams,
In your work,
And even in your rest.

E-YEH-SHURE

[1]From *I Am a Pueblo Girl*, by E-Yeh-Shure; copyright, 1939, by William Morrow and Company, Inc. By permission of William Morrow and Company, Inc.

Live and Learn

I. *The Young Scientist*

Danny Dillon had one ambition. Some day he would be a scientist, a great one and, needless to say, a famous one. His father and mother and his sister Jane were never permitted to forget Danny's dreams of his future. Every corner of the Dillon house bore evidence of Danny's ambition. In the most unexpected places there were collections of seeds and stones and minerals. His room overflowed with clay models of mountains, broken radio sets, bowls of decayed leaves, a small stuffed alligator, and a vast collection of pictures and charts and maps. "Live and learn" was Danny's motto, and he lived up to his motto.

The trouble with Danny was that he had not yet chosen a particular branch of science as his special interest. The world was so full of such wonderful things, as he had learned in a nursery rhyme, that he thought the Dillons should all be as happy as kings in a house littered with his experiments.

The Dillons were not as happy as kings, "I don't mind Danny's hamsters if they're in a cage," his sister Jane complained, "but, when fifteen of them gnaw their way loose and prowl around my room in the dark, I think he should have another hobby."

"Girls!" muttered Danny, but he built a new cage with a metal floor for his hamsters.

His mother voiced another protest. "May I ask you, Danny, why you put morning-glory seeds in the ice-cube tray?"

Danny had a ready answer, though it did not seem to calm her anger. "Water under motion is more powerful than air under motion," he explained. "Those poor little old seeds will grow stronger if they're first planted in ice."

"Maybe they will," said his mother. "I don't know. All that I can tell you is that we don't care for morning-glory seeds in our iced tea."

In school Danny was an average student but, with his deep interest in science, he sometimes neglected his other subjects. His teachers were amazed by his zeal, but often startled by the results of his work.

One teacher rebuked him. "You break more apparatus than any boy in the school," she said.

Danny paid for the damage he'd done out of his slim weekly allowance. "You have to live and learn," he sighed.

That very afternoon he went home to experiment making carbon dioxide from baking soda and vinegar. He mixed four parts of vinegar to one of baking soda. By lowering a lighted candle into the jar, he tested the gas which had been formed. It worked; the flame flickered and died. By that time Danny's interest had shifted to something else and he placed the bottle of carbon dioxide on a shelf in the garage and sought another scientific experiment.

That evening, as Danny's father was coming from the garage, he was struck by a rubber ball dropped from an upper window by his scientific son. The result was serious. Danny's father, with good reason, lost his temper. He rushed into the house and shouted at Danny, "Did you want to kill me?"

Danny was sorry, but he hastened to explain that the ball had been thrown in the interests of science. "I was only doing what Galileo did," he said. "It is said he dropped a ten-pound and a one-pound weight from the top of the Leaning Tower of Pisa to prove that gravity pulls all bodies to the earth at the same rate. I used only the baseball and a light rubber ball."

"I suppose I was lucky that you didn't have a ten-pound weight around," his father muttered.

"Sir Isaac Newton was the first to prove the laws of gravitation," said Danny, eager to discuss the subject.

"Did you ever hear of Galileo or Isaac Newton bouncing a ball on somebody's head?" asked his father scornfully.

Danny had to admit that he had never read of such an incident. All that he could remember was that Sir Isaac said that anything that is put in motion will keep on moving unless some force stops it. It seemed wiser not to repeat this to his father.

Danny did not stop learning, even though he often risked life and limb. Most of his neighbors were used to his experiments, but when a new family moved into the house across the street, they were startled one morning to see a whirling figure on top of the Dillon roof. They called Mrs. Dillon. When she went out and looked up she recognized Danny.

"Come down this minute," she ordered, for the wind was blowing half a gale.

Danny came down. "I was only checking the velocity of the wind," he said.

The Dillon house was at the top of a hill, and the roof seemed an excellent place to check wind velocity. The roof was a proving ground for many of Danny's studies. It was there that he had built his wind gauge, rain gauge, and other devices for his weather-bureau apparatus.

From the roof, too, Danny came to know the heavens in all their glory. He made a telescope and spent many hours gazing at the stars. He knew many of the stars, the planets, and the constellations by

266

name. He tried to interest his sister Jane by lending her his telescope. "That little cluster of stars is the *Pleiades*—" he started.

"The what?" asked Jane, shifting the telescope.

"The PLE-yah-dez," repeated the young scientist, pronouncing the word slowly. "They're known as the Seven Sisters. See how many of them you can count."

Jane sighed and returned the telescope. "I'd rather look at the moon," she said.

"No wonder nearly all scientific inventions and discoveries were made by men," said Danny. "I'll bet you don't even know where we get the terms *watt* and *volt* that you hear every day. Why don't you do some serious reading for a change and get acquainted with Mr. Watt and Mr. Volta?"

"Girls are scientists, too," Jane retorted. "I read in the newspaper about a girl who won first prize in a national science talent search. She got a trip to Washington and a scholarship to college."

"How did she do it?" Rivalry sharpened Danny's voice.

"How should I know?"

"Didn't the newspaper say what she did?"

"I don't remember."

Danny was disgusted. "How'll you ever get to college?"

Jane shrugged her shoulders. "Science isn't the only subject taught in college. I expect to major in languages."

II. *Danny Puts Science to Use*

So, most of the nights, Danny studied the heavens alone. Sometimes he would pretend that he was riding through space in a rocket ship. He would swing in imagination past Mercury, the smallest of the planets, past the thick clouds of gas that surround Venus, past the canals of Mars and the orbit of Jupiter. Comets would speed past, but what was a comet to a young scientist who was looking for bigger things?

One night on the roof, just as Jupiter appeared in the night sky and the flight of his rocket ship was about to begin, Danny saw a little flickering light leap upward from the side of the house.

It was no bigger than a firefly. At first Danny thought that it was one of the kind of beetles that can glow in the dark. He knew about beetles, too. He reminded himself of the five different chemicals that create a light in a firefly's body. He started to name them when suddenly he knew that this light did not come from any glowworm. "It's fire! Our house is on fire!" He was still shouting as he dropped through the trap door to the attic. "Fire! Fire!"

There was no answer. He raced down the stairs, past the empty bedrooms, down another flight of stairs, through living room, dining room, out into the kitchen. "Fire! Fire!" Then he remembered that his father and mother and his sister Jane had gone to the movies.

The smell of smoke filled the rooms. The telephone was in the hall, and Danny ran quickly, breathlessly retracing his steps. He dialed the number that stood in large type on the pad beside telephone numbers of the doctor, the druggist, and the police department. He gave their street and house address to the fire-department operator as the fumes of smoke grew worse. "Hurry! Hurry!" he cried.

Taking a short cut through the hall, Danny raced through the kitchen toward the steps that led to the garage. "That's where it is," he told himself. "It's a fire from rags!"

In the garage, in the center of the floor where the automobile usually stood, blazed a small fire. "There was an oil leak in the car last week," thought Danny, knowing that rags must have fallen into the pool. In the distance he could hear the siren of the fire engines, but reacting swiftly to the danger of the flames, Danny felt he could not wait. "It's oil! It's combustible! Maybe there'll be an explosion before they get here!"

Danny did some quick thinking. Now was the time to put his knowledge of science to the test, and he thought he knew the answer. He must not use water, for oil floats on water. So does gasoline, and this pool might be a combination of gasoline and oil. What should he use?

Then Danny knew. Blankets, sand, or carbon dioxide should be used to smother a fire like this. The nearest blanket was upstairs in the house. The sand was miles away. Carbon dioxide?

Carbon dioxide! Of course, he could use carbon dioxide. Hadn't he prepared a bottle just the other day? Hadn't it put out the flame of a candle? The bottle was still there, right on the shelf of the garage.

He plunged across the smoking garage and reached for his own fire extinguisher. "Carbon dioxide will put this fire out!" he said.

Danny poured a little of the liquid on the flame. No explosion followed. He poured a little more. The flame did not spread. As he worked, choked with fumes of smoke, he heard the fire engines draw up in front of the house and the shouts of the firemen. He called out to them and watched as they dragged their hose toward the garage.

"What are you doing?" a fireman shouted at him.

"I'm putting out the fire," Danny told him. "It's oil!"

Then firemen, equipped with fire extinguishers, raced toward him. Danny stepped aside and let them

finish the job. He had proper respect for firemen, but he wanted them to know that he was no amateur at this business, either. He'd wait until they were ready to leave to explain his interest.

In five minutes the fire was out, but excited neighbors filled the back yard. "Where are your father and mother?" one man shouted at Danny. He seemed to think that Danny had been responsible for the blaze.

A fireman heard him and spoke in Danny's defense. "Even this boy's parents couldn't have done a quicker job in checking this fire," he said.

With that praise Danny was content.

It took some time to tell the story to the Dillons when they came home from an unexciting movie. Mrs. Dillon said little, possibly because she feared that someone would ask how the rags happened to be in the pool of gasoline and oil. Jane was disappointed that she had ever left home. "I wish I could have been here," she said.

"Why?" said Danny, and added, "You couldn't have helped."

"But I'd have seen the fire engines," said Jane. "I love fire engines."

"Girls!" said Danny.

Danny's father said that he would give Danny a handsome present for being so quick-witted. "What would you like?" he asked.

Danny couldn't see that there was anything to make a fuss about in putting practical chemistry to work.

"Oh, gee," he said, with modesty, "it was nothing, Dad."

After all, the offer was a challenge. The world was so full of such wonderful things! Danny thought for a little while, silently, seriously. "How about money for some lead pipe that I could use as a weight for the bicycle wheel on the gyroscopic turntable?" he asked.

"It's a deal," said his father.

All the Dillons are proud of Danny, but they still wonder what in the world he is up to as he pounds frames and axles and rotors on what he calls his "stabilizing device." They do not know that, as he works, Danny is dreaming of the day when the aviation industry will place his name, *Daniel Dillon*, upon the roll of honor with the Wright Brothers and Langley and Sperry and the host of heroes who taught a wingless world how to fly.

273

List the names of six scientists mentioned in the story. Write a statement giving some information about each one. You may refer to a science book or the encyclopedia for help if necessary.

DIVIDING WORDS INTO SYLLABLES

Number your paper. Then find in the Word List the words described below and divide them into syllables. Use each word in a sentence.

1. A five-syllable word.
2. A four-syllable word with the heavy accent on the third syllable and the light accent on the first syllable.
3. A one-syllable word with a long-vowel sound.
4. A one-syllable word containing a diphthong.
5. A two-syllable word illustrating the principle that in a vowel digraph the first vowel usually has a "long" sound and the second vowel is silent.
6. A two-syllable word that illustrates an exception to the rule in number 5 above.
7. A three-syllable word with two suffixes.
8. A two-syllable word, accented on the first syllable, meaning "the most brilliant planet."
9. A homonym that is a one-syllable word.
10. A two-syllable word, accented on the last syllable.

Word List

ready	Venus	scornfully	oil
dialed	gale	Mercury	combination
extinguisher	explain	imagination	lead

Silver Ships

There are trails that a lad may follow
    When the years of his boyhood slip,
But I shall soar like a swallow
    On the wings of a silver ship,

Guiding my bird of metal,
    One with her throbbing frame,
Floating down like a petal,
    Roaring up like a flame;

Winding the wind that scatters
    Smoke from the chimney's lip,
Tearing the clouds to tatters
    With the wings of a silver ship;

Grazing the broad blue sky light
    Up where the falcons fare,
Riding the realms of twilight,
    Brushed by a comet's hair;

Snug in my coat of leather,
    Watching the skyline swing,
Shedding the world like a feather
    From the tip of a tilted wing.

There are trails that a lad may travel
    When the years of his boyhood wane,
But I'll let a rainbow ravel
    Through the wings of my silver plane.

MILDRED PLEW MEIGS

VI

Patriotism

Prayer for Help against Unjust Enemies

Fight, O Lord, against those who fight me;
  war against those who make war upon me.
Take up the shield and buckler,
  and rise up in my defense.
Brandish the lance, and block the way
  in the face of my pursuers;
Say to my soul,
  "I am your salvation."

PSALM 34

Pater Noster

Pa-ter no-ster qui es in cae-lis : san-cti-

fi-cé-tur no-men tu-um. Advé-ni-at re-

gnum tu-um. Fi-at volún-tas tu-a si-cut

in cae-lo, et in ter-ra.

Our Father, Who art in heaven,
Hallowed be Thy Name;
Thy kingdom come;
Thy will be done
On earth as it is in heaven.

The Maiden from the Oak Wood

Over five hundred years ago, the children of Domremy, a little village on the border in France, used to dance and sing beneath a beautiful oak tree. They called it "the Fairy Tree." Among these children was a girl named Joan, the daughter of French peasants. Joan sang more than she danced and, though she carried garlands like the other boys and girls and hung them on the boughs of the Fairy Tree, she was happiest when she took flowers into the parish church. There she would place them before the statues of Saint Margaret and Saint Catherine.

Wars have come and wars have gone in France, but the little house where Joan was born still stands. Under its thatched roof her mother taught her how to cook and sew and spin. Joan never learned to read or write, but it is not true, as popular legend would have us believe, that she spent her childhood caring for her father's cattle in the green fields of Domremy.

Joan was kind and gentle and honest, and all who knew her loved her. "She is a pious child," said the villagers, "and quiet beyond her years."

Joan lived in troubled times. For ninety years France had been at war with England. France had been without a king since Charles VI, the mad king, had died. His eldest son, also named Charles, lived in a far corner of France, protected by the strength of the loyal people of Orléans. In France, the eldest son

279

of the king was called the Dauphin, just as in England the eldest son of the ruler is called the Prince of Wales. The Dauphin laid claim to the royal title and called himself Charles VII although he had never been crowned in the great cathedral at Reims.

The Dauphin had no crown, no army, no money, no will to fight, but life was merry at his court. He feasted with his friends, even as the English laid siege to the stronghold of Orléans. "Will he do nothing to save Orléans?" cried his unhappy subjects, for they knew that if Orléans fell, France was lost.

One summer day when Joan was thirteen years old, she was out in her father's garden. The sunlight, the soft breeze, the fragrance of the wild flowers seemed the same as any other summer day. Suddenly Joan heard a voice. It seemed quite close to her. She looked up and, in a blaze of light, she saw Saint Michael and Saint Margaret and Saint Catherine. Frightened, she fell upon her knees as a Voice spoke to her.

"There is sorrow in France," the Voice said. "The day will come when you must go to the help of your country."

"But I am only a poor girl," Joan protested.

"God will help you," said the Voice.

In the garden, in the sunlight, Joan wept. How could she, a child of Domremy, save France from the invading armies, from the ships and the soldiers and the power of England?

Over and over, in sunlight and in starlight, the Voices came back to counsel Joan. "The Dauphin needs to be spurred into action," they said. "Tell him that you will help him to win back his throne."

"How can I, who cannot ride a horse or use a sword, be of help to the man who claims the throne of France but will not fight for it?" Joan asked.

"God will help you," said the Voices.

At that time there was an old prophecy, believed by many people, that France would one day be saved by a Maiden from the Oak Wood. There was an oak wood near Domremy and this prophecy, it has been said, had its influence in time upon Joan and later helped the French to believe in her.

When the girl was sixteen the Voices grew more urgent. "Present yourself to the captain of the garrison," they told her. "Ask him to escort you to the Dauphin. Then tell the Dauphin that you can lead him to victory because you are answering the call of God."

In the little church, beneath the statues of Saint Margaret and Saint Catherine, Joan prayed. Then, putting on the simple red peasant dress of Domremy, Joan set out for the garrison. There, with head high and eyes gleaming, she stood before the captain. She told him her name and her mission. She promised that the Dauphin should be crowned King of France in spite of his enemies, and that she herself would lead him in triumph to his coronation at Reims.

The captain laughed at her. "This girl is crazy," he said, and called out the guard. "Box her ears, and take her home to her father," he ordered.

Meanwhile the military situation of the Dauphin and his supporters was growing desperate. Orléans was tottering under the blows of the English and the complete defeat of the French seemed certain. Joan's Voices grew still more urgent: "Go! Go! Time is running out! It is your duty to lead the armies of France!"

"I do not know how to lead an army," Joan sobbed.

The Voices answered, "It is God Who commands it!"

The English armies came closer to Orléans. They surrounded Domremy. With flaming torches they advanced upon the village and set it ablaze. Only a few houses were left and, when Joan looked out from her father's garden toward the church, she saw nothing but a heap of smoking ruins. In the haze of smoke came the Voices: "Go! Go! Soon it will be too late!"

The winds of January were blowing against the smoldering ruins as Joan again set out for the French garrison. Again she talked to the captain, but with no better success. Around the garrison, however, and through the neighboring town, word spread that a maiden from an oak wood had come to save the kingdom.

"Someone must take her to the Dauphin," cried the citizens, fearful that their town would soon suffer the fate of Domremy.

"Someone must lead her to the prince," said the soldiers. Moved by Joan's faith, they believed in her, but the Dauphin was far away in his castle, and the citizens and soldiers knew well that she could not gain entry without permission from the captain of the garrison.

January passed, and February came. "Go to the garrison," the Voices demanded. "Tell the captain that this very day, at Orléans, the French have suffered a terrible defeat."

Joan went back to the captain. "Take me now to the Dauphin," she begged, "before the honor and glory of my country are lost forever."

He listened to her statement of the defeat of the French at Orléans. "How could you know of our

283

losses?'' he asked, but when official news came of the disaster, the cause of Joan gained ground. "Perhaps the girl is right," the captain confided to his men.

With hope nearly gone, Joan waited and prayed. One day, upon the road, she met a squire, a nobleman attached to the court of the Dauphin. He leaned down from his horse and spoke to the girl. "Well, my lass," he asked, "is our young king to be driven from France, and are we all to become English?"

"The Dauphin must act," said Joan. "I have begged the captain of the garrison to take me to the castle, but he will not listen to me. I know that I must go, for the Lord so wills it."

"Why do you say this?" asked the squire.

"Because no one in the world—neither kings nor dukes nor armies—can save France without me," said the Maiden from the Oak Wood.

"Can you fight?" asked the squire.

"War is not my calling," Joan told him. "I would rather stay home and sew and cook and spin, but the Lord has willed my destiny."

"And who is your Lord?" asked the squire.

"He is God," said Joan, and the Voices beside her said, "Now! Now!"

It was the squire who offered to take Joan to the Dauphin. The citizens of the garrison town raised the money to clothe the girl in proper raiment. For her they bought the clothes of a warrior—doublet, hose, surcoat, boots, and spurs. They bought her a horse, for the distance to the castle was great.

Desperate because of his country's need, the captain of the garrison consented. "Go, and take the consequences!" he told her, but he gave her an escort of three men-at-arms. Led by the squire, they set out upon the road.

"God keep you!" shouted the soldiers and the townspeople.

The enemy held the country through which they were to pass, so they had to travel by night. Joan's companions, alarmed, spoke of returning to the garrison, but Joan laughed at danger. "God will clear my path," she said. "For this end I was born."

On the twelfth day, Joan arrived at the court of the Dauphin. At first it looked as if she would not be received, in spite of the efforts of the friendly squire. Then more bad news came from Orléans. "Let her speak with the Dauphin," said his courtiers. "This may be our last chance to save France."

One evening, by the light of fifty torches, Joan was brought into the great hall of the nobles. Never in her life had she seen the Dauphin. Charles, to keep Joan from recognizing him, was dressed with less splendor than his attendants. "I don't want to be bothered with this girl," he complained. "She'll never know me in this simple robe."

Joan entered the room. With a single glance she saw and recognized the Dauphin. She knelt before him. "God give you a happy life," she said.

"I am not the Dauphin," he protested. "Over there is Charles VII, King of France." He pointed toward one of his nobles.

"You are he, gentle Prince, and no other," said Joan.

The Dauphin was startled. "What brings you here?" he demanded.

The girl still knelt. "The King of Heaven sends word to you, through me, that you shall be anointed and crowned," she said.

"Why should you, a peasant, be chosen by God to direct me?" The royal voice was shrill with disbelief.

She spoke with humility. "I do not know the reason," she said. "I only know that I have heard the Voices and I have seen the visions. They have told me that God has taken pity upon you and upon your people."

The Dauphin moved closer. Then he whispered, "Can you give me a secret sign?"

Joan had waited for this moment a long, long time. As he leaned down to listen to her message, Joan repeated a secret passed on to her by the Voices. "This is known only to God and you," she told him.

This message, "the secret of the king," was not revealed that night, or ever after. No one could know it but God and the Dauphin, and no one ever did.

"This girl speaks the truth," said Charles, the descendant of a long line of French kings. "Arm her at once. She must have many squires and pages and a chaplain. She must have armor and banners and a shining sword. We go to war against our enemies!"

Behind the altar of Saint Catherine in the castle of the Dauphin a sword was buried. The Voices spoke: "Order that the sword be dug from its ancient rust. Carry it into battle!"

The sword was found. Cleansed of its rust, it shone brightly in the light from the windows of the chapel of Saint Catherine. Joan lifted it high and saw the five crosses upon its sharp blade. "With this sword of God we shall save Orléans," she vowed.

"Make a standard for the Maid," ordered the Dauphin.

Softness of velvet and shimmer of gold! The holy names of Jesus and Mary! The images of kneeling angels and the imprint of the fleur-de-lis of France! The standard of Joan, the Maid of Domremy!

"Though I may be wounded by enemy shafts, though I may die by fire, the King of France will be crowned before the altar of God," cried Joan.

Ten thousand men-at-arms moved out ahead of her from the castle of the Dauphin. Swords flashed in the sunlight. "On to Orléans!" rose the cry. Joan, dressed in white armor, but wearing no helmet, sat erect upon a white charger. The horse leaped at her command, and she moved swiftly toward the head of the long line of troops. "Forward!" she called out. "As we share in toil, so shall we share in victory."

Marching forth to war, the soldiers sang a hymn to the Virgin. Orléans lay ahead of them. The coronation of the Dauphin at the foot of the altar of the great cathedral at Reims was in the future. The capture and trial and martyrdom of Joan of Arc lay before her. Centuries would pass before she would join the jubilant company of the mighty saints of God. On that April day, as the maiden from the oak wood led the armies of France toward victory, she only knew that the Voices who directed her had come from God, and that never again would she see the little village of Domremy.

Read quickly to find the paragraph that best answers each question below. On your paper, after the number of the question, write the page, the paragraph number, and the beginning and ending words of the paragraph where you found the answer.

1. How old was Joan of Arc when first she heard her Voices?
2. Who offered to take Joan to the court of the Dauphin?
3. What did the standard of Joan look like?
4. What great feat did Joan accomplish for her country?

"BEFORE" AND "AFTER"

From a simple peasant girl, Joan of Arc became the leader of a great army. Copy the sentences below. Then complete them to show the changes that took place in her. If you need help, look back in the story.

1, a. How Joan looked (think of her clothing) before she became a leader of an army: _____

b. How Joan looked after she was given an army to command: _____

2, a. What she did as a peasant girl: _____

b. What she did as the leader of an army: _____

3, a. How Joan felt when the Voices first spoke to her: __
_____

b. How she felt as she led the troops to war: _____
_____

Prayer of a Soldier in France

My shoulders ache beneath my pack
(Lie easier, Cross, upon His back)

I march with feet that burn and smart
(Tread, Holy feet, upon my heart)

Men shout at me, who may not speak
(They scourged Thy back and smote Thy cheek)

I may not lift a hand to clear
My eyes of salty drops that sear.

(Then shall my fickle soul forget
Thy agony of Bloody Sweat)

My rifle hand is stiff and numb
(From Thy pierced palm red rivers come)

Lord, Thou didst suffer more for me
Than all the hosts of land and sea.

So, let me render back again
This millionth of Thy gift. Amen.

JOYCE KILMER

Crown of Glory

I. *Siege of Vienna*

I am Gregor Kolski, a citizen of Poland, but now a student in the University of Vienna. More than a year ago I came here to study because the Rector, Father Lawrence, was giving a course not given then in my own country. In this year I saw the peril of the Christian world. I saw how the Christian world was saved from that peril.

Ever since I can remember, I have known that the Turks would one day reach out from their capital, Constantinople, to try to conquer our Christian countries. Slowly, like a creeping tide, they had taken cities, towns, and villages. Now the Turkish armies were nearing the gates of Vienna. Rumors had reached us that they were preparing to attack the city.

One morning in July Father Lawrence sent for me. "You are not in your own country, Gregor," he said. "You are in danger here which may not come to Poland. I have heard that the Moslems have made your king a promise that they will not invade Poland if Poland does not enter the war. If John Sobieski accepts that promise, there will be no war in Poland. Do you wish to go home now?"

"Our king will not remain at peace when the Christian world is in danger," I said. "Our king is a Catholic. He will fight for the rest of the Christian world, just as he would fight for Poland."

"Your king may love the Faith," said Father Lawrence, "but he has no reason to love Leopold, our emperor. Leopold has insulted John Sobieski, again and again."

"That is true, Father," I said, "but I know John Sobieski. He will fight for the Faith, even here in a land that has no love for him."

A few weeks later we awoke to find that the main army of the Turks had camped on one of the hills outside Vienna. Our lookouts on the roofs of the church towers reported that they could see thousands and thousands of tents in the great camp.

The Turks were approaching from the southwest. We thought their first heavy attacks would come on the gates of the Monastery and the Irish Convent. We did not realize then that they planned to surround the city. That would mean an attack upon the Cathedral of St. Stephen from all sides—and St. Stephen's was the center of our defense.

The Turks took a town across the Danube from Vienna. Now they could dig a mine under the river into our city. That was, we knew, our greatest danger. Our commander, although wounded by a Turkish arrow, remained at his post. He gave orders that no bell was to ring in the city. The great bell of the Cathedral of St. Stephen would ring, he said, as the signal that the Turks were at the city walls.

By that time we were almost starving. We were so weary that we could hardly go on with our duties, but

292

we all kept at our tasks. There came a day in August when disaster piled upon disaster. The great engineer who had held the gate at the Irish Convent was killed. So was the heroic leader defending the gate near the Monastery. The mayor died. Worst of all for us at the school, Father Lawrence was taken ill.

To my surprise, Father sent for me. I went to him, wondering what he would say to me. I found him in bed. He was weak, but, as always, brave. "I am going on a long journey, Gregor," he said to me, "and, before I go, I wish to send you on a shorter one."

"A journey, Father?" I asked, knowing how hard it was for anyone to go outside the walls.

"Once you told me," Father went on, "that you could speak Turkish. How well do you know it?"

"I learned Turkish before I learned Polish," I said. "My father was stationed at a fort on the Turkish border. I had a Turkish nurse."

"Have you forgotten what you learned?"

"One does not forget what one learns so young," I said.

Father Lawrence lifted himself on his elbow and stared at me as if he were reading my thoughts. Then he spoke again. "Gregor," he said, "I believe you are brave. That is why I am going to ask you to perform a task I would give to few young men. You must go to your king of Poland, John Sobieski."

"But how can I go, Father?" I cried.

"I do not know how you will go, Gregor, but I know that you will not refuse to try when you know that hope for Vienna, for all the Christian world, depends upon getting a message to your king. John Sobieski must reach Vienna before two weeks have passed if he is to save us, to save all Christians from the Turk."

"But that is not possible," I said. "Even if I were to run all the way to Krakow, he could not speed his army to be here in that time!"

"No," said Father Lawrence. "He could not do that if he were in Krakow, but he is no longer in Krakow. Days ago he led his army out of Poland. He has long known how desperately he is needed; but he waits until he is asked to come. The message to John Sobieski asking for his aid is the only hope of Vienna, the only hope of the Christian Faith in Europe."

Father Lawrence paused for a moment. "You are going to take that message, Gregor," he went on. "You will take to John Sobieski the letters from the commander and the Council of the city, asking his aid. You will tell him of our desperate situation and urge him to set out at once." He took a package from under his pillow. "Here are the letters. They are wrapped in oilskin so that they will not be blurred by the water when you swim the river. You must lose no time. Can you leave tonight?"

"Tonight," I promised. At the door I turned. "Will you give me your blessing, Father Lawrence?" I asked him. He gave it to me as I knelt. "It is a dying man's blessing, Gregor," he said. "I shall not be here when you return."

"I may not return, Father."

"If you do not, we shall meet the sooner."

II. *A Message to John Sobieski*

I went, as Father Lawrence had told me, to the commander's headquarters. There an officer took me down into one of the vaults of the cathedral where they had gone for safety. Other officers brought in strange-looking garments. They fitted me out in them so that, with my dark eyes and skin, I looked like the Turk I would pretend to be as I tried to make my way through the Turkish lines. They kept me in the cathedral until after dark. Then they led me to the Red Tower and opened a little gate. "God be with you," one of them said.

I stepped out into the darkness. I was within the Turkish lines, alone. For miles and miles I was to go through those lines, finding my way by sun and by stars, to the camp where John Sobieski waited for the message I carried. "God help me," I prayed, as I moved forward into the deep, summer night.

For a while I seemed all alone. Behind me lay the city, with fires burning here and there. Before me lay the first crossing of the Danube. I was feeling my way toward it when a group of Turkish horsemen rode by. I dropped into the cellar of a house that had been burned down, hiding until they had passed. Then I climbed out and crawled toward the river.

I had to take off my Turkish robes, wrap them in the oil-cloth I had brought to keep them dry, and hold them over my head as I swam through the dark water.

"God help me," I prayed again and again. God gave me guidance and I crossed the river safely.

My dark eyes and hair and my Turkish disguise helped me, and I sang a silly little Turkish song which I luckily remembered. I passed guard after guard, with none of them suspecting me, until I came to the leader's camp. There the guard took me before the Turkish leader so that I might tell what I had seen on the road. I told as little as I could to the fierce, magnificently dressed man who scowled at me. I trembled, but he did not keep me.

I took to the road again, keeping in the direction Father Lawrence had given me. I saw ruined villages, with fires still burning the houses. The way was long and difficult, but I came at last to the point which

Father Lawrence had marked on the map as the place I should find the Polish army.

Just as I was beginning to fear that I might never reach the place, I came upon it. From the top of the hill I saw the flag of Poland. My flag! I flung out my arms in joy, forgetting that I wore the dress of the enemy. A sudden order given in Polish reminded me. I turned to see a Polish soldier aiming his gun at me.

"Stop!" he ordered. I answered him in Polish, and spoke faster than I had ever talked before. "Take me to the king," I cried, "your king, my king, John Sobieski."

The soldier took me first to the captain. I had to plead all over again. The captain called other officers. Once more I spoke. At last I showed him the letters I carried. I had to take them out of the protecting oilskin to show the seals of the city of Vienna. Then the soldiers took me to the king.

John Sobieski was standing before a simple tent. He was a big man, tall and erect, with waving hair and flashing eyes. There was no splendor about him such as the emperor displayed, no courtiers attending him, no soldiers guarding him; but there was in him a kingliness so real that I sank down to one knee as I gave him the letters. When he had finished the reading, he spoke to me again. "Was the emperor in Vienna when these letters were written?" he asked.

"No, your Majesty," I said. "The emperor left the city with the first attack."

Slowly John Sobieski turned over the letters in his hand. "These are letters," he said, more to himself than to me, "from the men who are risking their lives every moment in the defense of Vienna. Though I would not listen to Leopold, I will listen to them. They ask me to come."

"At once, your Majesty," I had to say. "Unless you come at once, it will be too late."

"I will go at once," he said, as easily as if he were deciding to cross a street. He called an officer and gave an order. Then he turned back to me. "You will need other clothes if you march with us," he said.

"A uniform?" I cried. "A uniform of Poland?"

"A uniform," he said, and smiled. "Light blue, I suppose. The uniform of the staff?"

"Light blue," I said, "the blue of heaven."

The king sent me off with another officer, a youth hardly older than myself. The youth was an officer of

298

the Company of Prince James, the king's son, a boy of sixteen, who rode at his father's side. He told me that they had come through a hostile land, all on the chance that they might be needed. They had waited in vain for the emperor's message. Now, without it, they would move on to answer the call of the men who were holding Vienna.

Soon the army began to move forward. Back over the ground I had come moved the army of Poland. We had gone but a little way when a messenger from the Duke of Lorraine met us. The duke asked that the Poles meet him and his French army before advancing to the rescue of Vienna. Emperor Leopold would also be there with his army. Still Emperor Leopold sent no word to our king—but we moved forward.

We reached the meeting place on the same day that the Duke of Lorraine and Emperor Leopold arrived with their armies. Their number was greater than ours, but no one rode as did the men of our Polish cavalry. No one of the four kings and twenty-two princes there rode his horse as splendidly as did the king of Poland. Even the emperor looked small beside him.

A little late, Leopold gave praise to the man who had been great enough to forgive old wrongs to come to the aid of Vienna. "Even without your army," the emperor said, "we want you, John Sobieski."

The Duke of Lorraine, who had himself tried to take the throne of Poland, asked Sobieski to go before him, but Sobieski shook his head. "I left my royal dignity in Warsaw," he said. "I am only your friend and brother here. I follow you."

At last there came a day when John Sobieski could no longer follow. All the leaders—Emperor Leopold, the Duke of Lorraine, and the other princes who had come from all over Europe—all of them voted that the king of Poland was the man to lead the fight against the Turks.

That night, knowing that the battle would come on the morrow, I went late to the tent which had been set up for a church. There, in the dim light of the candles, I saw Prince James kneeling before the altar. He would, I realized, kneel there all night. Tomorrow, before the battle, he would be given his sword of knighthood.

The morning—it was the twelfth of September—came under a heavy mist. The light was gray as the army of Poland gathered before the altar. When Mass was finished, the king went with Prince James to the steps of the altar. For a moment or two he spoke to the prince, telling him the duties of knighthood. "You must be brave," the king said, "and you must be kind, and you must be good. You must always help the poor and the suffering. You must always love and fear God." Then he took off his sword, and placed its point upon the boy's helmet. "I dub thee knight," he said.

After the young knight had pledged allegiance to the king, John Sobieski turned to the army, and his voice rang high. "Warriors and friends!" he said. "Yonder

in the plain are our enemies in greater numbers than
when we defeated them in battle in our own country.
Today we have to fight them on foreign soil, but even
here on foreign soil we are defending our own country. We have to save today not a single city, not a
single country, but the whole of Christendom."

Sobieski paused then, looking over their faces, all
lifted to him waiting for his order. It came sharply
just as the sun burst through the heavy clouds to show
the Turkish forces below the hills. "I have but one
command to give," he said. "Follow me."

We Poles followed him, and the soldiers of many
other Christian nations followed us. Through those
hours before Vienna we forgot that we were of different
races, of different nations. We were Christians, fighting
for Christendom.

The Polish cavalry charged. The Turks held firm. Then at Sobieski's command, in order to trap the enemy, the cavalry retreated. The Turks followed them. Then the cavalry, with Sobieski at their head and the whole army at their heels, hurled themselves against the enemy and turned them back.

Before us the Turks gave way. They scattered like leaves in the wind over the wide plain. Even their leaders fled, destroying the treasures they could not take. Their commanding officer escaped with his life, but John Sobieski snatched up the Moslem banner, the Standard of the Prophet. On and on we swept, over the plain to the Danube, then over the Danube again to the walls of Vienna.

The next morning we entered the city. A German prince and his cavalrymen were the first within the walls. The gate of the Irish Convent opened to welcome them. The crowds ran so close to the horses that it took the Germans hours to move to the square. Never had any city shown such joy, for Vienna had given up hope of deliverance until, two nights before, the rockets from the mountains had told that help was at hand. Vienna flung wide her arms to all her deliverers, but it was for John Sobieski she waited.

He came, last of all, riding upon a tired horse, but with the light of happiness shining in his dark eyes. Men and women and children pressed close to him as he rode. "God bless you, God bless you, God bless you!" they cried over and over again. He bowed to

302

them, he smiled upon them; but when they began to cry out to praise him, he pointed to the spire of the cathedral. "Not I, but God helped you," he said. "I came, I saw, but it was God who won the battle."

There was a great Te Deum sung that morning. A victorious army and a saved people sang it. The emperor was there and the leaders of other nations. With them was John Sobieski. It was, others tell me, the most splendid service Vienna had ever known. I was not there. In the little chapel of the university, with those who were left of teachers and students, I was assisting at the Requiem Mass for Father Lawrence. Already he had gone upon his longer journey.

UNDERSTANDING THE AUTHOR'S MEANING

What did the author mean when he used the following expressions?

1. disaster piled upon disaster
2. fight on foreign soil
3. escaped with his life
4. Vienna flung wide her arms
5. a saved people
6. I dub thee knight
7. like a creeping tide
8. I took to the road again
9. they scattered like leaves in the wind
10. a kingliness so real
11. the whole of Christendom
12. finding my way by sun and by stars

303

Firm as the Boulders

Whenever I walk these hills,
I see again the faces of men
Who have walked this way before,
Those who loved the meadows
And the fields, who knew and felt
The heart-beat of the earth,
Whose wealth was sun and rain
And soil. These men were builders
Of a nation strong and deeply-rooted
As elms that have stood a century
Or more, firm as the boulders
Cropping out of the wild pastures,
Everlasting and invincible.

LANSING CHRISTMAN

The Bravery of Elizabeth Zane

On the spot where the city of Wheeling, West Virginia, now stands, a stockade was built and named Fort Henry in honor of Patrick Henry, the great patriot of Virginia. Close at hand were some twenty log cabins, the homes of the settlers.

It was a lovely autumn morning in 1776. The morning mist from the Ohio River had been chased away by the warm sun, and birds were chirping among the trees. But there was no joy in the little settlement, for at sunset on the day before a scout had come with evil tidings.

"That traitor Girty," he said, "with a large party of Indians, is making his way up the Ohio and is already within a few miles of the fort."

Every man, woman, and child sought shelter within the stockade. In the night, down the valley of the river, could be seen the blaze of a burning blockhouse and log cabins. At daybreak Captain Mason led out a few men to look for Indians.

A war whoop broke from a neighboring field, and without a moment's warning the savages hiding in the corn fell upon the little scouting party. When the smoke cleared away some of the men were seen fighting their way back to the fort, but more than half lay dead. Captain Ogle went to their rescue with twelve riflemen. Bullets and tomahawks thinned their ranks, and only a few got back to the stockade.

In the face of a hundred howling savages the big gate of the fort was shut and barred. Crowded together behind the high fence were about fifty women and children with fewer than twenty men and boys to defend them. The three leaders in the fort were the brothers Ebenezer and Silas Zane and Colonel Sheppard, all fearless Indian fighters.

Suddenly the war whoops stopped and there was deep silence. What had happened? The people in the stockade did not have to wait long for an answer. Simon Girty, the most hated white man on the frontier, was seen walking toward them, waving a white flag.

"Surrender the fort!" he shouted. "I have four hundred Indians here, and I'll take the fort in five minutes and kill every one of you."

"Surrender? No! We will never give up to you or to any other white traitor while there is one of us left to fight!" Colonel Sheppard answered.

Girty was angry. He shook his fist at the fort and, turning, waved his hand. With yells the Indians rushed to the attack. The little band of frontier people fought bravely. The men and boys used their long rifles with deadly effect. Some of the women made bullets, while others cooled the guns, loaded them, and passed them to the men at the loopholes.

Several times during the day, a rush was made to storm the fort. At sunset the savages returned into the thick woods, but they came back at midnight and made the darkness hideous with their war cries.

The terrible hours passed slowly. All the day before and all that night, without food, drink, or sleep, those brave men and women stood at their posts.

Early in the morning the Indians attacked the fort again. About noon they went again into the forest to plan some new mischief. Meanwhile the men looked sober and spoke together in low tones.

"The powder has almost given out," somebody said.

These words went quickly through the fort. The men and women looked at each other in despair.

"Not enough left for half a dozen rounds!"

What could even the bravest do without powder?

"There's a keg of powder in my cabin," said Captain Ebenezer Zane, "but it is sixty yards away. How can we get it?" To cross that space before the eyes of those savages meant death.

The Indians were sure to come back and make another attack. The settlers must have powder or give up the fort. If they surrendered, the men would be tortured at the stake and the women and children taken into captivity or put to death.

"We must have powder," Captain Zane said to the pioneers; "and there's none nearer than my cabin. Who will volunteer to go for it?"

Every man and every boy in that band of heroes wished to go.

"No, no, indeed! Not a man shall go; we haven't one to spare; let me go!" cried Elizabeth Zane, Captain Zane's younger sister.

In vain did they try to persuade her from attempting such a dangerous mission. "No, Betty, you must not run the risk!" cried all the men; "you'll be killed!"

"But I am going," Elizabeth said. "You have wasted time already. Look at those Indians creeping out of the woods."

The men and boys looked ashamed.

"Let me go; I can run as fast as any of you," said the girl. "If I am killed, I shall not be missed as a man would be. Somebody pin up my hair so it won't be loose for the Indians to grasp."

Carefully the big gate was opened just wide enough for Elizabeth to slip out. She gave one loving look at her brothers. Her dark eyes were shining, but in her face there was not a sign of fear as she walked slowly across the open space to her brother's log cabin.

The Indians lurking in the bushes saw the gate open and gazed in wonder to see the girl, bareheaded and with sleeves rolled up, quietly walk out of the fort as if for a morning stroll.

"Squaw! squaw!" they shouted, but did not fire a shot.

Elizabeth had now reached the cabin and found the keg of powder. In breathless silence the watchers at the loopholes saw the girl appear in the doorway with a keg of powder clasped in her arms. She stopped a moment and gave a quick glance at the fort, which seemed a long way off.

"Now it is death to my poor sister! Why did we ever let her go?" said Ebenezer Zane as he saw the young girl making ready to run back.

Pulling her skirts tight around her and hugging the keg, Elizabeth started for the fort as fast as she could run. The Indians set up a yell. They realized now what the girl was doing.

Crack! crack! crack! sounded the rifles of the savages. The bullets whistled past her, but not one hit her. Almost at the gate the excited girl stumbled and fell. Was she hit? No. She picked herself up and ran for her life. Ping! ping! sang the bullets around her; but in another moment the great gate was opened and Elizabeth fell into the arms of her brother, who stood ready to catch her.

"Three cheers for Betty Zane!" cried somebody, and they were given with a will.

With Elizabeth unharmed, and plenty of powder, they all took fresh courage. The worst, however, was over. Before sunrise the next morning mounted riflemen from other settlements came to the help of Fort Henry. Girty now gave up hope. After killing the livestock and setting fire to some cabins, the outlaw fled across the Ohio.

ALBERT F. BLAISDELL AND FRANCIS K. BALL

UNDERSTANDING A CHARACTER

Betty Zane showed many traits which were a part of her bravery. Find on pages 307–310 a sentence which shows that she possessed each of the following traits.

perseverance	calmness
determination	precaution
fearlessness	affection

DEFINITE OR INDEFINITE?

Copy the groups of words below on your paper. Write *D* before those that express an exact, or definite, number. Write *I* before those that express a vague, or indefinite, number.

___ some twenty cabins	___ fewer than twenty
___ within a few miles	___ five minutes
___ some of the men	___ several times
___ more than half	___ half a dozen
___ twelve riflemen	___ sixty yards
___ four hundred Indians	___ three leaders

Washington

He played by the river when he was young,
He raced with rabbits along the hills,
He fished for minnows, and climbed and swung,
And hooted back at the whippoorwills.
Strong and slender and tall he grew—
And then, one morning, the bugles blew.

Over the hills the summons came,
Over the river's shining rim.
He said that the bugles called his name,
He knew that his country needed him,
And he answered, "Coming!" and marched away
For many a night and many a day.

Perhaps when the marches were hot and long
He'd think of the river flowing by
Or, camping under the winter sky,
Would hear the whippoorwill's far-off song.
At work, at play, and in peace or strife,
He loved America all his life!

NANCY BYRD TURNER

311

This Is My Country

I. *The New Girl*

The new girl came into the sixth grade at St. Robert's School in the middle of the school year. Sister Margaret Rose introduced her. Her name was Rita Morena, and her desk was placed between Veronica Foster and Frances Donovan.

Rita was little, and dark, and quick of movement. She could solve arithmetic problems faster than any of the boys. She could read and write and speak well, although she sometimes used a Spanish word instead of an English word. She had a happy smile, but she did not show it often, in spite of the friendliness of Veronica and Frances. To them and to the others of the room it was plain that Rita Morena was, as they said, keeping to herself.

St. Robert's school was a lively place. Set in the heart of a California town in which was located a huge airplane factory, it carried through its day the spirit of the pastor, Monsignor Kelty. He had once been an Army chaplain, and he firmly believed in military observances. St. Robert's held assembly in the patio where the children sang a hymn, saluted the flag, and gave the pledge of allegiance.

Veronica, more alert than Frances, was the first to notice that Rita sang the hymn but did not salute the flag or repeat the pledge. She nudged the new girl with her elbow, but Rita looked at her blankly.

"We'll have to teach her. What would Monsignor say?" Veronica said.

"We'll talk to her after school," said Frances.

They did not find a chance for a few days. Every afternoon Rita brought to school her little sister, Dolores, who was in the second division of the crowded first grade. She took the child home after school, never staying for the talks and games of the other girls. Finally, however, her two classmates cornered her. Tactfully Frances asked her if she did not wish to sing in a Washington's Birthday entertainment.

"What would I sing?" Rita asked.

"Oh, maybe 'The Star-Spangled Banner,' if you can sing that last high note."

"No, thank you," said Rita, and hurried away from them.

"I think she wanted to do it," Veronica said.

"I think so, too," said Frances, "but she looked as if she didn't really believe us."

"Maybe it's because she's Mexican," suggested Veronica.

"What if she is?" asked Frances. "We've had Mexican girls in the Scouts, haven't we?"

"Maybe if we asked her to join the Girl Scouts—"

"I won't ask her to do anything," Frances said.

Both girls were very proud of being Girl Scouts. Frances was president of a troop and Veronica's mother was their troop leader. The group met once a week on Saturdays, usually at Veronica's house because it was easy for all the members to get there. Sometimes there was a special meeting after school, and Rita saw the girls hurrying back in their green cotton uniforms with green anklets and green caps. All of them wore dark-blue ties with Scout pins in the bows.

As she walked slowly homeward with little Dolores, Rita heard the girls singing "O Beautiful Banner." She knew both the words and the music, and she hummed with the singers. "Maybe I'll be a Scout some day," she told the little girl.

"Scout?" the child repeated. "What is a scout?"

"A Girl Scout belongs to a club. She goes to meetings with other girls," explained her older sister. "They sew together, and sell cookies, and they learn to do all sorts of things. Sometimes they go for long hikes in the country."

"I'd like that," said Dolores. "Will you be a Girl Scout, Rita?"

"I don't know," Rita said wistfully. "I hope so."

The longer she thought of it, however, the lower her hope sank. She was not only a new girl at St. Robert's, but she was the child of another nation. The school where she had gone before her family had come to this town had not been friendly to her people. Veronica and Frances were not like the American girls in that other school, but Rita had been too hurt to be sure she was now welcome. "You and I will go for a hike in the country some day," she promised Dolores.

II. *A Lost Child*

Monsignor Kelty had not noticed that the new girl failed to salute the flag. Sister Margaret Rose did not see the omission. Veronica and Frances kept noticing it, but refrained from advising Rita. Once Frances weakened in her determination not to ask the new girl to join the Scouts.

"We need a good singer," she told Veronica, "and she's certainly one."

"She'll refuse you if you do," said Veronica.

The Girl Scout troop was giving a play. Sister Margaret Rose had seen them rehearse and had told them that they might give the play in the school auditorium with all the children of the grades as their guests. "It is a very nice play," she said, "but you need a better singer for the last scene."

315

Frances, listening to Rita Morena as she sang the hymn at morning assembly in the patio, knew that Rita would be able to sing the song in the last scene very well. But she held back from asking her, just as Rita, knowing what she could do and wishing to do it, refrained from offering to do it. "They don't want a Mexican girl," she told herself, "and I'm Mexican."

The troop rehearsals took place in the sixth-grade room after school each afternoon. One afternoon Rita lingered to hear the beginning of the rehearsal as she went out to meet Dolores. The child was not at the yard gate, and Rita sat on the steps to wait for her. After a while she realized that the first-grade room had been dismissed before she had come out. But where was Dolores?

There was a main highway between the school and

the Morena home. Rita, remembering it, ran in fright lest Dolores would have trouble in crossing it. She came to the highway, but there was no sign of the child. Rita hurried home, hoping to find Dolores there, but the child was not there.

Rita hurried back to St. Robert's, pausing only to ask other children if they had seen her little sister. No one had seen Dolores. "She'll be waiting for me at the school," Rita thought, but Dolores was not there. In terror Rita began to cry. "I've lost her," she thought. "It's my fault. If I hadn't waited a little while in the room, I'd have been here when she came out. Then she wouldn't be lost."

The troop was coming out from rehearsal. Some of the girls looked curiously at Rita as they passed her. Veronica stopped. "What's the matter?" she asked, seeing the tears in Rita's eyes.

"Dolores is lost."

"Maybe she went home."

"No, I've been there."

"What is the trouble?" Frances came over to ask.

"Her little sister is lost," Veronica explained.

"Let's look for her," Frances, president of the troop, said. At once, in a loud, clear voice she called, "Scouts, assemble!" By twos and threes the members of the troop, scattering at the gate, returned. As the girls gathered around, Frances told them about Dolores. Then, turning to Rita, she asked what dress Dolores was wearing.

"A yellow dress."

While they were talking a woman in a large car drew up to the curb. "Oh, it's Veronica's mother, the leader of our troop," cried Frances.

"What is the matter?" Mrs. Foster asked.

Veronica told her. Immediately her mother spoke to the assembled Scouts. "We'll have to separate. Some of you go out to Bedford Street. No one is to go alone. Two or three of you keep together. Come back here when you've looked everywhere you can."

The girls went off, running. Turning to Veronica, Frances, and Rita, the troop leader said, "Get in the car, the three of you. We can get around faster this way."

Veronica took the front seat beside her mother. Frances sat with Rita. After a little while she put her hand over Rita's. "Don't worry," she said. "We'll find her. She can't have gone very far."

"She's so little," Rita sobbed.

"I know," said Frances. She put her arm around Rita's shoulder. "But we're all looking for her. Someone will surely find her soon."

Veronica's mother drove slowly through street after street, sometimes stopping the car to ask children if they had seen a little girl in a yellow dress. No one had until they came nearly to the end of Walnut Street. There a boy said that he had seen a little girl going out toward the mountain. "Why would she go there?" Veronica asked.

"She wanted to take a hike in the country," Rita said. "I told her I'd take her sometime."

The quick darkness of southern California was falling as Rita caught a glimpse of yellow close to the road. "There she is!" she cried joyfully, but when they overtook a tired and frightened child she scolded her almost fiercely. "What do you mean by running away?"

"Don't scold her," Veronica's mother said. She lifted Dolores to a place between Veronica and herself. "You're all right now, darling," she soothed the weeping child. "I'll take you home," she told Rita. "Where do you live?"

"First we have to find the Scouts," her daughter reminded her.

"We'll do that, too."

They drove again through the streets where they had looked for Dolores. Group by group they found the Scouts, tired girls who smiled at Rita and the younger child. "We're so glad you found her," all of them said. By that time Dolores was asleep, and Rita had long since dried her tears. She sat happily beside Frances who was even more happily telling her about the Girl Scouts. "You'll have to be one of us," she said. But, remembering the other school and the girls there, Rita sighed. "How can I be?" she thought, even as she thanked Frances and Veronica and Veronica's mother for their help. How could she be a Scout if she were not an American?

319

III. *The High Note*

More than ever the next morning she wished to join her classmates in saluting the flag. Looking out toward the low California mountains, she knew how much she loved the place. Watching the Girl Scouts, she wanted to cry out in gratitude to them for their help in finding Dolores.

"If only I could be one of them," she thought.

At recess Veronica turned to her. "We're having a troop rehearsal at my house after school this afternoon," she said. "Can you take Dolores home and come back to the meeting?"

"You mean you want me to be a Scout?"

"Sure," said Veronica. "Why not?"

"I'm Mexican," said Rita.

"What nonsense!" said Veronica. "We're friends and neighbors, aren't we? Anyhow, you're in the United States now. When did you leave Mexico?"

"I was never in Mexico," Rita said.

"You weren't?" Frances cut into the conversation. "Where were you born?"

"Down in the valley," Rita said, and named the little town.

"Why, that's California," Veronica said, and laughed. "You're good in history, Rita, and in arithmetic, but you aren't good in geography when you think the Imperial Valley is in Mexico."

"I didn't think that," Rita said, "but I thought I

was Mexican because the girls in the school there called me that. You mean I'm American—like you?"

"Like all of us," Veronica and Frances said at the same instant.

"Oh, that's wonderful," Rita said. "Sure, I'll come to the meeting. Is it a party? Do I bring anything?"

"Just bring yourself," Frances told her.

As she raced Dolores home after school Rita explained why she was happy. "I'm so happy," she told the child, "and you ought to be just as happy. We're Americans."

"All right," Dolores said.

"It's a wonderful country."

"Sure," said Dolores.

"And it's our country."

"Ours," the child repeated.

All the girls of the troop, dressed in their green uniforms, were waiting for her in Veronica's living room. They stood at a signal from Frances, then they moved in a line past Rita, each girl shaking hands with her. They formed a semicircle and sang:

"O beautiful banner, all splendid with stars,
That in the breeze is flying."

Then, solemnly, Frances explained to Rita the requirements for becoming a Girl Scout. She told her she must attend some of their meetings. Then, before too long, she could take the pledge that all girls make when they join the Girl Scouts.

Rita was a very happy girl when the day came for

her to take the Girl Scout pledge. Her friends were just as happy as they listened to Rita's clear voice proudly repeating the words:

"On my honor, I will try
To do my duty to God and my country,
To help other people at all times,
To obey the Girl Scout Laws."

"You're a Scout now," said Veronica.

The Scouts swung into the rehearsal of their play. Girl after girl repeated the lines of her part. Then the songs began, some of them well done, others poorly sung. Rita was silent until Frances asked her to join. Then her clear, lovely voice rang out in the room. "Oh, that's beautiful," the Scouts declared.

"Will you sing the last song in the play?" Frances asked her.

"Can I? Do I know it? What is it?"

" 'The Star-Spangled Banner.' "

"I know it, but I never sang it before. I did not think I had the right. But I will sing it now."

And Rita sang, high notes and all. The Scouts applauded when she had finished, and she blushed with pleasure. "Thank you, thank you, thank you," she kept saying.

The next morning, she wished to thank everyone at St. Robert's assembly, for she had saluted the flag, and sung with the others the national anthem of the United States. Happily she looked toward the low mountains, green now with springtime, and up at the blue sky. "God and my country," she repeated the words in the Scout promise. "How wonderful they are!"

She was, she thought, what she had always been, an American. Now she knew it, as she had not known it in that other school. This was her country. She would always love the Mexico of her father and mother, although she had never seen their native land. But this California was her own. Her heart lifted to a high note, even as her voice has lifted to the high note of "The Star-Spangled Banner."

"I'll teach Dolores," she thought, "and I shall help people who need help. This is my country, and I'm proud of it, and I want it to be proud of me."

Happily she fell into step between Veronica and Frances and marched toward the sixth-grade room.

Copy the pattern below on your paper. After each letter write a quality of a good Girl Scout that begins with that letter. There will be nine of them. Use your dictionary and write the definition for each quality.

G_____
I_____
R_____
L_____

S_____
C_____
O_____
U_____
T_____

SIMILAR MEANINGS

Rewrite sentences from the story in which you can substitute words of similar meaning for the following words and word-groups. Underline the word substituted and give the page number of the sentence.

1. active
2. large
3. inner yard
4. quicker
5. sang with closed lips
6. gladly received
7. practice

8. meeting
9. delayed leaving
10. great fear
11. with wonder
12. short view
13. seriously
14. promise

Freedom's Land

It is a mountain
My country,
It is a mountain and a river
Gold where the wheat has caught the sun.
It is a mountain and a river
And a people
Who have known the goodness
Of the spring holding earth.

It is a word
My country,
A word that is a river
And a plain,
A mountain,
And a dream,
And a song on a free man's lips.
It is a word and a song
And a people's dream.
It is my country.

NATHAN ZIMELMAN

325

VII

Justice

Human Wickedness and Divine Providence

O Lord, Your kindness reaches to heaven;
    Your faithfulness to the clouds.
Your justice is like the mountains of God;
    Your judgments, like the mighty deep;
    man and beast You save, O Lord.
The children of men take refuge
    in the shadow of Your wings.
For with You is the fountain of life,
    and in Your light we see light.

PSALM 35

Panis Angelicus

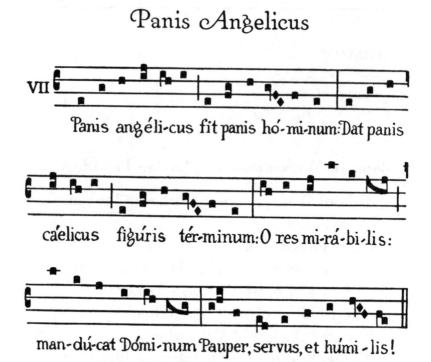

Panis angéli-cus fit panis hó-mi-num: Dat panis

cáelicus figúris tér-minum: O res mi-rá-bi-lis:

man-dú-cat Dómi-num Pauper, servus, et húmi-lis!

The angels' bread is bread for man,
The poor, the weak, the lowly can
Share heavenly bread because God gives
The bread in which Our Savior lives.

Saint of the Barbary Coast

I. *The Coast of Barbary*

The harbor of Marseille, a seaport of France, was filled with ships one summer morning in the year 1605. A young priest came out of an inn and walked toward the wharf.

Born in France, ordained in Spain, he had often gone back and forth over the high mountain passes that separated the two countries. He knew the weariness and hardships of the land journey which lay between him and his destination, Toulouse, a city in southern France. That was why, on this day, he was taking the advice of a traveler he had met at the inn. There, a gentleman had told him that the trip would be swifter, cheaper, and more pleasant by boat.

The priest made his way through narrow streets crowded with merchants and traders coming from a country fair. Sailors from the ships of many countries, dock workers, truckmen, jostled one another as they went about their business. A dozen languages sounded around him as he moved toward the wharf where his ship waited, with canvas set for sailing.

On the wharf an old sailor spoke to him. "You would be wiser to travel by land, Father Vincent," he told him. "In these days the Turks are lying in wait for every Christian ship that leaves the harbor of Marseille."

"I am going only a day's journey, Pierre," the priest said.

"What you propose to do is dangerous," the sailor muttered. "I have seen much happen in a day."

"So have I," said the young priest. "When I was a shepherd boy on my father's farm, I saw storms sweep down and in an hour change the whole face of the land."

"You will see more than a storm if you meet the Turkish pirates, those terrible sea robbers," the sailor said.

For some distance out of Marseille, however, the sailor's warning seemed foolish to Father Vincent de Paul. The sea was calm and as blue as the mantle of Our Lady. The sky was bright and clear. The sailors sang as they worked. A few passengers joined them

330

in the singing, but Father Vincent sat on a large coil of rope, saying his Office.

Then, suddenly, from the crow's-nest—the little inclosed platform set high on the mast where a lookout was always on watch—a cry came down to the deck. Instantly sailors and passengers leaped to the sides of the boat, staring out over the quiet waters.

"The Turks, the Turks!" rose a wild shout. "The pirates are upon us."

Desperately the pilot of the ship tried to find safety in the shelter of the shore. Desperately the crew and the passengers took up weapons to save themselves. Desperately they all fought the attack of the three Turkish ships which circled the little Christian vessel. The Christian sailors and passengers fought in vain.

Three sailors fell, killed by Turkish arrows. Twenty others, Father Vincent de Paul among them, were so wounded that they could no longer defend the ship. The three Turkish ships came alongside the boat from Marseille. Over the rails came the Turks, their curved knives high in their hands.

Then, enraged because the ship carried no treasure, the Turks killed the pilot and put the wounded men in chains. They robbed every man of all he had. They carried off to their own vessels all the ship's supplies. With the prisoners lying on the deck in the broiling summer sunlight of the Mediterranean, the pirates set sail for the Barbary Coast.

There, on the sands of Africa, they made the prisoners ready for the slave market of Tunis. They stripped each man of his clothes and possessions and gave him a loose-fitting garment of coarse cloth. Then they marched them for miles into the city.

At the city gate of Tunis, the Turks put chains around the wrists of their prisoners. They drove them, with whips, through the city streets, then took them to the slave traders. The slave traders threw aside those who were dying and took the rest to the slave market in the center of the city.

Father Vincent de Paul stood with the other prisoners as buyers inspected them, just as they would have inspected a horse or an ox which they wished to buy. Slave buyers opened the mouths of the prisoners to look at their teeth, pierced their wounds, made them run, trot, lift burdens. If the prisoners fell in weakness, the slave drivers lashed them cruelly with whips until they staggered to their feet again.

A fisherman bought the young priest, but Father Vincent was a poor sailor, and the fisherman sold him again, this time to a Moorish chemist. The chemist was not a hard master. Father Vincent's task was to keep the fires burning in a dozen furnaces. The Moor often talked to him as he worked. He came to like his slave and sought to win him to the Moslems. Finally he offered to share with Father Vincent his fortune and his knowledge, if the young priest would give up his Christian Faith.

Father Vincent refused the offer. "God kept in me always," he afterward wrote, "a belief that I should be saved. Because of my prayers, I firmly believe, I was saved."

Father Vincent was saved in a strange way. His master, the chemist, died, and the priest was sold to a farmer, who had been born in France and who had been a Christian but was now a Moslem. The farmer set his slave to work in the fields which he rented from the Sultan, the ruler of the Turks. It was a law of that country that no one but the Sultan could own any land. There, under the blazing sun of Africa, the priest toiled for his new master.

One day the Turkish wife of his master came to talk with her slave. "How do the people of France live?" she asked him. After Father Vincent had told

her something of the life of France, she said, "Sing praise to your God."

The priest thought of the children of Israel, prisoners in a strange land. With tears in his eyes he began to sing the psalm of the Jewish captives, "By the Rivers of Babylon." The Turkish woman listened to him. Then she turned away.

The next day she came back. "Tell me more about your God," she said.

Vincent told her. He told her of the glory of God. He told her of the kindness of God. He told her of Christ and of Mary. He taught her the "*Salve Regina*," the "Hail, Holy Queen."

"Queen of Heaven," she said. "Is a woman queen in your heaven?"

"Yes, a woman," Father Vincent said, "who once lived in the little village of Nazareth."

Day after day the Turkish woman returned to ask the priest to tell her more about God. One day she told the priest that she had said to her husband, "How could you give up faith in such a God?" Her husband had not answered her. Later the Turkish woman died. A little while afterward her husband came to Father Vincent.

"I am planning," he told his slave, "so that you and I shall go away from here. We will return to France. There I will do penance for my sin."

The master kept his word, although it was months later when he and Father Vincent sailed from the Barbary Coast in a little boat. They crossed the Mediterranean and came at last to France. There, before a great crowd, in the Church of St. Peter, the master declared his sorrow for his sin. Father Vincent de Paul had won his own freedom by his faith. He had also won another soul to Christ.

II. *In the Service of the Poor*

Memories of these years of slavery under the African sun always remained in the mind of Father Vincent de Paul. Because of these memories he never missed a chance to do a kindness to any man or woman or child who needed kindness. After his return to France he rose to a position of great trust and power as the confessor to a queen. After her death he was tutor, or instructor, to the children of one of the most important men of France. This important man was the warden of the royal galleys, those terrible prison ships where convicts lived in a slavery even worse than Vincent de Paul had known in Africa.

Father Vincent had already done great work for the poor, the neglected, the sick. He brought together groups of both men and women to continue and extend his work. He had aroused many of the poor to help one another. He believed that all the children of God should love one another. He taught the rich to seek out the poor. He taught the poor to understand the rich. He taught the rich to be kind. He taught the poor to be generous in their opinions of the rich.

No man could do much alone, Father Vincent said. He must work with his fellow men and for his fellow men. That was good sense. That was Christian charity.

Father Vincent de Paul organized associations, thirty of them. One was the great order of men, the Congregation of the Missions. Another was the Ladies of Charity, which included in its numbers ladies of the king's court, women of humble homes, wives of soldiers, shopkeepers, carpenters, and masons. These women went from house to house, caring for the sick, sweeping the rooms, giving food to the hungry. Still another association that Father Vincent started was the Daughters of Charity. With the aid of a saintly woman he founded this sisterhood, devoted to the work of charity.

"In the service of the poor," Father Vincent told the

Sisters, "put all else aside. In doing this you leave God only to find Him. The poor alone demand your time. Treat them well, with gentleness, with tenderness, with love; for they are your lords and masters, and mine."

These Sisters were angels of mercy in the hospitals of Paris. Working with the Sisters were the priests of the Congregation of the Missions, as well as the Lazarists, whom Father Vincent had established in the old hospital for the lepers, Saint-Lazare. The lepers suffered from a dreadful disease called leprosy.

All this work might have been enough for another man. It was not enough for the man who had been a slave in Africa. When Father Vincent learned that the men in the royal galleys suffered horrible hardships he went again to Marseille. This time he went to see for himself their condition so that he might plead for its improvement with the king of France and the warden of the galleys, who was in charge of all prison ships.

Vincent de Paul went without orders, without letters from the king. At Marseille he was horrified by the misery of the convicts. He saw the huge wooden clubs with which the officers beat the men. He saw the knots in the whips with which they lashed the unfortunates. He saw the filth, the disease, all around them. He saw men, chained to their places, working at oars that sent the boats out to meet enemies at sea. He saw the men, still chained, lying dead when the boats came back to Marseille.

There is a story that one day Father Vincent saw a convict weeping because he was being forced from his wife and children. The convict's despair was so great, his grief so awful, his sorrow for his crime so deep that Father Vincent went to the officer in charge of the galley and said, "Let me take this man's place!"

The officer hesitated, but at last, knowing that the priest was the warden's close friend, consented. The irons were still warm from the convict's body when Father Vincent de Paul put them on. He took his place on the bench and grasped the oar. Around him men groaned and wept as he worked with them to speed the galley.

For weeks Father Vincent lived the life of the man

whose place he had taken. Then the warden's wife, alarmed by the priest's absence, made inquiries which found him. He came back to Paris to tell her husband and the king what he had seen, what he had suffered, and to beg for mercy for the convicts.

There were few unfortunates in the France of his time whom Father Vincent did not help—the sick, the insane, old men and women, babies deserted by their parents, galley slaves and their families. He had known the greatest men and women of Paris. He had served four cardinals. He had been confessor to one queen. He had seen the wedding of another. He had talked long and often with a third queen. He had laughed with one great king. He had held another in his arms as the king died. He had seen the rising glory of the Grand Monarch, Louis XIV.

When Vincent de Paul died, great men and women mourned him. Half the nobility of France crowded into the Church of Saint-Lazare for his funeral Mass. For two hours the Bishop spoke of his life, his work. Then Father Vincent was buried beneath the choir of the church, while out in the streets of Paris, the poor, the sick, the lame, all the men and women whom he had helped, sobbed as they stood in the rain. "We have lost our friend," they said. "We have lost our father."

Only those whom he had helped most—the deserted children of the city—did not grieve for him. They did not yet know how much they had lost in losing Father Vincent de Paul.

MATCHING HEADLINES AND PARAGRAPHS

Match the following headlines with paragraphs of the story. On your paper write the headline and after it write the page and paragraph number to which it refers. The first one is given as an example.

1. Inspection of the Prisoners (*Page 332, paragraph 5*)
2. The Misery of Convicts at Marseille
3. Father Vincent at the Galleys
4. An Old Sailor's Advice
5. Father Vincent's First Masters
6. Father Vincent's Funeral

WRITING HEADLINES

Read the following sections of the story and on your paper write a good headline, or main idea, for each section.

1. Page 331, paragraphs 1–3
2. Page 333, paragraph 4, through paragraph 1, page 335
3. Page 336, paragraph 3, to end of paragraph 1, page 337

FINDING MEANINGS IN CONTEXT

As you read, do you realize that often words are defined, or explained, in the story? Locate the following terms in the story and write the meaning of each as it is given in the story, or context.

royal galleys	pirates
crow's-nest	Marseille
tutor	warden
Daughters of Charity	*Salve Regina*
Sultan	leprosy

Tilbury Dock, 1856

One of England's great wars was fought in the Russian Crimea, a district in the southeastern part of Europe. Twenty-three Irish Sisters of Mercy and Florence Nightingale, who had gone to the Crimea with them, helped to nurse the sick and wounded. After the War the Sisters returned to England, some of them on a ship with the Grenadier Guards, one of England's bravest and most famous regiments. The ship docked at Tilbury on the Thames River near London.

The people of London gathered to cheer
The heroes of Sevastopol
As the Grenadier Guards came home from war
In ships from Constantinople.
The Grenadier Guards stepped on Tilbury Dock,
Ready to march to the Tower,
When an order ran through their thinned, red lines
To set back their marching hour.

"We wait for the Sisters," the colonel said;
"They tended our sick, and they buried our dead.
They stood with us, fearless and unafraid,
Behind the charge of the Light Brigade.
Today, in England's triumphal hour,
They march before us to London Tower."

The Grenadier Guards gave the Mercy nuns,
Who nursed them at Sevastopol,
A cheer beyond any they ever heard
In streets of Constantinople;

341

But the London crowd at Tilbury Dock
Murmured in horrid groaning,
And from the streets picked the paving blocks
To hold in their hands for stoning.

"*We march with the Sisters*," the colonel said;
"*The Sisters of Mercy will march at our head,
Or the Grenadier Guards will not march at all
To Tower, or Palace, or even Whitehall.
Until the last of the Guards is dead,
We shall honor the Sisters*," the colonel said.

The band struck up with mighty roar
As the thinned, red lines stood ready,
And twelve black-robed Sisters passed through the ranks
That held for them, valiant and steady.
Then, falling in step to *Britannia Rules*,
And moving in courage solemn,
The Grenadier Guards marched to London Tower,
And the Sisters headed the column.

Long years have gone since those Grenadier Guards
Came home from far Sevastopol;
In other wars other Guardsmen marched
Through the streets of Constantinople;
But, still in barracks, the story is told,
With every Guardsman lifting his head
To say, "*We shall honor those Sisters twelve
Until the last of the Guards is dead.*"

Son of Thunder

Act I

CHORUS
Son of Thunder,
William Emmanuel von Ketteler,
by the grace of God the Bishop of old Mainz,
the city of the good Saint Boniface,
Ketteler, brave defender of the Faith,
Ketteler, champion of the rights of man,
Ketteler, fighter for the worker's cause,
was dying.

Scene

Just outside the door of the Cathedral of Mainz

Characters

HENRY, a tall old man in a faded coat and cap
BONIFACE, an old and weary factory worker of noble
birth
OTTO, a small and frail man, a storekeeper
CARL, a young man, recently come to Mainz
FREDERICK, the sexton of the cathedral

(*As the scene opens, the group of men are talking about their beloved Bishop who has been at the Cathedral for twenty-seven years.*)

OTTO: William Emmanuel von Ketteler, Bishop of Mainz! A great bishop, the greatest of our time here in Germany.

HENRY: What a life he has lived in his sixty-six years!

BONIFACE: Born, was he not, in a castle on Christmas

343

Day in 1811? They named him Emmanuel, which means "God with us." I am sure that his father, the Baron, never dreamed that a son of his would become the champion of the poor of the earth.

OTTO: They tell the story that his father was furious when William, then a young student, was wounded in a student duel. He would not let his son come home until the wound was healed.

BONIFACE: Well, his son has been in plenty of other duels since then, but they have not been duels with swords. They have been duels of words and wits. Like the knights of old, Ketteler has fought, not for himself, but for a cause.

CARL: How did the Bishop get into this cause?

HENRY: I think this is the story. Ketteler was a lawyer in a government job with a fine future when

his Prussian government said the Archbishop of Cologne had broken some state laws.

BONIFACE: That was nonsense, and everyone knew it.

HENRY: When Prussia arrested the old Archbishop, Ketteler resigned his job.

CARL: What did young von Ketteler propose to do?

HENRY: He went right off to study for the priesthood. In the Church he would find a way to serve God which he could not find in the government.

OTTO: You might have thought he would want a big city parish. Well, his first parish was a poor little place in the country. He himself asked for it. Everyone loved him, but he did not stay there long. He began to preach the cause of the poor, the working people of Germany. He was our champion. Soon a great city, Berlin, sent for him.

BONIFACE: Ketteler was brave. There had not been a Corpus Christi procession in Berlin for a long, long time, not since it had become a Protestant city. Father Ketteler formed a procession in his church, St. Hedwig's, and carried the Blessed Sacrament through the streets of Berlin.

HENRY: That was nearly forty years ago. Time goes fast, does it not, as one grows old? Through these years Ketteler never changed. He came to Mainz from Bingen on a steamer that was bright with flags and flowers. There were military bands to meet him. The whole city had a holiday.

BONIFACE: Princes and counts and barons came from

345

Austria and Bavaria and even from Prussia to do him honor. He spoke not to them, but to us, his people, here in Mainz. "I must be prepared to give my life for you, the flock of Christ," he said. "All I am and all I have belong not to me, but to you. I will give honor to the image of God in every man, woman, and child. I will do all in my power to rescue them from sin, and raise them to the dignity of princes of God's people. Whatever I possess till I die shall belong not to me, but to you."

HENRY: He kept his word.

OTTO: That was Ketteler.

CARL: When shall we find another like him?

(*One of the smaller church doors to the left of the group opens, and the sexton approaches the group.*)

SEXTON: Where are those boys? I sent them an hour ago to the telegraph office. They should be back by this time. I keep hoping—and yet I know the time for hope is past. The Bishop will not come back.

HENRY: Another Bishop will come to Mainz. He will be a good man, I know, perhaps a great man.

SEXTON: But I have been here twenty-seven years with my Bishop, and it will be hard for any other to be so dear to me. Let me tell you how he has lived. He was a baron and a bishop. Bishop of Mainz. Why, in the old Holy Roman Empire the Bishop of Mainz had the first vote in the naming of the emperor. With all that, my Bishop kept for him-

346

self only two little rooms—and how bare they are! And only twice, in all these years, has he used the table silver that belongs to the Bishops of Mainz. Had it been his own, he would have sold it long since and given the money to the poor.

HENRY: Through the Society of St. Vincent de Paul he has given them all he had to give, everything.

BONIFACE: The poor will miss him. I know that work like his is never done in vain; but I wonder, I wonder, who can take his place.

Act II

CHORUS

Never again would that great voice of thunder
that gave to him the name of Thunder's son,
rise in the meetings in the royal court,
in Cathedrals, in parish schools.

Scene

On a large porch

Characters

| ELIZABETH URSULA WILHELMINA | Elderly ladies who have been childhood schoolmates |

(*As the scene opens the elderly women are sitting on the porch drinking coffee.*)

ELIZABETH: I wonder if Sister Teresa knows that Bishop Ketteler is dying. Sister Teresa is not so young herself now, but she is as active as any of us. Ursula, do you remember the stories Sister

347

Teresa told us in school of the wonderful things that Bishop Ketteler was doing then for the people in Germany?

URSULA: I surely do remember them, and I'll bet Wilhelmina remembers them even if she wasn't at our school as long as we were. I recall especially the stories about knights and Sir Galahad and the Holy Grail. Do you remember when I asked Sister if there were any knights living in our time or if they belonged only to the Middle Ages?

WILHELMINA: Yes, I remember that because when Sister said that our own Bishop Ketteler was a knight I asked how he could be a knight when he didn't ride on a white charger or kill dragons.

ELIZABETH: And do you remember how Sister answered your question?

WILHELMINA: It is not hard to remember that because so often through the years I have seen such poverty and misery that I could not help thinking about Sister's telling us that these were the dragons the Bishop was trying to kill.

URSULA: Sister really painted a true picture when she spoke of poverty and misery as dragons working for King Injustice.

WILHELMINA: I remember how happy I was when my mother did not have to work in the factory. Our home was so much happier then.

URSULA: And I recall how happy we were when my little brother was not permitted to work in the mines.

ELIZABETH: When Sister Teresa told us those stories we thought that in a little while everything would be better.

URSULA: But when the school was locked up and Sister Teresa left I knew then that the dragons were still among the people.

ELIZABETH: Now the Bishop is dying, and they are still among us. Do you think that there will be anyone to fight them as the Bishop has?

WILHELMINA: Suppose we go over to the church now and pray for our beloved Bishop Ketteler, while the good monks are praying at his bedside in their monastery. I am so glad he had the happiness of an audience with our Holy Father, even if the pilgrimage to Rome was difficult for him. Saint Joseph, patron of a happy death, pray for him.

349

Act III

CHORUS

Through narrow streets, through little twisting lanes,
to factories of whirling wheels and looms,
to smithies where men pounded on the iron
for wagon wheels, to print shops, and cigar shops,
into the houses where pale women sewed
as if they never could catch up with time,
to schools and offices and every place
where men and women worked and children played,
sped on the news.

Scene
Hard-Heart's workshop

Characters

JAKE	HAROLD
GEORGE	LUTHER
CAROLUS	Several other workmen
JOHN	OLD HARD-HEART

(*As the scene opens, the workmen are silently pounding the iron and shaping the red-hot metal, when amidst the hammer beat one of them speaks.*)

HAROLD: Our Bishop is dying.

JOHN: And if he dies, we won't have anyone to fight for us. Then Old Hard-Heart will probably make us work from six in the morning till ten at night.

CAROLUS: It's bad enough now. I'm supposed to work from seven in the morning till six at night; but I have to be here at six every morning except Sunday, and I work every night till nearly eight. It

350

would be worse if it weren't for our beloved Bishop von Ketteler.

GEORGE: Something about Ketteler has always reminded me of the prophets of the Old Testament. Do you remember how Amos the Herdsman shouted at the men of Israel, "You who oppress the needy and crush the poor?" He told them that the day of the Lord would find them lifted up on poles or set on boiling pots. Our Bishop did not threaten, but his heart, like the heart of Amos, stayed with the poor.

HAROLD: Hard-Heart will probably cut our wages in half. I can hardly feed my family now. What will we do without Ketteler to defend us?

JAKE: Ketteler (*pause*). He's the best friend we workingmen have ever had. If he could have his way, we would have decent wages and decent hours and a decent way of living. He has worked for us and

fought for us and tried to help us. The least we can do is pray for him now that he is dying.

HAROLD: Our congregation said a special prayer for him yesterday at our church service. I think that's the first time our minister ever led prayers for a Catholic priest.

JAKE: Rabbi Obermann was talking about the Bishop after the Sabbath service. He said that Ketteler was a great man because he helped all the workingmen.

(*Old Hard-Heart yells from the neighboring room.*)

HARD-HEART (*in a mean, harsh tone*): You men, quit your talking and get to work. I don't pay you for talking about that man. You'll stay here tonight till you finish those wheels for Mr. Schultz.

JOHN: The people are all praying for him now at the Cathedral. He did so much for us workingmen. I think we ought to go now and try to help him.

LUTHER: I'm not a Catholic, but I'll go with you.

ALL THE WORKERS: I, too. Let's go.

(*The men put down their tools and they all walk out. As they leave, old Hard-Heart watches them in angry silence.*)

GEORGE (*to Hard-Heart*): And you will not take this hour out of our pay. You owe us far more than this hour we want to give to our true friend, the Bishop of Mainz.

(*Then the men walk hurriedly down the narrow street to the Cathedral.*)

352

Act IV

CHORUS

Then, through the narrow streets and twisting lanes
came hundreds, thousands, of the men of Mainz,
the women, and the children. Some of them wept.
Others, moved in a grief that went beyond all tears,
were dry-eyed. "He's dying," said their eyes.
They knew his death was glory to him,
but their own despair.
Who now could hurl the thunderbolts at wrong
when he, the Son of Thunder, was no more?

Scene
The living room of the Bachmann home

Characters
FREDERICK BACHMANN, a factory worker
GERTRUDE BACHMANN, his wife
KATHI, their daughter
FATHER KAMPER, the Bishop's secretary

(*Mr. Bachmann is resting after the day's work, Mrs. Bachmann talks with him as she knits a sweater for Kathi. Kathi is reading a book.*)

MRS. BACHMANN: Was this a busy day at the factory, Frederick?

MR. BACHMANN: Not too bad. We had a big order to ship to Berlin.

KATHI: I was busy today, Papa! I helped Mrs. Klein deliver her needlework to her customers after school was over.

353

Mrs. Bachmann: Poor Mrs. Klein! She works so hard. I wish there were some way we could help her, Frederick.

(*She is interrupted by a knock at the door.*)

Mrs. Bachmann: Kathi, please see who is knocking.

Mr. Bachmann: Yes, Gertrude, we must try to help Mrs. Klein. Remember how the Bishop helped us— what would we do if I didn't work at the factory?

Kathi (*at the door*): Father! Oh, Father Kamper!

Mrs. Bachmann: Can it be the Bishop's secretary?

(*The door is opened, revealing the Bishop's secretary standing there.*)

Mr. Bachmann: Come in, Father. It is so good to see you.

Mrs. Bachmann: It has been many weeks since we have received you into our home. Let me get you a warm drink.

Father Kamper: I hope I do not disturb you. It is a cold evening. (*With a smile*) I would certainly appreciate that warm drink, Mrs. Bachmann.

Mr. Bachmann: Come sit here by the fire and warm yourself. (*Turning to Kathi*) Kathi, stir up the fire.

Father Kamper (*also to Kathi*): And how are you, little one? Your cheeks have winter roses blooming in them.

Mrs. Bachmann (*coming from the stove*): Kathi is fine, Father, but her restored health is due to our good Bishop's kindness. I remember a few years ago when I was so ill and Frederick and I had nothing, nothing at all to give her. (*Turning to Kathi*) I was kneeling beside your bed praying, praying but wondering if God were hearing my poor prayer, when a knock came at the door, and the Bishop came. (*To the priest*) The Bishop sent a doctor; he sent food and clothes for us.

MR. BACHMANN: I will never forget how he came later to tell me he had found work for me at the factory.

FATHER KAMPER: And he considered it only justice. When will the world learn? When will men come to know that nothing but justice, the justice of God's law, can make all things right?

MRS. BACHMANN: He made the world better for us, and to think that now he is leaving us. What is the latest report of him?

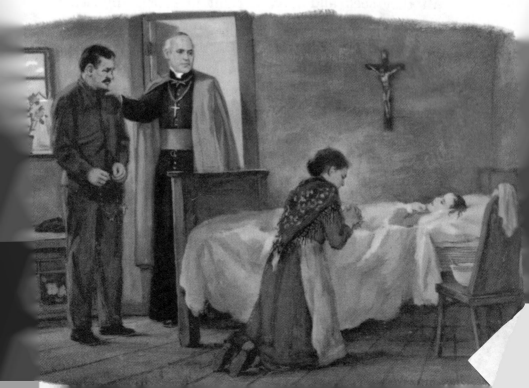

FATHER KAMPER: There is no chance of his getting better.

MRS. BACHMANN (*rising hurriedly*): The coffee must be ready now. Excuse me, please, Father.

KATHI: May I help, Mama?

MRS. BACHMANN: Yes, dear. Fetch a cup and saucer for the Father and Papa.

(*Mrs. Bachmann goes to the kitchen as the priest and Mr. Bachmann continue their conversation.*)

FATHER KAMPER: How is your job at the factory, Frederick?

MR. BACHMANN: Fine, Father. Our Bishop did so much to help the workers. We still do not have ideal conditions in our factories, but they are improving.

FATHER KAMPER: The only way the workers can win all they seek and have a right to seek is by peace and co-operation between their employers and themselves. The worker should be fair. The employer should be fair. (*With a sad shake of the head*) There does not have to be war between them.

MR. BACHMANN: I remember the day that I was at a workingmen's meeting. Bishop Ketteler was on his way to a meeting of the German Bishops, but he took the time to stop on his way and to speak to us.

(*Mrs. Bachmann enters with coffee.*)

MRS. BACHMANN: This will help to warm you, Father . . . Yes, I remember that day also, Frederick. You told us that evening what the Bishop said about higher wages, better working conditions, shorter hours, and days of rest for the workingmen. You told us, too, about women and young girls working in the factories. Thanks be to God that Kathi and I can stay here and make a good home for you, Frederick.

FATHER KAMPER: Mr. Bachmann, I came this evening to ask you to act as chairman of the committee of the St. Vincent de Paul Society. I know you are a very busy man, but you can do much good for the poor in this work.

MR. BACHMANN: I'll be happy to do all I can, Father. Perhaps in that way I can help to repay all the Society did for me many years ago when the Bishop loaned me money from the St. Vincent de Paul Society Fund.

(*Father Kamper rises to leave.*)

MRS. BACHMANN: We know you are very busy, Father, but we hope you can come soon again. We shall keep praying for our Bishop. May we please have your blessing before you go, Father? (*The priest gives them his blessing as they kneel.*) Thank you, Father, *auf Wiedersehen* and God bless you.

(*The priest leaves. Mr. Bachmann turns to Mrs. Bachmann.*)

MR. BACHMANN: How good Father Kamper is! We must thank God often for His wonderful priests.

(*Curtain closes.*)

357

Epilogue

Solo — While, far away in a Capuchin Monastery, the brilliant-robed angel of death hovers over the dying Bishop, the people of Mainz have finally gathered before the Cathedral. The Bishop's secretary steps forward to comfort them.

Father Kamper — Ketteler. I think Saint Michael will be glad to welcome him. For the Archangel knows that God's truth often needs fighters, fighters for the right. And he has fought for right. He fought for justice, God's justice shown by men to one another. He cried out for the rights of those who work—their right to hold together for security, their right to a living wage and better ways of living. The Bishop, could he live, might bring about fulfillment of our hopes. Now, by God's Will, the task must wait another.

(*The people voice their agreement to what he has said.*)

Chorus	Our brother of the ancient holy city of Boniface is going to his great reward.
Light	May Christ, Who called him, receive his soul; and may the angels lead him to the sight of God most High.
Medium	Upon this earth he has done good work and great work.
Dark	Within his voice, his mighty voice, sounded eternal truths. His was a voice of thunder ever lifted in a mighty cause, the welfare of the poor, children of Christ for whom Christ asked our justice.
Medium	He has led men a little nearer upon the way to God.
Dark	That was his mission. No cause of right is ever wholly lost. After him will come others who will take men nearer still, until at last they reach the perfect justice, God's Kingdom come to earth.
Light	Who will they be?
Medium	Who knows?
Dark	Someone will come.
Light	Some other voice be lifted.
L & M	Somewhere—
All	Sometime—
Chorus	In Mainz, in the old city of the Rhineland, the city of the good Saint Boniface, the bell of the cathedral slowly, slowly, began to toll. One, two, three, four, five, six.

Upon their knees within the street the people
   wept.
Ketteler, brave defender of the Faith,
Ketteler, champion of the rights of man,
Ketteler, fighter for the worker's cause,
Ketteler, mighty Son of roaring Thunder,
   was dead.

Never again in life would he return
to his gray city by the quiet Rhine;
but in the years to come would other men
of many nations and of many faiths
bear on the banner of his charity;
and from the throne of Peter two great Popes
would speak again his words to all the world.

That is the way of God. No one man ends
the work which he begins; but, if the work be
   good,
there will be other men to move it onward,
and though the clouds may darken the long road
of justice, yet the sun must shine again
somewhere, sometime.

The North Side of Pine Street

I. *Bad News for St. John's School*

The boys and girls in sixth grade of St. John's School could hardly wait for the bell to ring. There was much to talk about. This would be the last year they would ever spend in a classroom of the old building on Pine Street. The city planners needed the north side of Pine Street for a new expressway that would cross the city westward to the river. Before the summer was over, bulldozers and tractors would level all the buildings on the street on which St. John's had been standing for three generations.

Sister Mary Angela told the class about it. "St. John's is something of a landmark," she said. "It meant a great deal to your fathers and mothers and even to some of your grandparents. Tell them when you get home that the church is to remain, but the school must go." The church, as they knew, was on the south side of the street.

Richard Dunn, president of the Civics Club, rose from his seat. "There'll be a new school built here in the parish, won't there, Sister?" he asked.

Sister Mary Angela shook her head sadly. "There will be no school," she said.

As of one voice, the boys and girls cried out, "Why not?"

Sister explained. "The neighborhood has changed within the last ten years. Many families have moved

away and our enrollment has dropped to such a point that we haven't money enough to build a new school."

"Where will we go?" asked Monica Earl.

"There is St. Justin's," said Sister. "It's a splendid school."

"St. Justin's is more than two miles from here," Mary Cassidy protested. "We'd have to cross the railroad viaduct to get there."

Sister lifted her hand for silence. "A city grows and a city changes," she said. "We happen to stand in the path of progress, and we must think of the greatest good for the greatest number."

Nothing more was said during the school day, but now as class was about to be dismissed, the anger of the boys and girls in the room was rising. Not against Sister Mary Angela, for they could sense her regret.

Not against their pastor, Father O'Brien, for they were old enough to be aware of the heartbreaking battle he waged to support the church and school. Sometimes, they knew, it was hard to raise money enough to buy coal in winter. St. John's was a poor parish. Nearly every child in the school came from a home where lack of money was a real problem. Their anger now rose against a silent deadly enemy called Progress.

"Why did the city have to pick our street?" Eddie Carson complained as they reached the schoolyard.

"Why couldn't they build an expressway along the river?" grumbled Mary.

Monica tried to be reasonable. "Maybe the people who live across the river asked for it," she suggested.

"The people who live across the river don't vote in this city," said Richard Dunn. "What right have they to destroy our street?"

To the president of the sixth-grade Civics Club, civics meant politics. Knowledge of political methods had come naturally to Richard. His father and his grandfather had served as precinct captains for one of the major political parties. The boy knew the processes of city government from the first simple steps in a voting booth to the last hurrah of election night. "In politics you don't ignore the voters," he had learned.

The children parted at Waller Street. Alone, peering into every shop window, Richard walked along the north side of Pine. "I wonder if they've heard the news," he muttered to himself as he passed the familiar

places. He knew all the men and women who worked here—Mr. Sweeney in the drug store, Mrs. Grecco in her little candy and notion shop, Mr. Klein in the Shoe Emporium, Mr. and Mrs. Schultz in the bakery, Sam the laundryman, Charlie at his lunch counter. "Where'll they go?" he wondered. "What'll they do?"

His anxiety about the school and street stayed with him until dinner was ready. Then, as his father and mother and sisters and brothers sat down to eat, he exploded the news.

His mother was horrified. "St. John's School to be torn down!"

His father's face showed deep concern. "Oh, they can't do that!"

"The whole north side of Pine will be torn down, too," Richard added.

His father put down his coffee cup sharply. "That'll mean Charlie's place will go, and Sam's and—"

"And Mrs. Grecco's," said Richard.

"And Mr. Klein's store?" asked Peggy, Richard's sister, who knew the style and price of every shoe in Mr. Klein's window.

"And the place where the nice lady sells cookies?" cried Timmy, Richard's youngest brother.

A prophet of doom, Richard nodded soberly. "Everything will go," he said with finality.

The Dunns were strangely silent that night. The children were quiet. Richard's father held a newspaper, but he did not read. Richard's mother lifted a basket of unmended clothes, but she did not sew. Only once did she again mention the bad news. "St. John's was here when my mother was a girl," she said. "I hate to see it go."

By morning Richard had made the decision that action was needed to save St. John's and the north side of Pine Street. What could he do? Surely there must be some way of letting the city know that nobody in St. John's Parish was happy about the project. What was the best way to do this? Should it be left to Father O'Brien? to the Sisters? to the Ladies' Sodality? to the Parents' Group? to the shopkeepers of Pine Street? As he neared the school a quick flash of inspiration lighted his way. He rushed into the hall and up the stairs to the sixth-grade room. "The Civics Club! The Civics Club! That'll swing it!" he shouted.

365

Sister Mary Angela listened patiently to his plan. Then she sighed. "Others have spoken to the Mayor," she told the boy. "It's no use, Richard."

Richard, son and grandson of precinct captains, was not easily discouraged. Hadn't he seen pictures of the Mayor, pictures taken with children who had gone to him in other good causes? for the polio drive? for the Red Cross Blood Bank? for the United Nations? Surely the man in the City Hall would hear and heed the plea of children who were losing their beloved school. "You never know until you try," he told himself, and went to Sister Mary Angela's desk.

Again she listened. "I don't want to discourage you," she said, "but, before you speak to members of our Civics Club, ask Father O'Brien. You know that the club should engage in no project without his consent."

At noon Richard crossed the schoolyard to the rectory. "One more appeal cannot hurt us," said Father O'Brien, "but do not be too hopeful."

The Civics Club met that afternoon. "Who'll talk to the Mayor?" asked Eddie.

"We'll go together, in a body," said Richard.

"I'd be scared to talk to a Mayor," said Mary.

"I wouldn't," said Monica.

"Will the Mayor see us?" asked Eddie.

Richard, who knew his way about in politics, replied, "We can ask for an appointment."

"Let's try," the club members agreed.

Mary Cassidy penned the letter. She had to recopy it six times. Her penmanship was perfect the first time, but the club members suggested so many changes that she had to use all her good notepaper. Eddie Carson wanted to tell the Mayor the purpose of their visit. Richard didn't want to reveal the reason. "Maybe he'll brush us off if he knows ahead of time," he warned the club members. "Let's just say we want to discuss an important civic cause."

In due time their carefully worded letter brought a reply. "The Mayor will meet the Civics Club of the sixth grade of St. John's School on Saturday morning, April 14, at eleven o'clock in his office in the City Hall," it read.

Mary looked at the room calendar. It listed the feast days of all the saints. "April 14 is St. Justin's Day," she announced glumly. "We'll be marching yet over the railroad viaduct to St. Justin's School."

II. *"The Important Civic Cause"*

On an April morning, as the sun shone on Pine Street, the members of the Civics Club met at the bus stop. "What gives?" asked the bus driver as he came out of Charlie's lunchroom. "You're all dressed up as if you were going to call on the Mayor."

"We are," said Mary Cassidy.

"No kidding," said the bus driver, who knew every child on Pine Street.

"No kidding," repeated Eddie Carson.

"First time I ever saw you with a hat on," the driver told Mary.

"I wear it to church," she said.

"Sunday's my day off." He started the bus toward town.

Halfway toward the city, just as they could see the golden dome of City Hall rising above drab shops and factories, the bus driver stopped at a traffic signal. He looked around at the children. "What's taking you to see the Mayor?" he asked.

"We're trying to save the school," they shouted back at him.

The passengers grew interested. An old man sitting beside Richard listened to the story. "You youngsters are like the noble burghers of Calais," he said.

"*Kah LEH?*" Richard repeated. He had never heard of the incident in French history when six noble citizens of a French town named Calais offered themselves as a sacrifice to an invading army to save their people.

At Main Street the children left the bus. "Good luck," the bus driver called out.

The old man leaned out of an open window. "The noble burghers did a nice job, too," he said.

Up Main Street, past the County Building and the Law Courts, walked the boys and girls from St. John's. Confused, a little frightened by the morning rush of traffic on the busy street, they came to the doors of City Hall. Silently, holding together in a compact body, they moved toward the elevators. Richard's courage was ebbing as he asked the elevator operator, "Where's the Mayor's office?"

She gestured them all back into her car. "Second floor. Turn right. End of hall," she said briskly.

As they walked down the long corridor of the second floor, past doors that bore signs with names and titles of city officials, Eddie Carson slid into step beside Richard. "Remember that you promised to do the talking," he said.

A gray-haired woman sat at a desk in the Mayor's outer office. She spoke with crisp, businesslike brevity. "You'll have to talk quickly to the Mayor. He's a very busy man and he has another appointment in ten minutes."

"It won't take us long," said Monica.

A clock on a desk struck eleven and they were ushered forward. The Mayor, as they came into his room, took off his horn-rimmed glasses and held them in his hand. "What can I do for you?" he asked. His voice was kind, and his eyes were smiling.

There was a moment's pause. Then Richard gulped. There seemed to be a lump in his throat the size of an egg. "It's about St. John's School on Pine Street," he began, and then told the Mayor the story.

The Mayor reached into his desk and drew out a blueprint of the new expressway. "Let's see what is going to happen," he said. He put on his horn-rimmed glasses and peered at the chart. "You're right," he admitted.

"The school will be torn down," said Richard Dunn.

"So will the stores," said Eddie Carson.

"So will some old houses," chorused Mary Cassidy and Monica Earl.

"Everything will go," came a murmur of voices from the rest of the club members.

The Mayor put down the blueprint. Again he took off his glasses. "When I was a boy," he told them, "I lived in an old neighborhood in this city. I went to a school near my house. Today there is no trace of the house in which I lived nor of the school I attended. They're gone. In their place is a big factory, but men and women are working in that factory and they're earning decent wages to support their families and pay

370

for their children's education. I miss the old neighborhood, just as you will miss Pine Street, but time marches on and we must think of the greatest good for the greatest number of people."

"That's what Sister Mary Angela said," said Mary.

"But a highway—" Richard protested.

The Mayor looked serious. "I know that a highway isn't a factory," he admitted, "but have you stopped to think of the people who live across the river?"

Richard used his earlier argument. "The people on the other side of the river don't vote here," he said.

The Mayor shook his head. "You're a born politician, my boy," he said, and laughed a little, "but even though the city's politics may end at the edge of the river, there is something else that must go beyond."

"What, sir?" asked the children.

"Its name is Justice," said the Mayor. "Stop and think of the people across the river who must be at work in the city early in the morning. Don't they want to get home quickly in the evening to their children? Shouldn't we do something for them?"

"People on Pine Street have shops they have worked to build," said Richard. "What are they going to do without any customers?"

The Mayor gave Richard a puzzled stare. "They'll still have their customers," he said. "All they'll have to do is move to the other side of the expressway."

Eddie Carson found his voice. "What'll there be, sir, on the other side of the expressway? The school will be gone and pretty soon all the people of the parish will move to some other place."

"Why should they?" asked the Mayor.

"Why shouldn't they?" cried Mary. "It's two miles to the nearest Catholic school."

"Won't you have a new school?" asked the Mayor.

"Sister says we haven't money enough to build a new school. So many pupils have moved away already that we can't afford to build," Richard told him.

"But you'll have dozens of new pupils before long," said the Mayor.

"Where'll they come from?" cried the children.

"From the great big apartment project that is to be built just south of Pine Street," he said. "Didn't you know about it?"

"We never heard of it," said the children.

"In the new development," the Mayor went on, "there'll be space for modern stores that will be rented at a reasonable price. Your friends on Pine Street can move there. There'll be hundreds of apartments. There'll be a movie house and a filling station and—"

"Pardon me, sir," Richard interrupted. "Does Father O'Brien know these plans?"

"I wrote to him," said the Mayor, but he was frowning as he rang the buzzer on his desk. The gray-haired lady from the outer office came in. "When did my letter to Father Lawrence O'Brien go out to him?" he asked her.

"In last evening's mail, sir," she said. "He should receive it this morning."

"Father O'Brien will know about these plans this morning," said the Mayor. "It won't be long, I think, until you'll have a new school at St. John's."

"That'll be wonderful," said the children.

"And you'll have so many new parishioners that you'll be standing in the aisles on Sunday," he added.

"Your next appointment is waiting," said the gray-haired lady.

Again the club members thanked the Mayor. They bowed politely to the gray-haired lady and walked quickly out of the office. Then, racing against time, they sped down the long corridor. They did not wait for an elevator, but rushed down a flight of wide marble steps. Down Main Street they dashed, and whistled impatiently as they waited for a bus. When

373

it came, it was driven by the same driver. "What's the news?" he asked.

They told him. The church would be crowded on Sundays and holy days. There would be money enough to buy coal and perhaps enough money to build a new school some day. In the meantime, they might have to go to school in the parish hall, but Father O'Brien and the Sisters would find a way. As the bus stopped at the corner of Pine and Waller, they ran toward the rectory.

Father O'Brien was coming out of the doorway. His shoulders drooped a little in his worn black cassock. "Did you see the Mayor?" he asked.

"We did! We did!" Their voices rang with gladness. "Have you read your mail, Father?"

Father O'Brien looked surprised, but he hurried to the mailbox. To the children's relief they saw he drew out a long white envelope. Father opened the official document. He read it quickly and then, as if he could not believe its contents, he read it again. "A new apartment south of Pine Street," he quoted the Mayor. "A vast development that will spread across four city blocks."

"He means they'll build on the old baseball park, doesn't he, Father?" asked Eddie.

"That's the place," said Father O'Brien. He straightened his shoulders, and his smile was as bright as the sunlight of the April noon. To the children who watched him, he seemed surprisingly and suddenly young.

"You're glad, aren't you, Father?" asked Richard Dunn.

"I never was happier," he said, and added, "There are many things that make God's world a pleasant place in which to live, and one of the greatest of these is Justice."

Across the north side of Pine Street, soon to be leveled by bulldozers and tractors, the children plunged to tell the good news to Sister Mary Angela. Progress was no longer their silent deadly enemy. Across a city, across a parish, over a river toward a place where other people were living and working and dreaming high hopes for other children, Progress was marching hand-in-hand with Justice.

Write in your own words evidence from the story to prove the following statements.

1. The mayor was a just man.
2. The children were loyal.
3. Sister Mary Angela was an understanding person.
4. The bus driver was a kind person.
5. Sister Mary Angela advised the children wisely.
6. The bus passengers liked children.
7. The children loved and appreciated Father O'Brien.
8. The man on the bus was sympathetic.

UNDERSTANDING THE AUTHOR'S MEANING

Can you explain the expressions listed below? Number your paper from 1 to 14 and tell in your own words what each expression means.

in due time	businesslike brevity
prophet of doom	racing against time
"that'll swing it"	a born politician
"brush us off"	exploded the news
penned the letter	puzzled stare
gestured them back	flash of inspiration
courage was ebbing	"no kidding"

The Kingdom of God

The Kingdom of God
is not
the works of the mind of man
or the gathered treasures of art
or the churches built with hands.

The Kingdom of God
is the integrity
of a man's heart.

CARYLL HOUSELANDER

VIII

Unity

Praise of God, Israel's Deliverer

Come and see the works of God,
  His tremendous deeds among men.
He has changed the sea into dry land;
  through the river they passed on foot;
  therefore let us rejoice in Him.
He rules by His might forever;
  His eyes watch the nations;
  rebels may not exalt themselves.
Bless our God, you peoples,
  loudly sing His praise.

PSALM 65

Te Deum

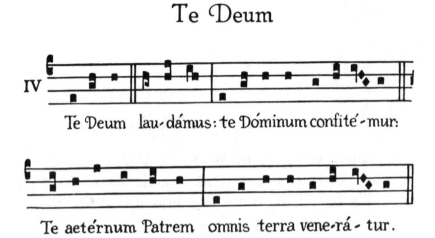

Te Deum lau-dámus: te Dóminum confité-mur.

Te aetérnum Patrem omnis terra vene-rá-tur.

We praise Thee, O God,
We acknowledge Thee to be the Lord.
All the earth doth worship Thee,
The Father everlasting.

Farewell to Spain

It was August, 1492. The ships, the *Santa Maria*, the *Niña*, and the *Pinta*, were ready for the sea. Martin Pinzon had built them. The ships had been inspected and declared fit for a sea voyage. Now, at the seaport of Palos, the three little ships were being loaded for their great adventure.

All day Ramon, the orphan boy from the convent of La Rabida, wandered about the town as crates of cargo were sped toward the docks. Barrels and kegs, sacks of flour and bolts of canvas, coils of rope and oil for the lamps, powder for cannon, and food for the crew were loaded into the holds. With them went crates of stuff for trading with natives beyond the unknown sea—crimson bells and shining beads, caps of red and scarfs of green, purple shawls and balls of colored glass.

All through the day Ramon caught some of the mood of the Palos crowd. It had filled him with fear. He heard whisperings in the crowds that filled the square. Threats were shouted along the water front. Isabella the queen might believe in Columbus. Martin Pinzon, the shipbuilder, and Friar Perez, the Prior, might believe in him, but to most of the men and women of Palos, Columbus was a madman.

Now in the August moonlight their anger against him had reached its height. The sailors who were to sail with Columbus joined the crowds, adding their shouts to the others.

Carlos was nearest to Ramon as the boy came to the *Santa Maria.* "What are they saying?" Ramon asked Carlos.

The sailor lifted his large tattooed arms. "You can hear them as well as I can," he said scornfully.

Ramon edged nearer.

Manuel, broad-chested, red-bearded, was shouting. "He says he is going to India. Everyone who has ever sailed the sea knows that you cannot reach the East by sailing west. We shall have to turn around and come back here."

Brown-skinned Marcos spoke. "He will never get enough sailors out of the taverns tonight to sail his ships on this crazy voyage."

Pedro spat into the water. "The town gates are shut now for fear we are going to desert the ship."

Cries went up from a dozen men.

"No one can stop us if we want to clear out of here!"

"The boats are too small for a voyage like this. They are tubs. They are deathtraps."

"Where are we going anyway?"

"I will tell you where you are going." A gypsy sailor with a red, knotted scarf about his head lifted his shrill voice. "I know where we are going. We are headed for a forbidden region on the sea where there are no laws of nature, where our compass will flicker, where we cannot plan the direction our ships shall take."

The protests became a roar. "We will never sail," they shouted, man after man. The gypsy went on. "There are monsters where we are going. We shall come to a ship's graveyard. When we get there, all that we shall find will be huge, gray heaps of slimy wreckage. Those are the ghosts of other ships. That is where we are going!"

"We shall be ghosts ourselves," sobbed Carlos.

"There is not enough gold in all India to pay us for our lives," muttered Marcos.

"Columbus can put me in jail," shouted Manuel, "but I will never leave home on a voyage like this. There are plenty of ships sailing for Iceland and England and France that need crews. I am picking the ship I sail on!"

"I am picking the captain!" Pedro's voice added to the roar. "If I am going to drown, it will be in some spot in the ocean that I know!"

Ramon was the first to see Columbus. Bright in the uniform of Admiral of the Ocean Sea, the Italian had come out of the cabin door of the *Santa Maria*, the door that was crowned with a statue of the Virgin Mary. Now he spoke, and his voice silenced the shouts and threats of the sailors.

"Why are you afraid?" he demanded. Before they could answer, he went on, "The ships are good ships. They are solid sailing vessels, made strong enough here in Palos to sail the deepest sea."

"They are too small," Carlos called out.

"The ships must be small, but no smaller than safety allows, to permit us to enter shallow harbors. All men of Palos know that Martin Pinzon would not send us to sea in unsafe ships."

384

"We do not trust you as a captain," Carlos shouted.

The Admiral smiled at him. "The queen trusts me," he said and drew from his pocket a sealed parchment. "I sail under her royal orders."

"What shall we get out of it?" Marcos cried.

Columbus moved nearer the rail and looked down on the mob. "To the first man who sights land I offer a purse of gold coins," he told them.

Pedro moved toward the ship; but Marcos cried again, "There is not enough gold in India to pay us for our lives!"

"Your lives?" the Admiral answered. "Why should you fear for your lives on these ships? You are men of Palos. These are ships of Palos, built in your own shipyards. You all know Martin Pinzon, the man who made them."

"We know him," said Carlos, "but we also know that he is not sailing on any of these ships."

"You are wrong," said the Admiral. "Martin Pinzon sails on the *Pinta*, and his brother sails on the *Niña*. Vincent Pinzon," he called, and the name went sounding through the darkness. "Don Diego! Martin Pinzon!"

Shadowy forms came out upon the decks. Three men moved through the moonlight to stand beside Columbus. Ramon recognized them, and so did the sailors; the Pinzons and Don Diego were the three men trusted by all of Palos, by every man who went out of Spain in ships.

385

"Will you tell these men," Columbus asked them, "if you believe our ships to be safe?"

"The ships are safe," said Don Diego.

"I made them," said Martin Pinzon. "I have asked the Admiral to take my brother and myself. What more proof do you need?"

"We sail with Columbus," said Vincent Pinzon. "Are we braver than all of you?"

"No!" cried Pedro. "No!" cried Marcos and Manuel and the gypsy. "No!" cried a dozen others, moving toward the *Santa Maria*. "I will go, I will go, I will go," they shouted.

One after another the sailors went aboard the ship. Only Carlos slid away from them, twisting and crouching beside the piles of the wharf. He came so close to Ramon that the boy could have touched him. Then the sailor was lost in the shadows.

On the deck the Admiral was calling the roll. Down the list he went while man after man, hearing his name, called, "Here!" When he read the name of Carlos, there was no answer. He read it again at the end of the roll. No one spoke. "We sail then," Columbus said, "with eighty-six men. We need eighty-seven. Is there anyone here to take his place?"

No answer came.

The Admiral turned to Marcos and gave him an order. Slowly a lantern moved up the mast of the *Santa Maria*. It must be, Ramon thought, a signal, for, in a little while, there came down the road the

386

sound of bells, the bells of the chapel of Santa Maria de la Rabida. As the sound of the bells drifted over Palos, people began to come out of the darkened houses. Men and women hurried to the wharf until a vast crowd stood behind the long pier.

Then, through the darkness rose a sound, strange for this hour of the night, the sound of wheels of carts and hoofs of horses. In the moonlight, over the road that was white now where it had been dusty and yellow in the sunlight, came a little procession. Only when it had come close to the wharf did Ramon know what it .was, a gathering of all the friars of La Rabida, come to say farewell to the man whom they trusted.

They leaped from the carts and plodded across the stones of the water front. There they formed into procession, led by the cross-bearer. Friar Perez, Prior

of the Convent, was wearing, over his dark robe, vestments of white and gold. Before him walked all the other friars of La Rabida.

Slowly, solemnly, as if they were going into their own chapel, they marched to the *Santa Maria*. "The Prior will say Mass here at midnight," someone said, and the word spread through the crowd. Quietly Ramon joined the procession.

Under the statue of the Virgin the procession moved into the cabin. There the Prior stepped to the little altar which had been built against the far wall. Two friars followed the Prior to serve him, but the Admiral held out his hands as if to plead for that privilege. Friar Perez nodded, and the Admiral took a place at the altar steps.

"Mass," thought Ramon, "is always the same." For years he had known the responses well. He had often served in the long ceremonies at the convent. Hundreds and hundreds of times he had listened to the Prior's voice as he had said *Credo* and *Lavabo*, *Sanctus* and *Pater Noster*. Here, in this midnight hour, upon a ship that would sail with the dawn out upon unknown seas toward unknown lands, the Prior's voice sounded strangely deep, and the Mass seemed strangely solemn.

The Admiral and Don Diego, the Pinzons, and a few of the sailors went to Communion. Ramon suddenly wished that he had gone to Confession during the afternoon instead of idling around the docks. Then he might have received Communion with these men. "I will go to Confession at the convent tomorrow afternoon," he promised himself, "and offer up my Communion for their safety."

Everyone in the little cabin knelt for the Prior's blessing. One by one, the sailors moved out to their tasks. The friars left the ship. The Prior was the last to go. Ramon was standing at the rail when the Admiral spoke to the priest.

"We shall need all the prayers you can say for us, Father," he told him. "We set sail on a perilous journey—and we are short a man already."

"Who has failed you?" the Prior asked.

"I do not know his name," the Admiral said.

"It is Carlos," said Ramon. "He ran away."

The Prior put his hand upon Ramon's head. "You would not run away if you had promised to go, would you?" he asked the boy.

"No, Father," said Ramon.

Then, suddenly, as if he saw a bright light shining where there had been no light, Ramon saw that he might go.

The friars had helped Columbus from the day he had come to La Rabida. They had fed and sheltered the friendless explorer and his son Diego, as they had fed and sheltered the orphan Ramon, who had been left at their gate so many years before. The friars had done all they could for those who needed help. Now it was time for Ramon to do something in gratitude.

The friars wanted Columbus to set out on this voyage. They wanted him to have all the men he needed, and he still lacked one man.

"Friar Perez," Ramon said, and, as the Prior looked down at him, he rushed into speech. "May I go with the Admiral if he will have me?"

"You, Ramon?" the Prior spoke in surprise. "You are very young."

"I am sixteen, Father. I am strong. I am skillful. I shall learn quickly. I know much of ships."

"Do you wish to leave Spain? To leave La Rabida and the friars there? Do you love us no longer?"

"I love Spain. I love Palos. Most of all, I love La Rabida. I had never, never thought of leaving you until now. But, O Father Prior, do you not understand that I wish to go because I do love you, because it is your wish that the Admiral have everything he needs?"

The Prior looked down at the boy. His kind eyes grew sad as he spoke to Columbus. "You have heard Ramon," he said. "He wants only to serve you because he thinks you need him. Here is faith. Here is courage. Do you want him?"

"I will take him," Columbus said, "if you wish him to go with me."

"We shall miss him," the Prior said. "Ramon has been the child of La Rabida. But, since he himself has asked to go, I think we shall all be glad that this boy, who has been so long with us, will be part of this great adventure. For God and Spain!"

"For God and Spain," the Admiral repeated.

Ramon knelt then for the Prior's blessing.

Just before dawn the bells of La Rabida rang again. The *Santa Maria* was setting sail, the *Pinta* and *Niña* following her. Out from the harbor of Palos, out into the gray Atlantic three little ships were going. They would never find the Orient lands they were seeking, lands of gold and ivory, of rubies and spices, but they would find a new land and, in finding it, change the world.

Ramon had no thought of this as he looked backward toward the coast of Spain, dim in the dawning light. He was saying good-by to all he knew, to all he loved, as he gazed afar off to the towers of La Rabida; but deep in his heart he knew that he had done right in giving to Christopher Columbus the one gift he had to give—himself. For La Rabida, for the friars who had given him all he had, he could have done no less.

As the sun rose, the coastline of Spain stood out sharply. In the distance the white walls of La Rabida gleamed. For a moment, as if he would stamp their memory upon his heart, the boy gazed at them. Then he turned toward the west. Before him spread the wide, gray Atlantic. He did not know—no one could know—how long or how far he would sail upon its lonely waters. Ramon only knew that he, like the friars of La Rabida and the queen of Spain, trusted Christopher Columbus, Admiral of the Ocean Sea.

RECOGNIZING WORD MEANINGS

Skim the story to locate the underlined words in the sentences below. Read the two sentences and on your paper write the number and letter of the sentence that uses the word with the same meaning as that in the story.

1, *a*. The teacher called the roll.
   b. Roll the ball to the baby.
2, *a*. John fastened the bolt on the door.
   b. The woman bought a bolt of silk.
3, *a*. The new rug was six inches short.
   b. Paul's father is a short man.
4, *a*. The tank will hold twenty gallons.
   b. They loaded the cargo in the hold.
5, *a*. The band played in the town square.
   b. The area of the table was four square feet.
6, *a*. The piles supporting the pier were strong.
   b. There were piles of cargo at the wharf.
7, *a*. The three ships were of uniform size.
   b. The band leader's uniform was beautiful.

A Ship Sails Out from Lisbon

1541

With the bells of Lisbon ringing,
And the choirs of Lisbon singing,
And the gulls of Lisbon winging
High above the river bar,
A ship sails out from Lisbon
To the Eastern lands afar.

With the king's high envoy staying
Under awnings, laughing, playing,
No one hears the sailors praying
With a black-robed Spanish priest.
The ship moves slowly southward
On her long way to the East.

With Atlantic trade winds leaping,
And a shipboard fever creeping
O'er a black-robed Spaniard sleeping
Only on a coil of rope,
The ship from Lisbon circles
Round the long Cape of Good Hope.

With the black-robed Spaniard bending
Over dying men, and tending
Little children with unending
Patience, love, and charity,
The ship sails on to Goa
Through the sultry Indian sea.

With the king's high envoy yearning
For his homeland, and returning
From the hard and cruel and burning
Lands of sullen nights and days,
The ship sails back to Lisbon;
But the black-robed Spaniard stays.

With the winds of China sighing,
And the gulls of China crying
Low above a martyr dying
On the lonely Asian strand,
A boy of China holds the cross.
In Francis Xavier's hand.

Tulip Time in Tenleytown

I. *Strange New World*

There were no Dutch children in Tenleytown before the Rossums came. There were children who had been born in other lands, and children of parents who had come from countries other than Holland. They all felt at home in Tenleytown when the Rossums, all seven of them, arrived.

At the drab railway station the Rossums stood out against the gloom of the town. For Tenleytown was a place of coal mines, of small factories, of rows of dull gray houses; and the Rossum children, although the mountain weather was cool, wore bright summer clothes. They all were yellow-haired, Minna and Lisa, the twins Peter and Jan, and little Hilda. They all stared happily with wide blue eyes as they trudged in single file behind their father and mother through the streets.

Someone showed them the way to the Convent of Our Lady of Peace. The Convent stood in the middle of town, a little way from the Catholic church and the school. The house had once been the home of a rich mine owner and, thanks to the care the Sisters gave it, held something of its one-time elegance, although the yard, which took up almost half of a city block, looked more than a little neglected. Within it, well to the back, was a cottage.

Two Sisters, one tall and thin, the other short and

stout, were standing at the gate of the yard as the Rossums came to it. "This is Mother Mary Margaret," the short Sister explained in Dutch, "and I am Sister Julianna. We welcome you. I also came from the Netherlands, but that was a long time ago." She smiled broadly at them, and the Rossums smiled back at her.

Mother Mary Margaret spoke in English. "We hope you will like your new home," she said. "We shall take you to it now, then later you will come to the convent for your dinner."

Sister Julianna translated what the other Sister had said. "We shall take you to the cottage," she added. "That will be your home."

The cottage looked tiny as they went into it, and Minna, the eldest of the children, wondered how they would all squeeze into it. But her mother cried out happily, and her father thanked the Sisters. "To-morrow," he told Sister Julianna, "I shall start work on the garden. It needs attention."

The Sisters were hardly out of the cottage when the elder Rossums began to explore the place and to make plans. "We must scrub," Mrs. Rossum said. "We must scour and scrub everything. The Sisters know. See, they have sent pails, and brushes, and soap. Minna and Lisa, take off your good dresses and put on your work clothes."

"The boys will help me in the yard tomorrow," said Mr. Rossum. "This afternoon we will go back to the railway station and see if our goods have come.

The train conductor said they would come on a later train."

"What shall I do?" asked little Hilda.

"We shall find something for you," said her mother.

The house was clean, but not as clean as Mrs. Rossum wished it to be. She aired the beds while Minna and Hilda scrubbed the floors, and Lisa dusted the furniture which needed no dusting since the Sisters had gone over it after the departure of the last tenant.

"We will make it look like our home in Holland," Mrs. Rossum told the children.

"Will the ocean come in here?" Hilda asked, remembering how the floods had destroyed their home and sent them out to this strange New World.

"We are a long way from the ocean," said her mother, "and God will take care of us here as He took care of us there."

The girls were tired when their father and the twins came back from the railway station. The driver of the truck helped them to unload trunks and packages, most of them burlap bags.

"What is in them?" Hilda asked her mother.

"Why, don't you know? They are the tulip bulbs."

"Can we have tulips—here?"

"Of course," Minna and Lisa chimed together. "Father can make tulips grow anywhere."

"Is this the right time to plant them?" Mrs. Rossum asked her husband.

"We will take a chance," he said.

Early the next morning he and the boys started to clear the yard. They worked all day while the girls found plenty to do in the house. Sister Julianna, coming in the late afternoon, praised all they had done.

"Are those tulip bulbs?" she asked Mr. Rossum eagerly when she saw the bags.

"Emperor Red tulips," he told her proudly.

"Oh, wonderful!" she cried. Then anxiously she added, "But will they grow here?"

"Why not?" asked the new gardener.

She watched as they started the planting. "Emperor Reds," she said in Dutch. "They will be beautiful here—if they grow."

"We will make them grow," said Mr. Rossum.

On Sunday the Rossums went to Mass, all together. Sister Julianna had told them to go to the Sisters' pew, the first in the middle aisle. In their best clothes and with new shoes squeaking, they went up the aisle in single file, all seven of them. Only Father O'Conner paid no attention to them. Everyone else in the church, from the Dixons who knelt in the pew across the aisle, to the choir in the back loft, looked at them with interest and curiosity. For the first time the Rossums felt that they were really strangers in Tenleytown.

The feeling stayed with the older children when they went to school on Monday morning. The grownups they met were kind, and the Sisters welcomed them, but they felt shy and uncomfortable with the other children.

Only Hilda, with her sunny smile and flaxen braids, made friends wherever she went. "Genevieve likes me," she told her mother one day. "Martha likes me," she said on another day, "and Veronica likes me, too."

"Everyone likes you," said her mother.

"I like everyone," said Hilda.

Winter was long and hard that year in Tenleytown. The Rossum children trudged through high snows on their way to and from school. They had little chance to play outdoors and so they remained apart from the town. The Sisters were more than kind to them. The children of the school were not unfriendly, but they did not do much to make the strangers feel at home in the town. There were times when the twins and the older girls longed to be back in Holland.

Because Lisa was a better student than Minna they were together in the sixth grade. Lisa liked social studies and recited easily the answers to questions in geography and history. It was Minna, however, who was the first to realize that some of the other pupils resented Lisa's manner of recitation. "You should not speak as if you knew more than others know," she warned her younger sister.

"But sometimes I do know more," Lisa said.

She showed it one day when Sister Mary Frances asked her to write on the board the names of six great European seaports, each one in a different country. Swiftly Lisa wrote Southampton, Antwerp, Rotterdam, Lisbon, Marseille, and Naples. Immediately Ellen, a classmate, cried out, "Lisa has a mistake, Sister. Antwerp and Rotterdam are in the same country."

"Oh, no," said Lisa quickly. "Antwerp is in Belgium, and Rotterdam is in the Netherlands. I know. I lived near Rotterdam."

"We all know you're not an American," Ellen said.

"I am an American now. I live here now in Tenleytown in the United States of America," answered Lisa quickly.

"Just the same—" Ellen began, but Sister Mary Frances hastily led the class into a discussion of sea routes.

"How could she say that I'm not an American?" Lisa asked Minna indignantly on their way home from school.

"She's right," said Minna. "We are not yet Americans."

"But I feel American now," Lisa protested.

"Everything takes time," said Minna wisely.

II. Banners of Neighborliness

Time dragged with leaden feet as winter moved toward springtime. The heaviest snow came in March, but as it melted green patches began to show on the hills beyond the town. Mr. Rossum, cutting down the odd jobs he had been doing in the neighborhood, began to spend every possible minute working in the big yard. Hilda trailed his footsteps, and one Saturday morning announced that the leaves of the tulip plants were coming above the ground.

"Soon we shall see the flowers," she told Sister Julianna.

"The Emperor Reds," said Sister Julianna.

One by one the green spikes pushed upward. Then,

suddenly, as if lured by the warmer winds of May, a mass of red blossoms appeared. "Look, look!" cried Hilda and brought Martha and Veronica and Genevieve to gaze at the crimson glory. Martha brought back her father and mother, and Genevieve and Veronica brought their sisters.

"Those tulips are beautiful," everyone said.

Sister Julianna brought all the Sisters to admire them. Children stood outside the fence, looking at the Emperor Reds, and men and women came through the gate to admire the beauty of the flowers.

"Emperor Reds," Mr. Rossum said proudly. "All the way from Holland. We brought them."

"Do you suppose I could get some for my place?" a neighbor asked the gardener.

"I will write to a friend in the old country and ask

him to send us more bulbs for planting this fall," said Mr. Rossum. "These bulbs are safe to come through the customs inspection."

Slowly at first, then more rapidly, requests for tulip bulbs poured in on the Rossums. "We shall have a large order to send to Holland," Mr. Rossum said to Sister Julianna.

Blossoming time was soon over, but he planned and worked for the next year. Lisa and Minna were in seventh grade and studying American history when the second planting of Emperor Reds blossomed, not only in the Sisters' yard, but in scores of other places in the town.

"See, we are spreading," said Minna.

They were indeed spreading, not only in the red flowers which proclaimed their influence, but in the friendliness which they were meeting. Even Ellen sometimes smiled at Lisa, perhaps because Lisa had changed her manner of recitation.

In the autumn a man came from City Hall. "The councilmen think that it would be a good plan to have flowers planted around the old building," he told Mr. Rossum. "How do I get the red ones? And how do I plant them?"

"I will help you," said Mr. Rossum.

Afterward, he told his wife and the children that he liked working with the man from City Hall. "I felt more American," he said, "because I was doing something for this new country of ours."

403

"We are Americans now, aren't we?" Lisa asked.

"Not yet, under the law," said her father, "but in a little while we shall be. We are Americans now, however, in our feeling, in our intention, and we should do something to show we are grateful."

"I think we are doing something," his wife said, "by being good, and kind, and busy, and friendly."

She showed her own friendliness to everyone she met, children who came to the cottage with her own children, and their elders who came asking about flower bulbs. "Everyone owes his neighbor a smile," she told Hilda and the twins and Lisa and Minna. "A cheerful good morning brightens the whole day, and it costs you nothing to give it." And the smiles of the Rossum children became as familiar in Tenleytown as their yellow heads.

In time the cottage got a new coat of paint and gleamed in the sun. With the help of the man from City Hall, Mr. Rossum painted the Sisters' convent. It was the big yard, however, which became the show-place of Tenleytown. Each spring it burst into bloom with the Emperor Reds. Even though other flowers blossomed later—lilacs and lilies and roses, daisies and bachelor buttons and geraniums—nothing aroused the admiration of the townspeople as did the tulips. "They are like flags," they said.

Each year the number of tulip beds grew until Tenleytown became known, all along the railway line, for the red flowers that welcomed the springtime. People who hardly knew them thanked the Rossums for the change in the look of the town. Opportunities opened for the family. Lisa won a scholarship to the Sacred Heart Academy. The twins found summertime and Saturday jobs. Mr. Rossum became gardener for a half-dozen places, one of them the big factory at the edge of town. "You see," he told his wife and the children, "everything comes good when you are right."

"See," said Sister Julianna, "what a man can do with a sack of tulip bulbs."

"And faith and a little work," said Mother Mary Margaret.

"A great deal of work," said Sister Julianna.

On the day when the Rossums received their final citizenship papers, Tenleytown celebrated. After they had taken the oath of allegiance to their new country,

everyone gathered on the lawn of the City Hall for the ceremony welcoming the new citizens. It was spring, and the Red Emperor tulips were in bloom. The flower beds which Mr. Rossum had planted so carefully blazed with color. The mayor stood in front of them as he spoke to the crowd.

"We wish to thank the Rossums," he said. "They brought to our country some fine gifts, the ability to work hard, patience, friendliness, faith in themselves and in us. And they brought beauty. Anyone looking at our town today sees that beauty, the red tulips which gleam and glow on every street. They have made our town not only more beautiful, but also a much happier place in which to live. We thank the Rossums who came from Holland to Tenleytown."

Today Tenleytown is still—at times—drab and dull with its old coal mines and its almost as old factories and its tall gray houses. But, some time in every year, there flashes across it a bright beauty that lifts the spirits of all who see it. Because of that beauty Tenleytown is growing a little brighter every year, with new factories and better houses and far better gardens.

As the Rossum children grow up, they can be justly proud of their father's skill and their mother's kindness. For it has made their town, like themselves, more truly American. It has brought together many people who were apart. Tulip time in Tenleytown is more than a show. It is a banner of neighborliness.

Copy each sentence on your paper. In the list below find the word or group of words that means the same or nearly the same as the underlined word in the sentence. Write the letter of the word or word group on the line at the right.

1. The children trudged through the snow.   _ _ _
2. The Rossums arrived at the drab railway station.   _ _ _
3. Little Hilda had blue eyes and flaxen braids.   _ _ _
4. The tulip bulbs were in burlap bags.   _ _ _
5. The older girls sometimes longed to be back in Holland.   _ _ _
6. Some of the pupils resented Lisa's manner of recitation.   _ _ _
7. Hilda trailed her father's footsteps.   _ _ _
8. Sister Julianna translated the conversation into English.   _ _ _
9. The tulips blossomed in scores of places.   _ _ _
10. Children came to gaze at the flowers.   _ _ _
11. The tulips were a mass of crimson glory.   _ _ _
12. The warm winds lured the blossoms.   _ _ _

a. to look with eagerness
b. light straw color
c. deep red
d. walked wearily
e. followed closely
f. felt indignant displeasure
g. a large number
h. dull; unattractive
i. wished very much
j. a coarse hemp fabric
k. interpreted
l. invited

Mother of Men

To you, our mother, Church of Our Lord and Savior,
  Jesus Christ,
we your children in this land of freedom,
give thanks for these, your gifts to us:

The faith you brought us.

From hills of Galilee and mount of Calvary,
through old lands around the blue Mediterranean,
came the Apostles of Christ—
Saint John, the Beloved Disciple;
Saint Paul, who saw the Light upon the road to Damascus;
Saint Peter, the rock upon which Christ founded you,
  His Church—
bringing the Gospel of Christ

to the mighty city of the West,
Rome of the Seven Hills.
There men and women and children
died gladly that the Faith might live.
Then out from Rome came missionaries,
monks, priests, bishops,
crossing wide seas, high mountains, braving far frontiers,
to bring the Faith to people of the West.
With the high blessing of Rome brave women worked,
nuns of the early orders,
and countless others,
to bring faith to their people,
people who were our people.
We must be true to that faith.

The freedom you brought us.
When wild barbarians overran the West,
you tamed them, taught them, led them on to God.
You showed them that the man
who casts off your law makes of himself a slave,
and the man who follows it makes himself truly free.
When Moslems threatened all of Christendom
you led on men to fight for a holy cause,
their freedom to serve God within the way
of His own choosing.
We must keep safe that freedom.

The chivalry you taught us.
Under the lilied banners of France
and the Saint George standards of England
you taught the strong to heed the weak.
For a little time you held back the dogs of war,
keeping the peace by the Truce of God.
You bade men use their swords only for justice,
and made the struggling world a better place.
We must keep alive that chivalry.

The learning you brought us.
Great mother of the world, you, Church of Christ,
knew that man always tries to lift his life
to something better, higher than the earth
on which he lives. You saw the shining wings
of skill which raise man up toward God.
You helped man spread them.

The greatest of all artists
worked the better for your guidance.
Long have you treasured the beauty of their art
and passed to us their work and their tradition.
We must serve God by any art we have.

The science you taught us.
From the earliest years of your history
you have striven to widen the horizons of your children.
Through the great experiments of Leonardo,
the patient trials of Louis Pasteur,
you showed the way to broader living,
and proved the laws of nature
were the laws of God.
We must keep on with seeking.

The patriotism you lighted in us.
You set the love of country in the hearts of men.
Joyfully the banished Jews, exiled in Egypt,
followed Moses to their own, the Promised Land.
Sadly men wept by the waters of Babylon,
grieving they would not see their homes again.
On English shores and holy hills of Ireland
you tamed the wild invaders of the North,
and made the nations.
Here, in the West, you lighted fires of homes
even as you lighted fires of faith.
We must keep the fires of patriotism burning.

The charity you brought us.
Always you, our mother, have remembered
the lesson of the Good Samaritan.
Through long years you have helped
the weak, the sick, the blind, the old, the lepers,
everyone who needed help.
Your great saints of charity
are but the leaders of your mighty army
of those who gave their all to help their brothers.
We must practice that charity.

The justice you brought us.
Teaching the Gospel of Our Risen Lord,
you have told all men:
"Love ye one another."
We are all equal, you have told us,
because we all are brothers and sisters
of Jesus Christ.
Because we all are equal we have this duty,
to treat all others as we should wish to be treated.
You have told us, too, our duty to our whole community
in social justice.
These duties, you have said, will be far easier
if we will truly love all other men,
even the men we do not know,
because we all are children of one God.
If we do this, the world will be the Kingdom
of God upon this earth.
We must live in that justice.

The unity you brought us.

Twelve men went out into a warring world
where armies clashed by night on bloody plains.
They bore no swords. They spoke in quiet words.
They taught the Word of Christ, and only asked
that men love one another.
But in a little while the Word they taught
blossomed in the hearts of men.
Across the world there ran the hope of peace,
the knowledge that all men are sons of God,
and the world moved into a brighter day.
We must forever keep that hope of peace alive.

For these great blessings of the grace of God,
we give to you, our mother,
Church of Our Lord and Savior, Jesus Christ,
our praise and honor in this land of freedom.

Glossary

A glossary is part of a dictionary. This glossary will help you to pronounce and to understand the meanings of the new or unusual words used in *This Is Our Heritage.*

The pronunciation of each word is shown by division into syllables, by an accent mark (if it has more than one syllable), and by respelling.

The following list shows you how each marked letter is pronounced by giving as an example the same sound in a word that you know. This is called a *pronunciation key.*

ā *as in* lāte   ī *as in* rīde   ū *as in* ūse
å *as in* al'wåys   ĭ *as in* ĭn   û *as in* û·nite'
ă *as in* ăm   ĭ *as in* pos'sĭ·ble   ŭ *as in* ŭs
ă *as in* ăp·pear'   ŭ *as in* cir'cŭs
ä *as in* ärm   ō *as in* ōld   û *as in* bûrn
à *as in* àsk   ŏ *as in* ŏ·bey'
â *as in* câre   ŏ *as in* nŏt   ōō *as in* mōōn
    ŏ *as in* cŏn·nect'   ŏŏ *as in* tŏŏk
ē *as in* hē   ô *as in* sôft   oi *as in* oil
ĕ *as in* ĕ·nough'   ô *as in* hôrse   ou *as in* out
ĕ *as in* nĕt
ĕ *as in* si'lĕnt   th *as in* that
ẽ *as in* mak'ẽr   th *as in* thin
ę *as in* hęre   tū *as in* natūre
    dū *as in* verdūre

ab'bot (ăb'ŭt). The head, or superior, of a community of monks.

ac'co·lade' (ăk'ŏ·lād'). An award.

ac·com'plish·ment (ă·kŏm'plĭsh-mĕnt). Completion in a satisfactory way.

Ag'a·tha (ăg'à·thà).

Ag'nus De'i (ä'nyŭs dā'ē). The Latin words for *Lamb of God.*

a·hoy' (à·hoi'). A word used as a greeting or to attract attention.

a·lert' (à·lûrt'). Watchful.

Al·ge'ri·a (ăl·jēr'ĭ·à). A French territory in northern Africa.

al·le'giance (ă·lē'jăns). 1. Loyalty and service owed to one's country and government. 2. Loyalty and service given to a person or thing.

al'ti·tude (ăl'tĭ·tūd). Height.

am'a·teur' (ăm'à·tûr'). One who is interested in an activity, but who does not engage in it professionally or for money.

a·mid' (à·mĭd'). Among.

---

lāte, alwåys, ăm, ăppear, ärm, àsk, câre, hē, ĕnough, ·nĕt, silĕnt, makẽr, hęre, rīde, ĭn, possĭble, ōld, ŏbey, nŏt, cŏnnect, sôft, hôrse, ūse, ūnite, ŭs, circŭs, bûrn, mōōn, tŏŏk, oil, out, that, thin, natūre, verdūre

A'mos (ā'mŏs). A Hebrew prophet.

am·phib'i·an (ăm·fĭb'ĭ·ăn). Any animal, such as a frog, which can live in water or on land.

an'ces'tor (ăn'sĕs'tĕr). A grandparent or other person far back in one's family line.

An'ge·lo (ăn'jĕ·lō).

a·noint' (à·noint'). To touch a person with oil as part of a ceremony.

an'them (ăn'thĕm). A song of praise, such as a patriotic or religious hymn.

an'thrax (ăn'thrăks). A disease which usually kills cattle or sheep.

An'ti·och (ăn'tĭ·ŏk). An ancient city in Asia Minor, visited by Saint Paul.

an'ti·tox'in (ăn'tĭ·tŏk'sĭn). A substance that is formed in the blood of a person who is ill with a germ disease and that helps in overcoming the disease.

Ant'werp (ănt'wûrp). A city in northern Belgium.

anx·i'e·ty (ăng·zī'ĕ·tĭ). Fear that something unpleasant or unfortunate may happen.

ap'pa·ra'tus (ăp'à·rā'tŭs). Necessary equipment used to do a particular kind of work or experiment.

Ap'pi·an (ăp'ĭ·ăn) **Way.** The oldest and most famous of the Roman roads.

ap·pren'tice (à·prĕn'tĭs). A person who is learning a trade or craft under a skilled worker.

A·qui'nas (à·kwī'năs), **Saint Thomas.**

A learned Dominican, patron of Catholic schools.

Aq·ui·taine' (ăk·wĭ·tān'). In olden times, a kingdom in what is now France.

ar'chi·tect (är'kĭ·tĕkt). A person who plans buildings and oversees their construction.

a·re'na (à·rē'nà). A place where public contests are held.

A'sia Mi'nor (ā'zhà mī'nẽr). A large peninsula in western Asia.

As·si'si (à·sē'zĕ). A town in Italy, famous as the place of birth and death of Saint Francis of Assisi.

at·tach' (ă·tăch'). To appoint a person to a particular position.

at·ten'tive (ă·tĕn'tĭv). Paying attention.

auf' Wie'der·seh'en (ouf' vē'dẽr·zā'ĕn). A form of farewell, meaning "Till we meet again."

Aus'tri·a (ôs'trĭ·à). A former kingdom in central Europe.

Bab'y·lon (băb'ĭ·lŏn). An ancient city where the Jewish people were held in captivity.

bade (băd). Ordered; commanded.

bag'pipe' (băg'pīp'). A shrill-toned musical instrument, used especially in Ireland and Scotland.

ban'ish (băn'ĭsh). To drive out from one's home.

bar·bar'i·an (bär·bâr'ĭ·ăn). A person who is not civilized.

Bar'ba·ry (bär'bà·rĭ) **Coast.** The countries on the north coast of Africa from Egypt to the Atlantic.

bard (bärd). In olden times, a man who composed and sang verses in honor of heroes; a poet.

Bar′na·bas (bär′nȧ·bǎs). A companion of Pauls on his first missionary journey.

bar′on (bǎr′ŭn). A member of the nobility; a lord.

bar′racks (bǎr′ǎks). A building or group of buildings in which soldiers live.

base (bās). The place on which a branch of the armed forces relies for its supplies.

Ba·var′i·a (bȧ·vâr′ĭ·ȧ). A large state in southern Germany.

Ba·yeux′ (bȧ·yōō′). A village in northern France.

Beck′et, à (ȧ bĕk′ĕt), **Saint Thomas.** A famous archbishop of Canterbury.

be·friend′ (bē·frĕnd′). To act as a friend to.

Bel′gi·um (bĕl′jĭ·ŭm). A kingdom of western Europe.

ben′e·fac′tor (bĕn′ē·fǎk′tẽr). One who gives a great gift.

Ber·lin′ (bûr·lĭn′). A large city in Germany.

Ber′na′dette′ of Lourdes (bĕr′nȧ′-dĕt′ ŏv lōōrd). A French peasant girl who was visited by Our Lady of Lourdes.

be·wil′der (bē·wĭl′dẽr). To confuse; to puzzle.

Bing′en (bĭng′ĕn). A town in Germany on the Rhine River.

block book. A book printed from wooden blocks.

Blon·del′ (blŏn·dĕl′). The friend and troubadour of Richard of the Lion Heart.

blue′print′ (blōō′prĭnt′). A photographic print, white on a bright-blue background, usually showing building plans.

bond (bŏnd). A binding promise.

Bon′i·face (bŏn′ĭ·fās), **City of Saint.** A name for Mainz in Germany, so called because of the work of Saint Boniface there.

bore (bōr). 1. Carried. 2. Gave; showed.

brev′i·ty (brĕv′ĭ·tĭ). Shortness.

Bri′an (brī′ǎn).

Brig′id (brĭj′ĭd), **Saint.** The patroness of Ireland.

Brit′ain (brĭt′n). A name for England.

Bri·tan′ni·a (brĭ·tǎn′ĭ·ȧ) **Rules the Waves.** A patriotic song of Great Britain.

brooch (brōch). An ornamental pin or clasp.

Bru′no (brōō′nō).

buck′ler (bŭk′lẽr). A small shield worn on the arm.

bull′doz′er (bōōl′dōz′ẽr). A tractor-driven machine for clearing land, road building, etc.

---

lāte, alwǎys, ǎm, ǎppear, ärm, ȧsk, câre, hē, ēnough, nĕt, silĕnt, makẽr, hẽre, rīde, ĭn, possĭble, ōld, ȯbey, nŏt, cŏnnect, sŏft, hôrse, ūse, ūnite, ŭs, circŭs, bûrn, mōon, tŏŏk, oil, out, that, thin, natų̄re, verdų̄re

417

Bu′reau of Im′mi·gra′tion (bū′rō ŏv ĭm′ĭ·grā′shŭn). A business office set up to help immigrants, or newcomers, to this country.

burgh′er (bûr′gẽr). A citizen.

Cal′ais (kăl′ā). A city in northern France.

Can′ter·bur·y (kăn′tẽr·bĕr·ĭ). A city in England. It has a famous cathedral.

can′vas (kăn′vàs). 1. A strong cloth used for making tents, sails, etc. 2. Something made of canvas, as, the sails of a ship.

cap·tiv′i·ty (kăp·tĭv′ĭ·tĭ). State of being a captive, or prisoner.

Cap′u·chin (kăp′ů·chĭn). 1. A branch of the Order founded by Saint Francis. 2. A religious of that Order.

car′bon di·ox′ide (kär′bŏn dī·ŏk′-sīd). One of the gases found in the air.

Car′lo (kär′lō). The Italian name for *Charles*.

Car′los (kär′lōs). The Spanish name for *Charles*.

Car′o·lus (kăr′ō·lŭs). The Latin name for *Charles*.

Cas·tile′ (kăs·tēl′). A former kingdom of Spain.

cav′al·cade′ (kăv′ăl·kād′). A procession of persons on horseback.

cav′al·ry (kăv′ăl·rĭ). Soldiers who are mounted on horseback.

cease (sēs). To stop; to come to an end.

ce·les′tial (sē·lĕs′chăl). Heavenly.

chal′lenge (chăl′ĕnj). A summons to fight.

cham′pi·on (chăm′pĭ·ŭn). A person who fights to defend another person or a cause; a defender.

chan′cel (chàn′sĕl). The part of the church reserved for the clergy.

charg′er (chär′jẽr). A war horse.

char′i·ot (chăr′ĭ·ŭt). In olden times a two-wheeled vehicle drawn by horses, used in war, racing, etc.

Char′le·magne (shär′lĕ·mān). An emperor, Charles the Great.

chem′i·cal (kĕm′ĭ·kăl). All things are made up of chemicals. Such things as water and salt are called chemical compounds.

chem′ist (kĕm′ĭst). A person who knows or works at chemistry.

chem′is·try (kĕm′ĭs·trĭ). The science which collects, studies, and explains facts about substances, what they are made up of, and what changes they undergo.

chiv′al·ry (shĭv′ăl·rĭ). The ideals of knighthood, such as bravery, honor, protection of the weak, etc.

Chris′ten·dom (krĭs″n·dŭm). 1. The whole body of Christians. 2. The church. 3. That part of the world in which Christianity prevails.

Ci′ma·bu′e (chē′mä·boō′å). An Italian artist.

civ′il (sĭv′ĭl). 1. Of or relating to citizens. 2. Courteous; polite.

clam′or (klăm′ẽr). Loud and continued noise.

clan (klăn). A group of families, all descended from one person.

cleanse (klĕnz). To make clean.

clime (klīm). A region of the earth.

clus'ter (klŭs'tẽr). A number of things of the same kind, growing, or collected, together.

Co·logne' (kŏ·lōn'). A city in western Germany.

com·bus'ti·ble (kŏm·bŭs'tĭ·b'l). Apt to catch fire; easily burned.

com'et (kŏm'ĕt). A bright heavenly body, usually having a long cloudy tail and traveling around the sun.

com·mune' (kŏ·mūn'). To come into spiritual understanding.

Com'mu·nist (kŏm'ŭ·nĭst). A member of a political party which seeks to control both religion and private enterprise.

com·pact' (kŏm·păkt'). Closely united or packed; solid; firm.

con·cern' (kŏn·sûrn'). Worry or anxiety.

con·fide' (kŏn·fīd'). To entrust a secret.

Con·fi'te·or (kŏn·fē'tē·ôr). The Latin word for I confess.

Con'or (kŏn'ẽr).

con'se·quence (kŏn'sĕ·kwĕns). A result.

Con'stan·ti·no'ple (kŏn'stăn·tĭ·nō'-p'l). The former capital of Turkey.

con'stel·la'tion (kŏn'stĕ·lā'shŭn). Any stars in the sky which seem to form a group.

con·vert' (kŏn·vûrt'). To change in religious belief.

con'vert (kŏn'vûrt). One who has changed one's religion.

con'vict (kŏn'vĭkt). A person serving a prison term.

con·vict' (kŏn·vĭkt'). To prove or find guilty of an offense.

con·vince' (kŏn·vĭns'). To persuade.

Cor'mac (kôr'măk).

cor'o·na'tion (kŏr'ŏ·nā'shŭn). The act of crowning.

Cor'pus Chris'ti (kôr'pŭs krĭs'tē). The Latin words for Body of Christ. The Feast of Corpus Christi is in honor of the Eucharist.

coun'cil (koun'sĭl). A group of persons who are called together to give advice.

coun'sel (koun'sĕl). Advice given, especially by a wiser person.

cour'ti·er (kōr'tĭ·ẽr). A member of a king's court.

crafts'man (krȧfts'măn). One who is skilled, especially in work with the hands.

Cre'do (krā'dō). The Latin word for I believe, the first words of the Creed.

Cre'mer (krā'mẽr), Father. The vicar of the Church of St. Stephen in Mainz.

crest (krĕst). The top.

---

lāte, alwăys, ăm, ȧppear, ärm, ȧsk, câre, hē, ĕnough, nĕt, silĕnt, makẽr, hẽre, rīde, ĭn, possĭble, ōld, ŏbey, nŏt, cŏnnect, sŏft, hôrse, ūse, ûnite, ŭs, circŭs, bûrn, mōon, tŏŏk, oil, out, that, thin, natŭre, verdŭre

419

Cri·me′a (krī·mē′à). A peninsula in southern Russia. It was the scene of the Crimean War between Russia and England.

crow's′-nest′ (crōz′nĕst′). A platform set high on the mast of a ship for a lookout.

Cru·sade′ (krōō·sād′). One of the Christian armies which went to the Holy Land to regain it from the Turks.

Da·mas′cus (dà·măs′kŭs). A city of Syria, one of the most ancient cities of the world.

Dan′ube (dăn′ūb). A great river in Europe.

Dau′phin (dô′fĭn). At one time, a title of the oldest son of the king of France.

daze (dāz). A bewildered state caused by fear, grief, etc.

de·scend′ant (dē·sĕn′dănt). A person who descends from a particular ancestor, as, a *descendant* of a king.

des′ti·na′tion (dĕs′tĭ·nā′shŭn). The place set for the end of a journey; the goal.

des′tine (dĕs′tĭn). To be intended.

des′ti·ny (dĕs′tĭ·nĭ). The fate or lot of a person.

de·vice′ (dē·vīs′). Something made or thought up to bring about a desired result.

dis·course′ (dĭs·kōrs′). Conversation; talk.

dis′cus (dĭs′kŭs). A heavy round plate to be hurled as a trial of strength and skill.

dis·placed′ per′son (dĭs·plāst′ pûr′-s'n). A person driven from his native land because of race, nationality, religion, or political beliefs.

doc′u·ment (dŏk′ū·mĕnt). A written or printed paper giving information.

Do·min′i·can (dô·mĭn′ĭ·kăn). A religious of the Order founded by Saint Dominic.

Dom′re·my′ (dôn′rẽ·mē′). The birthplace of Joan of Arc.

Don′al (dŏn′ăl).

Don Di·e′go (dŏn dĕ·ā′gō).

dou′blet (dŭb′lĕt). A close-fitting garment for men. It covered the body from the neck to the waist or a little below.

drab (drăb). Dull and monotonous.

drafts′man (dràfts′măn). A person who makes plans, sketches, etc., for construction work.

dub (dŭb). To make a man a knight by striking him lightly with a sword.

Dür′ren·stein (dōō′ràn·shtīn). The name of a mountain in Austria; also, the castle located on it.

earl (ûrl). A nobleman.

ebb (ĕb). To decline or fall to a low point.

em′er·ald (ĕm′ẽr·ăld). A deep-green precious jewel or stone.

E·mil′i·a (ē·mĭl′ĭ·à).

Em′i·nence (ĕm′ĭ·nĕns). A title of honor, applied exclusively to a cardinal of the Catholic Church.

em·po'ri·um (ĕm·pō'rĭ·ŭm). A store, usually carrying many kinds of articles.

en·gage' (ĕn·gāj'). To take a part in doing something.

en·slave'ment (ĕn·slāv'mĕnt). Making slaves of.

en'try (ĕn'trĭ). 1. The act of entering. 2. A place by which entrance is made.

en'voy (en'voi). A person who is sent upon a mission; a messenger.

ep'i·logue (ep'ĭ·lŏg). A speech, short poem, etc., spoken by an actor after the close of a play.

e·pis'co·pal (ē·pĭs'kŏ·păl). Of or relating to a bishop.

e·quip' (ē·kwĭp'). To furnish for some special purpose.

es'cort (ĕs'kôrt). A person or a group of persons accompanying another, as an honor, or as a protection.

es·cort' (ĕs·kôrt'). To accompany anyone as a mark of honor or courtesy, or as a protection.

e·ter'nal (ē·tûr'năl). Lasting forever; having no beginning or end.

E·van'ge·list (ē·văn'jĕ·lĭst). A writer of any one of the four Gospels—Matthew, Mark, Luke, or John.

ev'i·dence (ĕv'ĭ·dĕns). Proof.

ex'ile (ĕk'sīl). Forced removal of a person from his native country.

ex·pect'ant (ĕks·pĕkt'ănt). Waiting hopefully; looking forward to.

ex·pose' (ĕks·pōz'). To leave without care or shelter.

ex·press'way' (ĕks·prĕs'wā'). A superhighway.

fal'con (fôl'kŭn). A swift-flying hawk.

fal'ter (fôl'tĕr). 1. To move or act in an unsteady manner. 2. To hesitate.

fare (fâr). To journey.

Fi'an (fē'än). A hero army of Ireland.

fick'le (fĭk''l). Changeable.

fi·nal'i·ty (fī·năl'ĭ·tĭ). The quality of being final or decisive.

Fin'bar (fĭn'bär).

fir'ma·ment (fûr'mà·mĕnt). The heavens.

flaw'less (flô'lĕs). Without fault.

fleur'-de-lis' (flûr'dĕ·lē'). A design suggested by the iris flower and used as an emblem of France.

Flor'ence (flŏr'ĕns). A city in Italy, a famous center of art.

ford (fōrd). To wade across a river or stream at a shallow spot.

fore'most (fōr'mōst). First in time, order, place; most advanced.

Found'lings (found'lĭngz) **Home.** A home established for the care of babies whose parents have deserted them.

---

lāte, alwâys, ăm, ăppear, ärm, ȧsk, câre, hē, ĕnough, nĕt, silĕnt, makĕr, hēre, rīde, ĭn, possĭble, ōld, ȯbey, nŏt, cŏnnect, sŏft, hôrse, ūse, ūnite, ŭs, circŭs, bûrn, mōon, tŏŏk, oil, out, that, thin, natŭre, verdŭre

Fran'cis of As·si'si (à·sē'zē), **Saint.** The founder of the Franciscan Order.

Fran·cis'can (frăn·sĭs'kăn). A religious of one of the Orders founded by Saint Francis of Assisi.

Frank (frănk). A term used by Moslems, etc., to describe a European.

fri'ar (frī'ẽr). A member of a religious Order.

ful·fill'ment (fŏŏl·fĭl'mĕnt). Carrying into effect.

Gael'ic (gāl'ĭk). Of the Gael, as the people of Ireland and Scotland are sometimes called.

Gal'a·had (găl'á·hăd), **Sir.** A knight of the Round Table, who found the Holy Grail.

Gal'i·le'o (găl'ĭ·lē'ō). An Italian scientist.

gal'ley (găl'ĭ). A large low vessel, moved either by sails or oars.

gar'land (gär'lănd). To decorate with wreaths of leaves, flowers, etc.

gar'ri·son (găr'ĭ·sŭn). 1. A body of troops stationed in a fort. 2. A place where troops are stationed.

gauge (gāj). An instrument for measuring or testing something.

gen·er·a'tion (jĕn·ẽr·á'shŭn). The usual length of time (about thirty-three years) accepted as the difference in age between parent and child.

Gen'e·vieve' (jĕn'ĕ·vēv'), **Saint.** The patron saint of Paris.

gen'ius (jēn'yŭs). A very gifted person.

ges'ture (jĕs'tŭr). A motion of one's body or limbs to express a feeling or give emphasis to a statement.

Geth·sem'a·ne (gĕth·sĕm'á·nē). The garden outside of Jerusalem which was the scene of the agony and arrest of Jesus.

Giles (jīlz).

Giot'to (jŏt'tō). A famous Italian painter, architect, and sculptor.

Gir'ty (gûr'tĭ), **Simon.** An American soldier who turned against the Americans and became a leader of Indian raiding parties.

glee'ful·ly (glē'fŏŏl·ĭ). In a joyous or merry manner.

glum'ly (glŭm'lĭ). In a gloomy manner.

Go'a (gō'á). A Portuguese colony in India. It contains the tomb of Saint Francis Xavier.

goad (gōd). Something that stirs or urges on.

God'frey (gŏd'frĭ). A leader of the First Crusade.

God'speed' (gŏd'spēd'). A farewell wish for success.

gold'smith' (gōld'smĭth'). A person who makes things of gold.

gos'ling (gŏz'lĭng). A young goose.

gran'deur (grăn'dŭr). Magnificence.

grat'i·tude (grăt'ĭ·tūd). Being grateful; thankfulness.

grav'i·ty (grăv'ĭ·tĭ). The force that pulls all things on the earth toward the center of the earth.

Great Char'ter (chär'tẽr). *See* Magna Carta.

Greece (grēs). A country in south-eastern Europe.

Greg'o·ry (grĕg'ŏ·rĭ), **Saint.** A great Pope of the Church.

Gren'a·dier' (grĕn'à·dẽr') **Guards.** A regiment of the British Army.

grim (grĭm). Stern and determined.

guer'don (gûr'dŭn). Reward.

guild (gĭld). A group of men, all of whom make by hand the same kind of goods.

guin'ea (gĭn'ĭ) **pig.** A small animal, much used in scientific experiments.

Gu'ten·berg (goo'tĕn·bĕrk), **John.** The German inventor of printing from movable type.

gy'ro·scop'ic (jī'rŏ·skŏp'ĭk). Like a gyroscope. A gyroscope is a heavy rotating wheel which resists being turned, thus keeping the controls of an airplane steady.

haze (hāz). Light smoke in the air.

ha'zel (hā'z'l). A tree, the wood of which was used for making strong clubs, or staffs.

heed (hēd). To give careful attention.

her'ald (hĕr'ăld). A person who carries messages and makes announcements.

herb (ûrb). A seed plant that has more or less tender stalks and stems.

he·ro'ic (hĕ·rō'ĭk). Very brave; courageous.

his·to'ri·an (hĭs·tō'rĭ·ăn). A person who writes or knows much about history.

hoard (hōrd). To store away.

hold (hōld). 1. The act of holding. 2. The part of a ship below decks where the cargo is stored.

Ho'ly Grail (grāl). The cup used by Our Lord at the Last Supper.

Ho'ly Ro'man Em'pire. An empire made up of the German-speaking peoples of Central Europe. It lasted from 800 A.D. to 1806.

Ho'ly Sep'ul·chre (sĕp'ŭl·kẽr). The tomb of Our Lord.

hose (hōz). 1. A flexible pipe for carrying water or other liquid. 2. Close-fitting coverings for the legs and waist.

hos'tile (hŏs'tĭl). Unfriendly; belonging to the enemy.

hov'er (hŭv'ẽr). To flutter about.

hu·man'i·ty (hù·măn'ĭ·tĭ). The human race.

Hu'mer·y, Con'rad (hū'mẽr·ĭ, kŏn'răd).

hu·mil'i·ty (hù·mĭl'ĭ·tĭ). Freedom from a proud manner.

hurl (hûrl). To throw with great force.

---

lāte, alwăys, ăm, ăppear, ärm, àsk, câre, hē, ĕnough, nĕt, silĕnt, makẽr, hẽre, rīde, ĭn, possĭble, ōld, ŏbey, nŏt, cŏnnect, sŏft, hôrse, ūse, ûnite, ŭs, circŭs, bûrn, moon, took, oil, out, that, thin, natũre, verdũre

hy′dro·pho′bi·a (hī′drò·fō′bĭ·à). A very fatal disease of dogs and other animals.

I·ca′rus (ĭ·kär′ŭs). The boy who, according to Greek legend, flew too near the sun.

Ice′land (īs′lănd). A large island of the North Atlantic Ocean.

I′dle·wild′ (ĭ′d'l·wĭld′) **Airport.** The world's largest airfield, located near New York City.

ig′no·rance (ĭg′nò·răns). Lack of knowledge.

ig·nore′ (ĭg·nōr′). To refuse to take notice of.

im′mi·grant (ĭm′ĭ·grănt). A person of foreign birth who enters a country for the purpose of making his home there.

im′mi·gra′tion (ĭm′ĭ·grā′shŭn). The act of coming into a strange country for the purpose of living there.

Im·pe′ri·al (ĭm·pēr′ĭ·ăl) **Valley.** A large valley in southern California.

im′print (ĭm′prĭnt). Something stamped or printed.

in·dig′nant (ĭn·dĭg′nănt). Angry because of treatment believed to be unfair.

in′fi·nite (ĭn′fĭ·nĭt). Without limits of any kind; endless.

in·ject′ (ĭn·jĕkt′). To force some fluid, drug, etc., into a part of the body or the blood.

in·oc′u·late (ĭn·ŏk′ů·lāt). To insert into the skin disease germs or chemicals which enable the body to be safe from disease, as, to *inoculate* a child with a polio shot.

in′sti·tute (ĭn′stĭ·tūt). An organization to promote learning, art, etc.

in·teg′ri·ty (ĭn·tĕg′rĭ·tĭ). Soundness; purity; honesty.

in·ten′tion (ĭn·tĕn′shŭn). Something that is intended; purpose.

in·vade′ (ĭn·vād′). To enter with force for the purpose of taking possession.

in·vin′ci·ble (ĭn·vĭn′sĭ·b'l). Incapable of being conquered.

I′ris (ī′rĭs). A girl's name.

I′ron Cur′tain (ī′ẽrn kûr′tĭn). A term used to describe the restrictions imposed by the Communists to keep the people of the countries controlled by them from communication with the free countries.

Is′a·bel′la (ĭz′à·bĕl′à). A queen of Spain.

Is′ra·el (ĭz′rà·ĕl). 1. The Jews. 2. An ancient kingdom in Palestine. 3. A modern nation.

is′sue (ĭsh′ū). To print and circulate.

It′a·ly (ĭt′à·lĭ). A country in southern Europe.

Ja′son (jā′sŭn).

jeer (jēr). To make fun of.

Jen′ner (jĕn′ẽr), **Edward.** An English doctor, discoverer of vaccination.

Je·rome′ (jĕ·rōm′), **Saint.** A Father of the Church who translated the Bible into Latin.

Jo′a·chim (jō′à·kĭm), **Saint.** Father of the Blessed Virgin Mary.

Joan′ of Arc′ (jōn′ ŏv ärk′), **Saint.** The saint who led the French to victory against the English, but was captured and burned as a witch.

jos′tle (jŏs″l). To push roughly.

joust (jŭst). A combat on horseback between two knights with lances.

ju′bi·lant (jōo′bĭ·lănt). Shouting with joy.

Ju′pi·ter (jōo′pĭ·tēr). 1. The Roman god of the heavens. 2. The largest of the planets.

ju′ry (jōor′ĭ). A group of persons chosen to decide from the evidence presented at a trial what the facts are.

jus′ti·fy (jŭs′tĭ·fī). To prove to be right.

jus′tice (jŭs′tĭs). The practice of dealing fairly with others; complete fairness; just action.

Ket′tel·er, von (fŏn kĕt′ĕl·ēr), **William Emmanuel.** Bishop of Mainz.

Kil·dare′ (kĭl·dâr′). A county in Ireland.

knight′hood (nīt′hŏŏd). The rank, honor, or dignity of a knight.

Kol′ski, Gre′gor (kōl′skĕ, grā′gôr).

Kra′kow (krà′kŏŏf). A famous city in Poland.

Ky′ri·e (kē′rĭ·ē). The Greek word for *Lord.*

lab′o·ra·to′ry (lăb′ō·rà·tō′rĭ). A room or building where experiments and scientific tests are carried on.

lack (lăk). Need of something.

lad′en (lād″n). Loaded.

la·ment′ (là·mĕnt′). To mourn greatly.

lance (làns). A long-handled weapon with a sharp steel point.

Lang′ley (lăng′lĭ), **Samuel.** An American scientist, one of the first to study aviation and to carry on the work of the Wright brothers.

Lang′ton (lăng′tŭn), **Stephen.** Archbishop of Canterbury and Cardinal.

La Ra′bi·da (lä rä′bē·dä). A Franciscan convent in Palos, Spain.

La·va′bo (lä·và′bō). The Latin word for *I shall wash.*

law′suit′ (lô′sūt′). A case before a court of law.

lay (lā). A song.

Laz′a·rist (lăz′à·rĭst). An Order devoted to the care of the sick.

leg′end (lĕj′ĕnd). An old story that is widely accepted as true, but cannot be proved to be so.

---

lāte, alwăys, ăm, ăppear, ärm, àsk, câre, hē, ĕnough, nĕt, silĕnt, makēr, hēre, rīde, ĭn, possĭble, ōld, ôbey, nŏt, cŏnnect, sŏft, hôrse, ūse, ūnite, ŭs, circŭs, bûrn, mōon, tŏŏk, oil, out, that, thin, natûre, verdûre

Lein'ster (lĕn'stēr). One of the early kingdoms of Ireland, now a province.

Le'o·pold (lē'ŏ·pōld). 1. Ruler of Austria at the time Vienna was attacked by the Turks. 2. Ruler of Austria at the time of the Third Crusade.

lep'er (lĕp'ēr). One suffering from a dreadful disease of the skin.

lep'ro·sy (lĕp'rŏ·sĭ). A dreadful disease of the skin.

lest (lĕst). For fear that.

Light Bri·gade' (līt brĭ·gād'). An English regiment, famous for an heroic charge made against the enemy during the Crimean War.

lin'tel (lĭn'tĕl). A beam, stone, etc., across the top of an opening, as of a door, to carry the weight of the building above it.

Lis'bon (lĭz'bŭn). An important city in Portugal.

loft (lŏft). A balcony where the choir is seated.

Lon'don (lŭn'dŭn). The capital and largest city of Great Britain.

loom (lōōm). A frame or machine used for weaving cloth.

loop'hole' (lōōp'hōl'). A small opening through which guns may be fired.

Lor·raine' (lŏ·rān'), **Duke of.** A French duke who joined forces with Sobieski to come to the aid of Vienna.

Lou·is' (lōō·ē'), **Saint.** A king of France.

Lu'ci·a (lū'shĭ·à). A girl's name.

lure (lūr). To tempt or lead away.

lute (lūt). A stringed musical instrument, played by plucking the strings with the fingers.

mad'der (măd'ēr). A plant from the roots of which a bright-red dye is obtained.

Mag'na Car'ta (măg'nà kär'tà). The Great Charter, signed by King John, and guaranteeing certain rights to Englishmen.

mag·nif'i·cent (măg·nĭf'ĭ·sĕnt). Splendid; richly decorated.

Mainz (mīnts). A city in Germany.

Mal'ek (măl'ĕk).

man'kind' (măn'kīnd'). The human race; all men.

Man·uel' (mä·nwĕl'). A Spanish name.

man'u·script (măn'û·skrĭpt). 1. A book written by hand. 2. A written paper, book, etc. 3. Writing, not print.

Mar'cos (mär'kŏs). The Spanish name for *Mark*.

Mar'cus (mär'kŭs). The Greek name for *Mark*.

Mars (märz). 1. The Roman god of war. 2. One of the planets.

Mar·seille' (mär·sĕ'y'). A seaport in France.

ma'tron (mā'trŭn). A woman who is in charge of some place; as, a *matron* of a hospital.

Med'i·ter·ra'ne·an (mĕd'ĭ·tĕ·rā'-nĕ·ăn) **Sea.** A great inland sea, inclosed by Europe, Asia, and Africa.

men-at-arms (měn ăt ärmz). Armed soldiers.

Mer'cu·ry (mûr'kû·rǐ). 1. A Roman god. 2. The smallest of the planets.

Mes·si'as (mě·sī'ǎs). The expected king and deliverer of the Jews; the Christ.

mi'crobe (mī'krōb). A germ; an animal or plant so small that it can be seen only with the aid of a microscope.

mi'cro·scope (mī'krŏ·skōp). A scientific instrument which enlarges the size of objects seen through it.

mi·la'dy (mǐ·lā'dǐ). A noblewoman or gentlewoman.

min'strel (mǐn'strěl). An entertainer, usually a singer.

mold (mōld). A hollow form from which something takes its shape.

mon'arch (mŏn'ẽrk). A person who is the supreme ruler.

mon'as·ter'y (mŏn'ǎs·tẽr'ǐ). The building or group of buildings in which a community of monks or nuns dwell.

Moor'ish (mo͝or'ǐsh). Of, or relating to the Moors, a people of northern Africa.

mor'al (mŏr'ǎl). Virtuous, good, as, a *moral* life.

Mo·re'na (mŏ·rē'nȧ).

mor'row (mŏr'ō). The next following day; tomorrow.

mor'tal (môr'tǎl). Causing death; causing spiritual death, as, a *mortal* sin.

Mos'lem (mŏz'lěm). One who believes in the religion founded by Mohammed. Most Turks, Arabs, etc., follow this religion.

moun'tain·eer' (moun'tǐ·nẽr'). A person who lives in a mountain region.

Na'ples (nā'p'lz). A large seaport in Italy.

nave (nāv). The central part of a church running lengthwise.

Ne'ro (nē'rō). A Roman emperor, who cruelly persecuted the early Christians.

Neth'er·lands (něth'ẽr·lǎndz). A name for Holland.

New'ton (nū't'n), **Isaac.** An English scientist.

Ni'co·lette (nǐ'kȧ·lět).

Night'in·gale (nīt'ǐn·gāl), **Florence.** An English army nurse.

Ni'na (nē'nyä). The name of one of the smaller ships of Columbus.

Nor'man (nôr'mǎn). A person from Normandy, an old province of France.

No·tre Dame' (nō·tr' dȧm'). The French words for *Our Lady,* the Virgin Mary—used especially in names of French churches.

---

lāte, alwȧys, ăm, ǎppear, ärm, ȧsk, câre, hē, ěnough, nět, silěnt, makēr, hēre, rīde, ǐn, possǐble, ōld, ŏbey, nŏt, cǒnnect, sŏft, hôrse, ūse, ûnite, ŭs, circǔs, bûrn, mo͞on, to͝ok, oil, out, that, thin, natůre, verdůre

427

ob·serv'ance (ŏb·zûr'văns). Act of observing a rule, law, or custom, etc.

O'do (ō'dō). Bishop of Bayeux.

Of'fer·to·ry (ŏf'ẽr·tŏ·rĭ). The part of the Mass during which bread and wine are offered to God with prayers.

O·lym'pi·a (ŏ·lĭm'pĭ·à). A plain in Greece where the Olympian games were held every fourth year.

O·lym'pus (ŏ·lĭm'pŭs). A mountain in Greece. In olden times, it was supposed to be the home of pagan gods.

or'bit (ôr'bĭt). The nearly circular path of the earth or any other body around the sun.

or·dain' (ôr·dān'). To administer the sacrament of Holy Orders.

O'ri·ent (ō'rĭ·ĕnt). The East; eastern countries, especially those east of the Mediterranean.

or'i·gin (ŏr'ĭ·jĭn). The beginning, or cause, of a thing.

Or'lé'ans' (ôr'lā'än'). A city in France.

out'skirts' (out'skûrts'). The outlying parts of a town.

Pad'u·a (păd'ụ̄·à). A very old city in Italy.

pa'gan (pā'găn). A worshiper of false gods.

page (pāj). A boy in training for knighthood.

Pa'los (pä'lōs). The seaport in Spain from which Columbus sailed.

Pan'ge Lin'gua (pän'jĕ lēn'gwä). The first words of a hymn in honor of the Blessed Sacrament, *Sing My Tongue.*

Pan'is An·gel'i·cus (pän'ēs än·jĕl'ē·kōōs). The Latin words for *bread of angels.*

pa·py'rus (pà·pī'rŭs). A paper made from a grasslike plant by the ancient Greeks and Romans.

par'al·lel (păr'ă·lĕl). Moving in the same direction, but always the same distance apart.

parch'ment (pärch'mĕnt). The skin of sheep, goats, etc., prepared so that it can be written on.

Pas'teur' (päs'tûr'), **Louis.** A French scientist.

pas'teur·ize (păs'tẽr·īz). To treat a fluid, such as milk, so that certain germs in it are killed.

pat'ent (păt'ĕnt). A writing that secures to an inventor, for a number of years, the exclusive right to make, use, and sell his invention.

Pa'ter Nos'ter (pä'tẽr nŏs'tẽr). The Latin words for *Our Father.*

pa'ti·o (pä'tĭ·ō). A courtyard.

Pat'mos (păt'mŏs). An island, off the coast of Greece, the place of Saint John's exile.

Pe'dro (pā'drō). The Spanish name for *Peter.*

Pe'rez (pā'rāth), **Friar.** The prior at La Rabida.

per'se·cute (pûr'sĕ·kūt). To cause people to suffer because of their beliefs, especially religious beliefs.

per′se·ver′ance (pûr′sĕ·vēr′ăns). The act of keeping at something in spite of difficulties.

Per′sia (pûr′zhà). A kingdom in southwestern Asia, now called Iran.

Pic′ar·dy (pĭk′ĕr·dĭ). A former province of France.

pierce (pērs). To stab.

Pierre (pyâr). The French name for *Peter*.

pil′grim·age (pĭl′grĭ·mĭj). The journey of a person who travels to a holy place or shrine as an act of religious devotion.

Pin′ta (pĭn′tà). The smallest of the three ships of Columbus.

Pin·zon′ (pēn·thōn′), **Martin** and **Vincente.**

Pi′sa (pē′zà). An Italian city.

plan′et (plăn′ĕt). One of the nine bodies in the solar system which revolve around the sun.

Ple′ia·des (plē′yà·dēz). A certain cluster of stars, named by the Greeks for seven sisters whom they believed were changed into a group of stars.

plod (plŏd). To move or travel slowly but steadily.

pluck (plŭk). 1. To pull off or out. 2. Spirit, courage.

Pol′ish (pōl′ĭsh). Of or relating to Poland, its language, or its people.

Polish Exile Army. An army organized to fight with the free countries of Europe after the fall of Poland during World War II.

pol′i·ti′cian (pŏl′ĭ·tĭsh′ăn). A person who is actively concerned with party politics.

pol′i·tics (pŏl′ĭ·tĭks). Activity in the affairs of parties which control or seek to control the management of government business.

post ex·change′ (pōst ĕks·chānj′). A store that sells goods to members of the armed forces and certain other approved persons.

pre·cau′tion (prĕ·kô′shŭn). Caution or care.

pre′cinct cap′tain (prē′sĭngkt kăp′tĭn). A person in charge of a district set off for election purposes.

prel′ate (prĕl′ĭt). A clergyman of high rank, such as a bishop.

pri′or (prī′ĕr). The superior of a community of monks.

priv′i·lege (prĭv′ĭ·lĭj). A right or liberty granted to a person as a favor.

proc′ess (prŏs′ĕs). Method.

pro·claim′ (prŏ·klām′). To announce publicly; to declare.

proph′e·cy (prŏf′ĕ·sĭ). A saying of a prophet revealing to other men the truths made known to him by God.

---

lāte, alwâys, ăm, ăppear, ärm, àsk, câre, hē, ĕnough, nĕt, silĕnt, makĕr, hēre, rīde, ĭn, possĭble, ōld, ôbey, nŏt, cŏnnect, sôft, hôrse, ūse, ūnite, ŭs, circŭs, bûrn, mōon, tŏŏk, oil, out, that, thin, natūre, verdūre

proph'et (prŏf'ĕt). 1. One who foretells future events. 2. With a capital (*The Prophet*), among Moslems, Mohammed, the founder of their religion.

pro·pose' (prŏ·pōz'). To have as a plan.

pros'pect (prŏs'pĕkt). That which may be probable.

Prov'i·dence (prŏv'ĭ·dĕns). God, as the loving Father of all human beings.

Prus'sian (prŭsh'ăn). Belonging to Prussia, a state in Gemany.

Pu·las'ki, Cas'i·mir (pŭ·lăs'kĭ, kăz'-ĭ·mĭr). A Polish patriot who served and died in the American Revolution.

pur·su'er (pĕr·sū'ĕr). One who chases another.

pyre (pīr). A heap of wood, etc., on which a dead body is burned.

quar'ter (kwôr'tĕr). 1. Twenty-five cents in United States money. 2. A division of a town, city, or country; a special district.

rab'bi (răb'ī). A teacher of the Jews.

ra'bi·es (rā'bĭ·ĕs). Hydrophobia, a fatal disease attacking dogs and other animals.

rai'ment (rā'mĕnt). Clothing; garments.

Ra·mon' (rä·mōn'). The Spanish name for *Raymond*.

rap'ture (răp'tụr). A deep, joyous feeling.

Ray'mond' (rā'môn'). A commander of a large army during the First Crusade.

re·act' (rĕ·ăkt'). To act or change as a result of something.

realm (rĕlm). 1. A region. 2. A kingdom.

re·bel'lion (rĕ·bĕl'yŭn). An uprising.

re·buke' (rĕ·būk'). To scold or criticize severely.

re·cep'tion cen'ter (rĕ·sĕp'shŭn sĕn'-tĕr). A place set aside where newcomers may be greeted, their papers checked, etc.

re·frain' (rĕ·frān'). To hold oneself back.

reg'i·ment (rĕj'ĭ·mĕnt). A body of soldiers commanded by a colonel.

Reg'i·nald (rĕj'ĭ·năld), **Brother.** A Dominican friar.

Reims (rēmz). A city in France, famous for its beautiful cathedral where the kings of France were crowned.

ren'der (rĕn'dĕr). To give in return.

rep'tile (rĕp'tĭl). A snake, lizard, or the like.

Re'qui·em (rē'kwĭ·ĕm). A Mass for the repose of a departed soul.

re·sent' (rĕ·zĕnt'). To feel angry and displeased.

re·sound' (rĕ·zound'). To be proclaimed far and wide.

re·tort' (rĕ·tôrt'). To reply angrily, sharply, etc.

re·veal' (rĕ·vēl'). To make something known.

Rich'ard (rĭch'ẽrd) **of the Lion Heart.** A king of England.

Rhine (rīn). A river in Europe, flowing from Switzerland to the North Sea.

Rob'bia, del'la (dĕl'lä rōb'byä). An Italian sculptor.

Ro·ber'to (rō·bĕr'tō). The Italian name for *Robert.*

rock'et (rŏk'ĕt) **ship.** An airplane operated by a rocket engine which works on the same principle as a firework rocket.

ro·mance' (rō·mǎns'). A tale of noble deeds.

ro'tor (rō'tẽr). A part that revolves in a stationary part.

Rot'ter·dam' (rŏt'ẽr·dăm'). A seaport in Holland.

Sab'bath (săb'ăth). 1. In the Jewish calendar, Saturday, the seventh day of the week, kept for rest and worship. 2. Among most Christians, Sunday, the first day of the week, kept for rest and worship.

Saint-La·zare' (san lă·zär'). A hospital established for the care of lepers.

St. Peter's. The basilica adjoining the Vatican in Rome. It is the largest church in the world, and the place where religious ceremonies of world-wide importance take place.

Sainte Cha·pelle' (săn shà·pĕl'). The chapel which Saint Louis built for the Crown of Thorns.

Sal'a·din (săl'à·dĭn). A leader of the Moslems.

sal'a·man·der (săl'à·măn·dẽr). A lizardlike animal.

sal·va'tion (săl·vā'shŭn). The saving of a person from sin or from the punishment of sin.

Sal've Re·gi'na (säl'vä rä·jē'nä). The Latin title for the prayer *Hail, Holy Queen.*

Sa·mar'i·tan (sà·măr'ĭ·tăn). A person who is ready to help strangers in trouble, as was the Good Samaritan in the Bible.

sanc'tu·ar·y (săngk'tṳ·ẽr·ĭ). 1. A sacred place. 2. A place of refuge or safety.

Sanc'tus (sănk'tōōs). The Latin word for *holy.*

San'ta Ma·ri'a (sän'tä mä·rē'à). The name of Columbus's largest ship.

sap'phire (săf'īr). A bright-blue precious jewel or stone.

Sar'a·cen (săr'à·sĕn). A Moslem, especially one who fought the Crusaders.

Saul (sôl). The name of the Apostle Paul before his conversion.

scourge (skûrj). To whip; to lash.

Scrip'tures (skrĭp'tṳrz). 1. The books of the Old Testament, of

---

lāte, alwăys, ăm, ăppear, ärm, àsk, câre, hē, ĕnough, nĕt, silĕnt, makẽr, hẽre, rīde, ĭn, possĭble, ōld, ōbey, nŏt, cŏnnect, sŏft, hôrse, ūse, ûnite, ŭs, circŭs, bûrn, mōōn, tŏŏk, oil, out, ~~that~~, thin, natṳre, verdṳre

the New Testament, or of both.
2. The Bible.

seal (sēl). Something which is a proof of a paper's genuineness.

sear (sēr). To burn.

sem'i·cir'cle (sĕm'ĭ·sûr'k'l). Half of a circle.

se'rum (sē̦r'ŭm). A fluid used to prevent or cure diseases.

Se·vas'to·pol (sĕ·văs'tŏ·pôl). A seaport on the Crimea.

sex'ton (sĕks'tŭn). An official in a church who takes care of the building and property.

shaft (shȧft). 1. A deep, narrow pit leading into a mine. 2. A weapon, such as a spear, arrow, lance, etc.

sheep'fold' (shēp'fōld'). A pen, or place of shelter, for sheep.

shil'ling (shĭl'ĭng). A silver coin of England, of about the same value as the United States quarter.

siege (sēj). The placing of an army around or before a fortified place to force its surrender.

sire (sīr). A title of respect in addressing a king or ruler.

sit'u·a'tion (sĭt'ū·ā'shŭn). State; circumstances.

slaugh'ter (slô'tẽr). To kill.

smith'y (smĭth'ĭ). The workshop of a person who works in metals.

smote (smōt). Struck hard with the hand or a weapon.

smol'der (smōl'dẽr). To burn and smoke without flame.

So·bies'ki (sŏ·byĕs'kĕ), **John.** A great patriot and king of Poland.

soothe (sooth). To quiet, comfort.

South·amp'ton (south·ămp'tŭn). A seaport in southern England.

spec'ta·cle (spĕk'tȧ·k'l). An impressive public display or show.

Sper'ry (spĕr'ĭ), **Elmer.** An American electrical engineer and inventor. One of his most famous inventions is the gyroscopic stabilizer for ships and airplanes.

squire (skwīr). 1. A shield-bearer or armor-bearer for a knight. 2. A title often given to a landowner.

sta'bi·liz·ing de·vice' (stā'bĭ·līz·ĭng dē·vīs'). Something made to hold an object firm or steady.

staff (stȧf). 1. A stick, pole, or rod used for any of various purposes, such as to support or to hold up, etc. 2. In the army, a group of officers whose duties are to plan and manage army affairs.

stall (stôl). A booth where goods for sale may be shown.

stand'ard (stăn'dẽrd). 1. A banner. 2. An upright support.

Stan'is·laus (stăn'ĭs·lȧs).

states'man (stāts'măn). One skilled in public affairs and the art of government.

Ste'fan (stĕ'fän).

Ste'phen (stē'vĕn), **Saint.** The first Christian martyr, stoned to death.

striv'en (strĭv'ĕn). Tried hard; made great efforts.

strong'hold' (strŏng'hōld'). A fort.

stuc'co (stŭk'ō). Plaster used in coating walls.

sul′tan (sŭl′tăn). The ruler of the Turks.

su′per·sti′tion (sū′pĕr·stĭsh′ŭn). An unreasoning fear of nature caused by ignorance.

su·preme′ (sŭ·prēm′). Highest in rank or authority.

sur′coat′ (sûr′kōt′). An outer coat or cloak, worn by a knight over his armor.

surge (sûrj). An onward rush; as, the *surge* of a great crowd.

tact′ful·ly (tăkt′fŏŏl·lĭ). Saying or doing things in such a way as to avoid hurting a person's feelings.

ta′per (tā′pĕr). A candle.

tap′es·try (tăp′ĕs·trĭ). A heavy hand-woven cloth, often with figures woven into it, used as a wall hanging, etc.

Ta′ra (tä′rà). A town in Ireland where the High King lived.

tat·too′ (tăt·tōō′). To put permanent patterns or figures on the skin by pricking and coloring it.

tav′ern (tăv′ẽrn). An inn.

Tar′sus (tär′sŭs). The birthplace of Saint Paul.

Te De′um Lau·da′mus (tā dā′-ōōm lau·dä′mōōs). A hymn of praise, the Latin words for *We praise Thee, O Lord.*

ter′mi·nal (tûr′mĭ·năl). The station, office, buildings, etc., at the end of a railroad or air line.

Ter·ri′nus, Lu′ci·us (tĕr·rē′nŭs, lū′shĭ·ŭs).

Thames (tĕmz) **River.** The river on which London is located.

thatch (thăch). A covering for a roof made of straw, reeds, etc.

thrice (thrīs). Three times.

thun′der·bolt′ (thŭn′dẽr·bōlt′). A flash of lightning and the thunder that follows it.

ti′dings (tī′dĭngz). News.

Til′bu·ry (tĭl′bẽr·ĭ) **Dock.** A dock on the Thames River in London.

Tim′o·thy (tĭm′ō·thĭ). A convert of Saint Paul.

Ti′tus (tī′tŭs).

Tou·louse′ (tōō·lōōz′). A city in southern France.

tour′na·ment (tŏŏr′nà·mĕnt). In olden days, a contest for a prize between mounted armored knights.

Tow′er (tou′ẽr). A large collection of buildings, at one time a fortress, on the banks of the Thames in London.

tra·di′tion (trà·dĭsh′ŭn). Beliefs that are handed down from one generation to another.

trib′ute (trĭb′ūt). An act showing respect, loyalty; especially, praise.

---

lāte, alwăys, ăm, ŭppear, ärm, àsk, câre, hē, ēnough, nĕt, silĕnt, makẽr, hẽre, rīde, ĭn, possĭble, ōld, ōbey, nŏt, cŏnnect, sŏft, hôrse, ūse, ūnite, ŭs, circŭs, bûrn, mōōn, tŏŏk, oil, out, that, thin, natûre, verdûre

433

tri·um'phal (trī·ŭm'făl). In honor of a triumph, a victory, a success.

trou'ba·dour (trōō'bá·dŏŏr). In olden times, a poet-musician, who composed songs, usually about love and romance.

tu·ber'cu·lous (tŭ·bûr'kŭ·lŭs). Affected with tuberculosis, a serious disease.

tum'bler (tŭm'blẽr). 1. A person who does acrobatic tricks. 2. A drinking glass.

Tu'nis (tū'nĭs). A Barbary state in North Africa.

Turk (tûrk). A Mohammedan, especially one living in Turkey.

tu'tor (tū'tẽr). An instructor; one in charge of the studies of a pupil.

type (tīp). A block of metal or wood which is so shaped as to produce a letter, figure, etc., when pressed against a suitable surface.

un·sci·en·tif'ic (ŭn·sī'ĕn·tĭf'ĭk). Not based on scientific laws or reason.

ur'gent (ûr'jĕnt). Calling for immediate attention.

Ur'su·la (ûr'sŭ·lá).

u'su·ry (ū'zhŏŏ·rĭ). Too high a rate of interest charged for a loan.

vac'cine (văk'sēn). A fluid containing weakened or dead germs used in vaccination.

vain (vān). 1. Without success. 2. Proud of one's looks.

val'iant (văl'yănt). Boldly brave.

vat (văt). A large container for liquids; a large tub or barrel.

vault (vôlt). 1. A burial chamber, usually beneath the main floor of the church. 2. A steel room in which valuables are kept.

ve·loc'i·ty (vē·lŏs'ĭ·tĭ). The speed at which a thing moves.

Ve'ni Cre·a'tor (vĕ'nē crā·ä'tôr). The opening words and name of a hymn asking the aid of the Holy Spirit.

Ve'nus (vē'nŭs). 1. The Roman goddess of beauty and love. 2. One of the planets.

ver'dant (vûr'dănt). Green as fresh grass.

Vex·il'la Re'gis (vĕk·sĭl'á rē'jĭs). The Latin words for *the banner of the king*.

vi'a·duct (vī'á·dŭkt). A bridge for carrying a road or railroad over a gorge, highway, etc.

Vi·en'na (vē·ĕn'á). The capital of Austria.

vig'or·ous (vĭg'ẽr·ŭs). Full of strength.

Vin'cent de Paul (vĭn'sĕnt dĕ pôl), Saint.

Vin'ci, Le'o·nar'do da (vēn'chē, lä'ŏ·när'dŏ dá). A great painter, sculptor, architect, engineer, and scientist of Italy.

volt (vōlt). The unit of electrical pressure.

Vol'ta (vôl'tä). An Italian scientist, one of the first to study electricity. The volt is named in his honor.

vow (vou). 1. To make a solemn promise, especially to God. 2. Any pledge or promise.

wage (wāj). 1. To engage in, as a war. 2. Pay for work.

Wales (wālz), **Prince of.** The title given to the oldest son of the English king.

wane (wān). To grow smaller or less.

ward'en (wôr'd'n). A chief keeper, as, the *warden* of a prison.

wares (wârs). Goods; merchandise.

War'saw (wôr'sô). The capital of Poland.

War'wick (wôr'ĭk). A county in England.

wa'ter front. Land, or a section of a town, that fronts on a body of water.

watt (wŏt). The unit of electrical power.

Watt (wŏt), **James.** A Scottish engineer and inventor   The watt is named in his honor.

West'min'ster (wĕst'mĭn'stẽr). The place where English rulers are crowned.

White'hall' (hwĭt'hôl'). A street in London which is bordered by government offices.

whol'ly (hōl'lĭ). Entirely.

Wil'hel·mi'na (wĭl'hĕl·mē'nà).

wind'ing gown (wīnd'ĭng gown). A robe in which a dead body is wrapped for burial.

Wind'sor (wĭn'zẽr). The place where King John met the people for the signing of the Magna Carta.

Xav'i·er (zāv'ĭ·ẽr), **Saint Francis.** A Spanish missionary priest.

yearn (yûrn). To be filled with longing; to desire eagerly.

Yid'dish (yĭd'ĭsh). A language used by Jews in many countries.

zeal (zēl). Ardent and active interest.

Zi'ta (zē'tà).

---

lāte, alwăys, ăm, ăppear, ärm, àsk, câre, hē, ĕnough, nĕt, silĕnt, makẽr, hẹre, rīde, ĭn, possĭble, ōld, ôbey, nŏt, cŏnnect, sŏft, hôrse, ūse, ûnite, ŭs, circŭs, bûrn, mōōn, tŏŏk, oil, out, that, thin, natụre, verdụre

To the Teacher

This Is Our Heritage (New Edition) is the sixth-grade reader of the FAITH AND FREEDOM SERIES. It introduces 1192 new words and maintains a large percentage of the words taught in the preceding books of the series. New words which occur only in the poetry are italicized in the list below. The teacher should not require mastery of these words. Except for these italicized words, not more than six new words appear on any page. Words followed by a heavy black dot indicate words which are pronounced and defined in the glossary.

Word List

8. _ _ _

9. *verdant* •
   staff •

10. *visible*
    begotten

11. quarter •
    Jupiter •
    Mercury •
    cripple
    slender

12. Israel •
    Messias •
    crucified
    Saul •
    Tarsus •
    rabbis •

13. mob
    garments
    ignorance •
    Damascus •
    Palestine

14. hatred
    dost
    persecute •
    Barnabas •
    befriended •

15. proclaimed •
    stunned
    centuries
    justified •
    jeers •

16. _ _ _

17. anger
    erect

healed
Olympus •
Greece •

18. surrounded
    protests
    limb
    vigorous •
    discus •
    supreme •

19. salvation •
    uproar
    height

20. gesture •
    indicated
    slaughtered •
    clamor •

21. traitor
    spat
    lamenting •
    superstitions •

22. eternal •
    garlanded •
    hem
    Antioch •

23. martyrdom
    bruised
    pattern
    occurred

24. *goad* •

25. Patmos •
    Jason •
    Greek
    Olympia •
    wrestling

26. Marcus •
    thus
    accompany

27. tone
    sprang
    staggered

28. misery
    denied
    affection
    slavery
    begun

29. huts
    despising

30. bony
    brilliant
    hollow
    released
    therefore

31. Creator

32. _ _ _

33. _ _ _

34. spite
    rank
    seized

35. ceased •
    exhausted

36. _ _ _

37. reed
    papyrus •
    Evangelist •

38. peninsula
    influenced

437

39. *shalt*
    falter •

40. senator
    Lucius •
    Terrinus •
    divorce
    Emilia •
    Titus •

41. Judea

42. _ _ _

43. hunger
    district
    poverty
    Senate

44. prophecy •

45. mankind •
    Simon

46. wisdom

47. Nero's •
    stucco •

48. shield

49. Iris •

50. madness
    wrung

51. pyre •
    halt
    balconies
    tigers
    peril

52. burdens

53. tomb
    Appian •
    idled
    attended
    arena •
    constantly

54. converts •
    scorn
    delayed

55. arrival
    cleansing •

56. obedience
    chariots •

57. crucifixion
    test
    approaches
    vast
    empire

58. _ _ _

59. *winding-gown* •
    throng
    fluttered
    bore •

60. primroses
    Stefan •
    European

61. invaders •

62. relief
    conceived
    rye
    Barbara

63. braids
    bobbing
    clenching

64. Bernadette •
    Vision

65. Agatha •

66. Crusades •
    Moslems •

67. _ _ _

68. tribute •
    responses
    pang

69. _ _ _

70. elders

71. _ _ _

72. _ _ _

73. *amid* •
    thorn

74. _ _ _

75. *refuge*
    encamp
    waged •
    dwell

76. *Vexilla Regis* •
    flesh

77. Ascension
    Orient •
    Mediterranean •
    minstrels •
    Notre Dame •
    Sainte Chapelle •

78. Malek •
    bade •

79. Dominicans •
    Franciscans •

80. vacant
    embroideries
    Persia •
    acquaintances
    slyly

81. Confiteor •
    Kyrie •
    Offertory •
    Sanctus •
    Pater Noster •
    Agnus Dei •

82. awnings
    doves
    friar •
    sandaled
    Thomas
    Aquinas •

83. anxiety •

84. intend
    weapon

85. dodging
    hounds
    pursuers •

86. nave •
    confusion

87. chin
    knowledge

88. cautiously
    puppet
    jugglers

89. _ _ _

90. desperate
    recognized

91. Pentecost

92. guilty
    defending
    Reginald •

93. misfortunes
    ruin

94. Blanche
    mortal •
    muslins
    courtiers •
    slight
    frail

95. dignity
    sire •

438

439

144. squires •
rustling
paws
prowling
chamber

145. thrust
privilege •

146. credit
vats •

147. absence

148. *hearth*
shimmer

149. Blondel •
romance •
troubadours •
lute •
Gethsemane •
Holy Sepulchre •

150. jousts •
tournaments •
knighthood •
fling
lance •
temper

151. fleur-de-lis •
bid
Godspeed •

152. indignantly •
companions
youth
Saladin •

153. Leopold •
Austria •
vow •

154. imprisoned
Dürrenstein •
ford •
tavern •

155. strummed
thrice •

156. furiously
earl •
traits
chart

157. efforts

158. *lintel* •
boughs
tapers •
Picardy •
Aquitaine •
Castile •

Charlemagne •
didst
link

159. apartment
fund
rehearse
cigar
Nick
barber

160. curb
rehearsal
Martie
slacks
gymnasium

161. bike
Crockett

162. awards
bats
cameras
courteous
strode
photographer

163. startled
accomplishments •
tennis
racket
tingle
daze •

164. perseverance •
applause
focused
bulb
grin
unnatural

165. applauded
reverse
hoarded •
glazed
whooped

166. courageously

167. timidly

168. agony
modest
smart-aleck

169. janitor
matron •
grimly •

170. organized
hobby
flushed
flared
laden •
fuss

171. attentively •

172. accolade •

173. helmet's
crest •
moral •
midst
fares •
Holy Grail •
chancel •
guerdon •
commune •
valiant •

174. _ _ _

175. *firmament* •
handiwork
imparts
discourse •
resounds •

176. *Pange Lingua* •
excelling
destined •
redemption

177. Tara •
Brian •
Donal •
Leinster •
clans •
Fian •

178. Conor •

179. talents
trench
hazel •

180. confident

181. Brigid •
Kildare •

182. ambition
bond •

183. Scriptures •
Irish
monasteries •
manuscripts •

184. Jerome •
emeralds •
sapphires •
merely
Britain •

185. advanced
bounds
Testament
abbot •

440

441

236. alas
    ventured
    instructing

237. solve
    shrugged

238. genius •
    stammered

239. prospects •

240. *flawless* •
    rapture •
    altitude •
    realms •

241. Watson
    professor
    laboratory •
    battery
    spilled
    acid

242. patent •
    connect

243. crank
    transmitted
    conversation
    published
    parallel •
    compare

244. crazy
    adjusted
    vain •

245. interferes
    disgust
    convinced •
    troublesome

246. breathe
    astonish

247. syllable
    conversational
    sufficient

248. actually
    dictionary
    definition

249. *glittering*
    swaying
    breed
    veins

250. microscope •
    anniversary
    Pasteur •
    dragons
    explorers

251. tubes
    apparatus •
    conqueror
    microbes •
    germs
    disease

252. operations
    pasteurize •
    vaccines •
    antitoxins •
    institutes •
    issued •

253. chemistry •
    bewildered •

254. sour
    chemicals •
    temperature
    process •
    civilized

255. unscientific •
    remedies
    curing
    Jenner •
    smallpox
    anthrax •

256. vaccinated
    according
    injected •
    inoculated •

257. hydrophobia •
    rabies •
    horrible

258. infected
    zeal •
    serum •

259. pinprick
    guinea pig •

260. benefactor •
    Algeria •
    origin •
    contributed
    humanity •
    alert •

261. _ _ _

262. *chanting*

263. Dillon
    evidence •
    motto
    littered
    hamsters
    gnaw

264. cube
    average
    slim
    allowance
    carbon dioxide •
    vinegar

265. Galileo •
    Pisa •
    gravity •
    Newton •

266. bouncing
    velocity •
    gauge •
    devices •
    planets •
    constellations •

267. Pleiades •
    terms
    watt•
    volt •
    retorted •
    rivalry

268. rocket •
    Venus •
    Mars •
    orbit •
    comets •
    beetles

269. attic
    dialed
    pad
    fumes

270. reacting •
    combustible •

271. extinguisher
    equipped •

272. amateur •
    defense
    handsome
    quick-witted
    practical

273. gyroscopic •
    axles
    rotors •
    stabilizing •
    Langley •
    Sperry •

274. accent
    vowel
    diphthong
    principle
    digraph
    suffixes

443

444

corridor
brevity •

370. ushered

371. politician •

372. _ _ _

373. pardon
parishioners

374. _ _ _

375. document •

376. sympathetic

377. *integrity* •

378. _ _ _

379. unity
tremendous
rebels
exalt

380. *acknowledge*

381. Niña •
Pinta •
Pinzon •
Palos •
La Rabida •
cargo

382. mood
Isabella •
Perez •
Prior •
tattooed •
Manuel •

383. gypsy
forbidden
region

compass
monsters

384. wreckage

385. parchment •
Don Diego •

386. aboard
crouching

387. plodded •

388. Lavabo •

389. _ _ _

390. _ _ _

391. _ _ _

392. gallons
area

393. Lisbon •
gulls
envoy •
Goa •

394. sullen
Xavier's •

395. tulip
Tenleytown
Rossums
Minna
trudged
elegance

396. Julianna
Netherlands •
translated

397. conductor
tenant

398. burlap

399. squeaking
O'Conner
loft •
social

400. resented •
Southampton •
Antwerp •
Rotterdam •
Naples •
Belgium •

401. spikes

402. lured •

403. _ _ _

404. intention •
lilacs
bachelor buttons
geraniums

405. _ _ _

406. _ _ _

407. unattractive
hemp
fabric

408. Calvary

409. _ _ _

410. barbarians •
casts
truce

411. tradition •
striven •
banished •

412. Samaritan •
ye

413. clashed